SPELLING

By Sound and Structure

For Christian Schools

SPELLING

By Sound and Structure

Teacher's Manual

8

Rod and Staff Publishers, Inc.
PO Box 3
Crockett, Kentucky 41413

Telephone (606) 522-4348

Printed in USA

ISBN 978-07399-0585-2

Catalog no. 16891

6   7   8   9   —   29   28   27   26   25   24   23   22   21   20

Acknowledgments

We acknowledge the everlasting God, the Lord, besides whom there is none else. His blessing made the writing and publishing of this book possible.

To the following persons we express gratitude: The writers, Verna Mast and Amy Herr; the reviewers, Vernon Weaver, Lester Weaver, and various others; and the editor, Marvin Eicher. We are also indebted to numerous people who assisted in the work by helping in related projects along the way, by providing finances, by encouraging those working most directly with it, and by interceding in prayer for the work.

We are grateful to the writers and publishers of the materials that were consulted for reference in preparing this book.

–The Publishers

TABLE OF CONTENTS

INTRODUCTION

The main purpose of any spelling course is to teach pupils how to spell words correctly. Earlier books in this series seek to accomplish that purpose by focusing on phonetic patterns. In grades 7 and 8, the focus shifts to word elements—the roots, prefixes, and suffixes that make up words. Studying these elements will help students understand why words are spelled as they are.

The study of word elements can be fascinating. Who would have guessed, for instance, that *ample* and *plenteous* have the same root, or that *trifling* and *trivial* are not related? Knowing the meanings of roots and affixes will also help to expand the students' vocabularies.

The teacher should remember, however, that *learning to spell* must always have the primary emphasis in this course. Spelling test scores should carry the most weight in report card grades. If a student misspells a word on a spelling test, he should write it correctly at least ten times. Any spelling word misspelled in an exercise should be counted wrong. These and other means will help to keep the focus on learning to spell.

A large percentage of our common vocabulary is made of word elements that come from Latin and Greek. Therefore, the lessons in this book teach the meanings of numerous Latin and Greek roots, prefixes, and suffixes. This is the purpose of Parts A and B of the lessons.

Each lesson also has two other parts. Part C is a review section that exercises phonetic and word-building concepts that are taught in earlier years of this course. (There is no Part C in the six-week review lessons.) Part D is a section on the history of the English language. This part of each lesson explains some of the reasons for the modern spellings, pronunciations, and meanings of many English words.

In addition to Parts A, B, C, and D, a Speller Dictionary has been included. This specialized dictionary has been condensed to fit the needs of the students as they do the exercises throughout the book; however, a classroom dictionary will also be needed.

A good understanding of phonics, word elements, and the history of the English language should make a significant contribution to the spelling ability of the students.

Weekly Lesson Plans

Four-Day Plan	Three-Day Plan	Two-Day Plan
Day 1 Study Spelling Words Parts A and B	**Day 1** Study Spelling Words Parts A and B	**Day 1** Study Spelling Words Parts A and B
Day 2 Test 1	**Day 2** Part C	Test 1
Day 3 Part C	Test 1	**Day 2** Part C
Day 4 Test 2	**Day 3** Test 2	Test 2

The pupils can do Part D when they have time throughout the week, or the teacher can assign that part on a certain day. The more able pupils in particular should be required to complete Part D.

Weekly Spelling Tests

The weekly lesson plans suggest two tests for each lesson.

For Test 1, the new and review words should be tested in the order they are listed in each lesson. You will need to supply your own sentences for this test. Following Test 1, the pupils can easily exchange papers and check each other's tests. Record no scores from Test 1. The purpose of this test is to give practice in spelling the words and to see where the pupils need more drill.

For Test 2, the order of the spelling words should be scrambled, and you may use the oral test sentences that are provided for each lesson. You will likely want to check and score Test 2 yourself. The results of Test 2 should be recorded.

Review And Final Tests

Every sixth lesson reviews the words from the preceding five lessons. Fifty test words are provided for each of these review lessons. These words are selected from the preceding lessons to illustrate the structure and phonetic patterns taught in those lessons. Test words were selected to cover a wide difficulty range.

Page 224 gives a suggested list of fifty words to use as a final test at the end of the year. These words were selected from most of the lessons in the book and also cover a wide difficulty range.

Suggestions For Additional Spelling Lessons

If you complete the lessons in this book before the school year has ended and you want additional spelling lessons, these suggestions may help you.

Words for the Lessons

From the categories listed here, select ten, fifteen, or twenty words for each lesson, and write them on the board. For each lesson you could also choose a few words to review from previous lessons.

- names of food
- names of animals
- names of nearby cities or towns
- names of countries
- names of rivers
- words misspelled on assignment papers
- homonyms

Exercises for the Lessons

The pupils should first copy the words correctly on paper. Then assign any or all of the following.

- Write the words in syllables.
- Fit the words together crossword puzzle style.
- Write the words alphabetically.
- Write the words five times each.
- Use the words in sentences.
- Print the words, drawing a blank for every vowel. Exchange papers, and write the words correctly.

BIBLIOGRAPHY

Ayers, Donald M. *English Words From Latin and Greek Elements.* Tucson: University of Arizona Press, 1965.

Baugh, Albert C. *A History of the English Language.* New York: Apppleton-Century-Crofts, Inc., 1963.

Hanna, Hodges, Hanna. *Spelling: Structure and Strategies.* Boston: Houghton Mifflin Co., 1971.

Merriam Webster. *The Merriam-Webster New Book of Word Histories.* Springfield: Merriam-Webster Inc., Publishers, 1991.

Nist, John. *A Structural History of English.* New York: St. Martin's Press, 1966.

Reader's Digest. *Success With Words.* Pleasantville, New York: The Reader's Digest Association, Inc., 1983.

The New Encyclopaedia Britannica, 15th edition.

Etymology Resources

Webster's Third New International Dictionary. G&C Merriam Co., 1971

The American Heritage Dictionary. Boston: Houghton Mifflin Company, 1985, 1993

Funk & Wagnalls Canadian College Dictionary. Fitzhenry & Whiteside Limited, 1986

The Random House College Dictionary. Random House, Inc., 1975

Funk & Wagnalls New Standard Dictionary of the English Language. Funk & Wagnalls, 1963

SPELLING WORDS

This alphabetical list contains all the NEW WORDS and REVIEW WORDS taught in this book. The numeral after each word indicates the lesson in which the word is taught. In addition to learning these words, the pupils learn to spell many related words in the exercises.

A

abandon 2
abolish 7
abhor 1
abnormal 1
absolute 2
abstain 5
abstinence 7
abstract 16
abundance 20
acceptable 21
access 9
accommodate 10
accommodation 3
accompanied 21
accompany 27
accordingly 1
acknowledgment 13
acquaintance 5
actor 4
additional 16
address 10
adjourned 27
admission 3
adolescence 7
adoration 3
advisable 10
advisory 4
aeronautics 8
alarm 27
algebra 20
allegiance 14
alligator 28
alligators 22
alloys 1
all right 17
Almighty 23
alto 32
amateur 26
ambitious 28
amphibian 3

ample 5
amuse 14
amusement 5
amusing 20
Anabaptist 22, 29
analysis 22
anarchy 23
anatomy 22
angel 21
anoint 27
anointing 16
Antarctic 8
anticipate 19
anticipating 8
anticipation 3
antiseptic 8
anxiety 23
apologize 5
apology 10
apostasy 10
apostolic 13
apostrophe 10
appendicitis 16
appetite 15
applicant 25
application 3
approximately 13
aquarium 31
architect 25
arguing 8
arising 11
armor 15
arrangements 32
arthritis 16
artificial 32
artistic 13
ascend 19
ascension 14
ascertain 13
asphalt 9
assessment 22

associated 28
assurance 13
asterisk 27
atheist 9
athletic 13
atone 17
attached 29
attendant 25
attorney 9
audience 14
auditor 4, 14
authority 16
autograph 16
auxiliary 4
available 26
avocado 29

B

bananas 10
barbarous 28
barbecue 28
bass 32
beaten 22
beggar 4, 15
behavior 15
beige 26
believable 10
benediction 4
beneficial 4
benign 4
bestow 2
biennial 7
binoculars 7
biography 3
biology 3, 5
bookkeeping 5
bored 16
borne 20
boulevard 27
bouquet 26
breadth 8
brilliancy 14

brochure 26
buffalo 32
bumblebees 1
bureau 27
buyer 15

C

cafeteria 28
calorie 15
camouflage 26, 27
campaign 27
cancellation 3
candidate 10
canoe 33
canvass 7
canyon 29
capacity 11
capitalism 29
carbohydrates 19
cardiac 13
career 26
caribou 33
carton 7
catalog 10
cataract 10
category 10
caution 3
cease 5
ceased 14
celestial 2
centipede 7
ceremony 10
certainty 23
certificate 13
certify 13
challenge 15
chaperon 26
characteristic 13
chauffeur 26
chemical 5
chocolate 33
chord 20

LATIN AND GREEK ROOTS

This list contains all the Latin and Greek roots taught in *Spelling by Sound and Structure,* Grade 8. Each root is followed by its meaning and the number of the lesson in which it is taught.

Lesson Roots

Latin

audi (hear) 14
bene (well) 4
bi (two, twice) 7
cal (heat) 15
cent (hundred) 7
cert (sure) 13
cīvi (citizen) 17
curr, curs (run) 19
dīv (God) 2
du (two) 8
fōrma (shape) 11
frīg (cold) 15
littera (letter) 16
lūmin (light) 14
magn (great) 9
mal (bad) 4
mini (small) 9
mod (measure, manner) 10
mort (death) 3
oct (eight) 7
ple (fill) 5
popul (people) 17
pract (do) 23
qual (what sort) 9
quant (how great) 9
quart (fourth) 7
scend (climb) 19
scrib, script (write) 16
speci (kind, appearance) 11
struct (arrange) 11
tri (three) 8
uni (one) 7
urb (city) 17
verb (word) 5
vīta (life) 3

Lesson Roots

Greek

arch (begin, lead) 25
bio (life) 3
caco (bad) 4
chron (time) 10
deca (ten) 8
dēmos (people) 17
dyna (power) 23
eu (well) 4
gen (produce, begin) 25
geō (earth) 22
gnos, not (know) 13
graph (write) 16
hydro (water) 22
logos (word, study) 5
macro (large) 9
micro (small) 9
metron (measure) 10
not, gnos (know) 13
patho (feeling, suffering) 3
penta (five) 8
philo (love) 21
phōno (sound) 14
phōto (light) 14
physio (growth, nature) 22
pneuma (spirit, breath) 20
polis (city) 17
psychē (soul, mind) 20
schēma (shape, form) 11
sōma (body) 20
sophos (wisdom) 21
tetra (four) 8
theo (God) 2
therm (heat) 15
typo (impression) 11

AFFIXES

This list contains all the prefixes and suffixes taught in *Spelling by Sound and Structure,* Grade 8. Each affix if followed by its meaning or source and the number of the lesson in which it is taught.

Prefixes

a-, an- (without) 9
ana- (again, up) 22
anti- (against or contrary to) 8
apo- (away) 10
bi- (two, twice) 7
cata- (down) 10
dia- (through, across, apart) 11
en-, em- (on, in) 19
ex-, ec- (out) 19
epi- (upon, over) 20
meta- (between, after) 11
para- (beside, near) 21
peri- (around) 21
syn-, sym- (together) 9

Suffixes

-ac (affected by, like) 13
-ance (act, state, or quality of) 14
-ancy (act, state, or quality of) 14
-ant (one who) 25
-ar (one who) 4
-ary (pertaining to) 4
-ast (one who has or does) 25
-eau (French ending) 27
-ee (one who is) 26
-eer, -eur (one who) 26
-efy (make, become) 33
-ence (act, state, or quality of) 14
-ency (act, state, or quality of) 14
-ent (one who) 25
-ety (condition or quality) 23
-fest (German ending) 31
-heit (German ending) 31
-ic (affected by, like) 13
-ical (affected by, like) 13
-ify (make, become) 33
-ion (act, state, or quality of) 2
-ism (act, doctrine, system) 29
-ist (one who has or does) 25
-ite (that which, one who) 15
-itis (disease or inflamation of) 16
-ity (condition or quality) 23
-ize (make, become) 33
-oir (French ending) 27
-ois (French ending) 27
-ology (study or science of) 5
-or (one who) 4
-ory (pertaining to) 4
-osis (condition, process) 17
-otic (producing, characterized by) 17
-ous (full of, quality of) 28
-sion (act, state, or quality of) 3
-tion (act, state, or quality of) 3
-ty (condition or quality) 23
-y (condition or quality) 23

PUPIL
LESSONS

LESSON
GUIDES
and
ANSWER
KEYS

1 LESSON

NEW WORDS

abhor
alloys
bumblebees
engagement
exploring
fascinating
infallible
initiation
inspiration
justified
materially
overreactions
perished
precaution
process
reconcile
recovered
representatives
scheduled
unlikely

REVIEW WORDS

abnormal
accordingly
contrition
secretary
sincerely

A.   UNEARTHING THE ROOTS

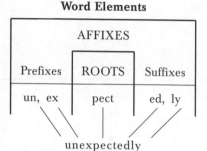

Word Elements

AFFIXES		
Prefixes	ROOTS	Suffixes
un, ex	pect	ed, ly

unexpectedly

The diagram above shows how *word elements* are put together to make words. The most basic element is the *root;* it contains the primary meaning of the word. Elements that can be attached to the beginning of a root are called *prefixes,* and those attached to the end of a root are called *suffixes.*

1. Make a diagram like the one above. Find the spelling words with the following roots and divide them into their separate elements, placing each element under the correct heading as shown for *unexpectedly.*

   hor   gage   plor   fall   spir   act
   cess   cile   cover   like   norm   cord

2. Write the NEW WORD that is better described as a compound word than as a word with a root and some affixes.

There are two kinds of suffixes: inflectional and derivational. Inflectional suffixes are used to change words from singular to plural (*chair, chairs*), from present tense to past tense (*jump, jumped*), and so forth.

Derivational suffixes usually change verbs to nouns (*sing, singer*), nouns to adjectives (*mountain, mountainous*), adjectives to adverbs (*gentle, gently*), and so forth. The word *unexpectedly* has both kinds of suffixes. There are many more derivational suffixes than inflectional suffixes.

3. Copy these hints as a help to remember the difference between inflectional and derivational suffixes.

   a. A word with an *in*flectional suffix *in*herits the same part of speech as its root word.

   b. A word with a *d*erivational suffix has a *d*ifferent part of speech than the word it is *derived* from.

Understanding word elements and how they are put together will be a great help to you in learning the spellings and meanings of new words. As you understand words better, you can also understand the Bible better.

Lesson 1

(Total points: 87)

Notes on Part A

This is an introduction to the study of word structure. If your students have been through Grade 7 of this series, the concept will be review.

Define *prefix, root,* and *suffix* as word elements. *Roots* as handled in these lessons are often not recognizable English root words, but the core of a word as it comes from an older language. Exercise 1 lists some of these roots for the students.

Antidisestablishmentarianism is an extreme example of multiple affixes. The root word is *establish* (which comes from the Latin root *stabilis,* meaning "stable"). *Disestablishment* came into use in the early 1800s with particular reference to the Church of England and its relation with the government. Derivatives of the word grew as the controversy was debated in following years: *disestablishmentarian, antidisestablishmentarian, antidisestablishmentarianism.*

Exercise 1: You may want to begin the exercise on the chalkboard to show the students how to use the diagram. (See Answer Key.)

Answer Key—Part A (15 points)

1.
AFFIXES

Prefixes	ROOTS	Suffixes
ab	hor	
en	gage	ment
ex	plor	ing
in	fall	ible
in	spir	a tion
over re	act	ion s
pro	cess	
re con	cile	
re	cover	ed
un	like	ly
ab	norm	al
ac	cord	ing ly

2. bumblebees

3. a. A word with an *in*flectional suffix *in*herits the same part of speech as its root word.

   b. A word with a *d*erivational suffix has a *d*ifferent part of speech than the word it is *derived* from.

Lesson 1 Test Sentences

1. *inspiration* Sunshine gives *inspiration* for a hike. *inspiration*
2. *exploring* How about *exploring* some animal trails? *exploring*
3. *initiation* That was my *initiation* to wildlife study. *initiation*
4. *justified* At first Job *justified* himself. *justified*
5. *abhor* Later he said, "I *abhor* myself and repent." *abhor*
6. *contrition* God honors such *contrition. contrition*
7. *recovered* Job *recovered* his former wealth and more. *recovered*
8. *infallible* God's judgments are *infallible. infallible*
9. *reconcile* Can you *reconcile* the conflicting reports? *reconcile*
10. *abnormal* An *abnormal* rainfall ruined the asters. *abnormal*
11. *bumblebees* Six *bumblebees* clustered on the insect trap. *bumblebees*
12. *perished* They *perished* in the fluid inside. *perished*
13. *materially* The *materially* rich can be paupers in spirit. *materially*
14. *sincerely* We should *sincerely* seek the kingdom of God. *sincerely*
15. *accordingly* The rest of life will harmonize *accordingly. accordingly*
16. *unlikely* It is an *unlikely* event that we will see a bear. *unlikely*
17. *alloys* New *alloys* were used to build the barges. *alloys*
18. *process* The *process* is explained in this news report. *process*
19. *overreactions* Overreactions cause new problems. *overreactions*
20. *precaution* A little *precaution* can save lives. *precaution*
21. *secretary* The school *secretary* filed the reports. *secretary*
22. *engagement* His new *engagement* was guiding tours. *engagement*
23. *representatives* Safety *representatives* visited the mine. *representatives*
24. *fascinating* I found a *fascinating* book in the attic. *fascinating*
25. *scheduled* Sickness delayed the *scheduled* trip. *scheduled*

B.   AFFIXING AFFIXES

1. Write four NEW WORDS that are plurals made by adding -*s*.
2. Which of your answers for number 1 have two suffixes?
3. Write six spelling words that follow this rule: "Drop the final *e* in a word before adding a suffix beginning with a vowel." After each word, write the form with the final *e*, following this pattern: *exploring—explore*.
4. a.   Write the NEW WORD with the adjective-forming suffix -*ible*.
   b. Write the REVIEW WORD with the adjective-forming suffix -*al*.
   c. Write one spelling word with the suffix -*ment*, and one with the suffix -*ary*.
5. Write four NEW WORDS that have inflectional suffixes showing past tense.
6. For these exercises, use words you wrote as answers for number 5.
   a. In which word was *y* changed to *i* before the suffix was added?
   b. Which word also has a prefix?
7. Write four spelling words with the derivational suffix -*ly*.

C.   SOUND, STRUCTURE, AND MEANING

1. Write four spelling words that have the /ôr/ sound.
2. Write the NEW WORD in which one *g* sounds /g/ and one *g* sounds /j/.
3. Write the REVIEW WORD in which /ī/ of the root word changed to /i/ when the suffix was added.
4. Write the NEW WORD with two /sh/ sounds spelled *ti*.
5. Write NEW WORDS that are antonyms for these words.
   a. boring   b. antagonize
6. Write *process* two times, and mark the first vowel in two different ways to show how it may be pronounced. (See the Speller Dictionary.)
7. The *etymology* of a word is the history of its source. The Speller Dictionary gives the etymology of many words at the end of the entry. Look up *perish* in the Speller Dictionary.
   a. Write the Middle English (ME) word that *perish* comes from.
   b. Write the Old French (OF) word that was the origin of that Middle English word.
   c. Write the Latin (L) word that was the source of the Old French word.
   d. The Latin word is a combination of the Latin prefix *per-* and the Latin root *īre*. Write the meaning of this prefix and root.
8. Write one of these spelling words to match each etymological meaning.
      abhor   alloys   precaution
   a. To beware before.
   b. To shudder or shrink from.
   c. To bind to.
9. a.   Write the definition of *fallible*.
   b. What NEW WORD is the opposite?
10. The Speller Dictionary lists a doublet for *alloy*. Doublets are two different words that come from the same root. Write the doublet of *alloy*.
11. a.   Which doublet in number 10 refers to a joining of people?
    b. Which doublet refers to a joining of metals?
12. *Alley* is a completely different word with a different root. Write the definition for *alley*.

Notes on Part B

    This section refreshes general acquaintance with suffixes and how they work. The exercises give guidance on where to find the answers. When the directions call for NEW WORDS, make sure the answers are from the NEW WORDS list. Sometimes they call for REVIEW WORDS. When it says "spelling words," the answers may come from either part of the list, and likely include some from both.

Answer Key—Part B (32 points)

1. alloys, bumblebees, overreactions, representatives

2. overreactions, representatives

3. exploring—explore
   fascinating—fascinate
   initiation—initiate
   inspiration—inspire
   scheduled—schedule
   contrition—contrite

4. a. infallible
   b. abnormal
   c. engagement, secretary

5. justified, perished, recovered, scheduled

6. a. justified   b. recovered

7. materially, unlikely, accordingly, sincerely

Notes on Part C

    This section reviews phonetic details, vocabulary, and dictionary skills, often focusing on some key to help remember correct spelling.

    Exercise 7 traces the etymology of *perish*. Exercise 8 uses the etymological meaning of some spelling words.

Answer Key—Part C (24 points)

1. abhor, exploring, abnormal, accordingly

2. engagement

3. contrition

4. initiation

5. a. fascinating   b. reconcile

6. prŏcess, prōcess (Accept unmarked short *o*, as shown in Speller Dictionary.)

7. a. *perishen*
   b. *periss-*
   c. *perīre*

    d. to go away (Accept *away, to go.*)

8. a. precaution
   b. abhor
   c. alloys

9. a. capable of failing
   b. infallible

10. ally

11. a. ally
    b. alloy

12. a narrow street

D.   LANGUAGE LINEAGE

THE BIBLE IN OUR LANGUAGE

The original Old Testament was written in the Hebrew language, and the New Testament was written in Greek. Both testaments were translated into Latin by Jerome in the fourth century. For a thousand years, this was the Word of God, while much of church life became a formalized system using the Latin Scriptures that most common people could not understand.

In the late 1300s a priest, John Wycliffe, resolved to give the English people the Bible in their own language. Amid intense opposition,* he translated the New Testament from the Latin version of Jerome and distributed copies in manuscript form. In the early 1500s, William Tyndale worked at translating the New Testament from the original Greek into English. The printing press of his day multiplied many copies despite opposition from the authorities. In 1535 Miles Coverdale, an English bishop, produced the first complete English Bible. His version was based on a German translation, Jerome's Latin, and Tyndale's English; and it was printed in Germany.

But opposition finally turned to favor. In 1537, printers in England published the Thomas Matthew Bible, which was based on Tyndale's and Coverdale's versions. Miles Coverdale produced another Bible in 1539 as a revision of the Matthew Bible. This volume was so large that it became known as the Great Bible and was used chiefly in churches. Several other versions followed, each based on some previous translation.

And then King James I authorized a work that was to become the standard English Bible for centuries afterward. About fifty of the most eminent scholars of the day were organized into six teams, and a portion of the Bible was assigned to each. From the original Hebrew or Greek, with consideration of other current translations, every man worked through a translation of the portion assigned to his team. Then he met with the other team members to compare the results and agree upon a final form. This draft was sent to each of the other groups for approval or adjustment. Finally a select committee went over the whole again. The first edition of the King James Version was printed in 1611, and with time it became recognized as the masterpiece of all English translations.

*See Lesson 60 of Rod and Staff's Eighth Reader.

Exercises

1. Name the Bible translator for each time given, and tell what version he translated from.
   a. fourth century
   b. fourteenth century (1300s)
   c. early sixteenth century
   d. 1535
   e. 1537
   f. 1539
   g. 1611

2. Give two reasons why the King James Bible is more reliable than the translations of the 1500s.

Notes on Part D

This table lists some basic information about most of the early English Bible translations.

English Bible Translations

Chief Translator	Date	Basis for Translation	Notes
Caedmon	680	Jerome's Latin	Not true translation, but stories in poetic form. (See Grade 7 of this series, Lesson 19, *Language Lineage*.)
John Wycliffe	1380	Jerome's Latin	First complete English Bible; handwritten.
William Tyndale	1525	Original Greek	15,000 New Testaments printed, many bought to be burned.
	1530	Original Hebrew	Portions of Old Testament.
Miles Coverdale	1535	Luther's German Jerome's Latin Tyndale's English	First complete English Bible from the printing press.
Thomas Matthew	1537	Coverdale's Tyndale's	First Bible to be printed in England. *Thomas Matthew* is pen name for John Rogers.
Miles Coverdale	1539	Matthew's	Called the Great Bible, this large book was chained to the desk in each church in England.
William Wittingham (editor)	1557 NT 1560 OT	Coverdale's	This Bible had verse divisions and Roman type; called the Geneva Bible.
Parker and Bishops	1568	Coverdale's Great Bible	Called the Bishops' Bible.
Gregory Martin	1582 NT 1610 OT	Latin Latin	Done by English refugees at Rheims, France. Done at Douay, France; called Douay-Rheims (Catholic).
Committee of Scholars	1611	Hebrew, Greek English translations	King James Version

The translations in the 1530s give the impression of a seesaw. Was each man trying to refute or correct something in the other's work? Imagine the wanderings of doctrine if a long succession of translators each based his work only on the one that preceded his. The King James committee was the first in a long time to go back to the original languages. This statement commonly appears on the title page of the King James Version: "Translated out of the original tongues and with the former translations diligently compared and revised by his majesty's special command."

For over two hundred years the King James Bible was unchallenged. In the twentieth century, numerous attempts were made to modernize the Bible, one of the complaints being that the King James language was antiquated and hard to understand.

Modern translations offer a variety in style and expression, but they can also hide some subtle snares in doctrine. Such doctrinal implications sometimes outweigh improvements that may be gained in clarity of language.

Answer Key—Part D (16 points)

1. a. Jerome, from original Hebrew and Greek
   b. John Wycliffe, from Jerome's Latin
   c. William Tyndale, from original Greek
   d. Miles Coverdale; from German, Jerome's Latin, and Tyndale's English
   e. Thomas Matthew, from Tyndale's and Coverdale's English
   f. Miles Coverdale, from Matthew's English
   g. fifty scholars, from original Hebrew and Greek

2. The King James Version was translated by many scholars working together. It was translated from the original languages.

LESSON 2

A. UNEARTHING THE ROOTS

ROOT	MEANING	EXAMPLE
Latin *div*	= God	divine
Greek *theo*	= God	theocracy

NEW WORDS

abandon
bestow
celestial
divinity
editorial
enthusiastic
exhausted
guarantee
icicles
leisure
mutual
necessity
ridiculous
ruined
suspicion
swamps
temporal
theology
underrate
wretched

REVIEW WORDS

absolute
communion
companion
onion
opinion

1. a. Someone who is possessed of God is likely to be ___*
        rather than indifferent. (An asterisk means that the
        answer is a spelling word.)
    b. Give the etymological meaning to this word.
        (Etymological meanings are definitions in normal
        print following the italicized foreign words.)
2. The Greek word *atheos* means "denying the gods." What
    related English word do we use when speaking of some-
    one who does not believe in God?
3. The Israelites were not satisfied with their government
    of (theocracy, democracy), but desired a king instead.
4. One NEW WORD with a Latin root means "a divine being;
    God." Write the word and its root.
5. One meaning of *divine* is "to foretell the future by using
    signs or magic." Who did this for money in Micah 3:11?
6. The Lord wants His children to trust Him for the future.
    In Deuteronomy 18:14, the Israelites were forbidden to
    hearken to what two kinds of people?
7. One NEW WORD with a Greek root means "teachings about
    God." Write the word and its root.
8. Write the phrase in 2 Peter 1:4 that means "nature of God."
9. In preparing to serve in a certain religious field, some peo-
    ple attend a school of divinity. Why would they do that?
10. What is the best book of divinity or theology that you
    can study?
11. Luke wrote his Gospel to a man whose name means "friend
    of God" (Luke 1:3). Write this man's name, and draw a
    line to divide it into the parts that mean "God" and "friend."
12. In the name *Theodore,* the last syllable means "gift."
    What is the meaning of *Theodore?*
13. In the etymologies of words with the *div* and *theo* roots,
    the word *god* is not capitalized. When Paul was at Athens
    (Acts 17), what phrase did he find written that tells us
    the Greeks worshiped many gods?

Lesson 2

(Total points: 67)

Notes on Part A

Selected Words With Lesson Roots

Words in this lesson's list are in boldface. A number in parentheses after a word indicates that the word is in the spelling list of another lesson.

L *div:* **divinity,** divine

Gk. *theo:* **enthusiastic, theology,** atheist (9), theism, theist, theistic, theocentric, theocracy, theologian

Grade 7 of this spelling series teaches many Latin roots. This book deals with some Latin and some Greek. The root language is identified in the box where the roots are listed, but distinction in the exercises is only incidental. Many lessons have roots from both languages, often with the same meaning. The relationship of these two languages in the Indo-European language family is diagramed in Lesson 9 of Grade 7.

Many exercises in this course refer to the Bible. All answers assume that the KJV was used.

Answer Key—Part A (17 points)

1. a. enthusiastic
   b. god-possessed

2. atheist

3. theocracy

4. divinity, *div*

5. the prophets (of Zion)

6. observers of times, diviners

7. theology, *theo*

8. divine nature

9. (Sample answer) At such a school they would study about God and divine things.

10. the Bible

11. Theo/philus

12. Gift of God

13. "TO THE UNKNOWN GOD"

Lesson 2 Test Sentences

1. *divinity* Miracles showed the *divinity* of Jesus. *divinity*
2. *exhausted* He became *exhausted* as any other human. *exhausted*
3. *leisure* Jesus and the disciples had no *leisure* to eat. *leisure*
4. *suspicion* Walter Reed had a *suspicion* about mosquitoes. *suspicion*
5. *swamps* He ordered the *swamps* to be drained. *swamps*
6. *ridiculous* Ignore his *ridiculous* comments. *ridiculous*
7. *theology* It takes more than *theology* to serve the Lord. *theology*
8. *communion* Communion with God is important. *communion*
9. *mutual* The *mutual* encouragement is vital. *mutual*
10. *abandon* Never *abandon* your commitment. *abandon*
11. *guarantee* God's faithfulness to you is a *guarantee*. *guarantee*
12. *onion* Mother added *onion* flakes to the stew. *onion*
13. *ruined* Susan thought it *ruined* the supper. *ruined*
14. *wretched* Perhaps she felt *wretched* from her cold. *wretched*
15. *necessity* Amos saw the *necessity* of organizing his closet. *necessity*
16. *bestow* He decided to *bestow* some things on his brothers. *bestow*
17. *underrate* Does he *underrate* the value of a keepsake? *underrate*
18. *temporal* Our *temporal* possessions will perish. *temporal*
19. *editorial* Printing goes faster than *editorial* preparation. *editorial*
20. *opinion* Every book reveals the *opinion* of the writer. *opinion*
21. *absolute* The frosty dawn broke with *absolute* stillness. *absolute*
22. *icicles* A fringe of *icicles* trimmed the balcony. *icicles*
23. *enthusiastic* My neighbor is an *enthusiastic* star gazer. *enthusiastic*
24. *celestial* Orion strides along the *celestial* equator. *celestial*
25. *companion* Canis Major is his *companion*. *companion*

B.   AFFIXING AFFIXES

1. Write spelling words ending with *-ion* to match these etymological meanings.
   a. The act of watching from below.
   b. The act of supposing.
2. In which spelling word was a final *e* omitted before the suffix *-ion* was added?
3. Write the spelling word that is a related form of *company*.
4. Write the spelling word in which *-ion* is not a suffix.
5. Use the noun-forming suffix *-ion* to write words with these meanings.
   a. The act of discussing.
   b. The state of being separate.
   c. The state of being confused.
   d. The act of completing.
   e. The act of resurrecting.

Noun-forming Suffix

SUFFIX	MEANING	EXAMPLE
-ion	act, state, or quality of	communion

6. Write two NEW WORDS that are plural forms ending with *-s*.
7. Write two NEW WORDS that are verbs with the inflectional suffix *-ed*.
8. Write the NEW WORD that is an adjective with the suffix *-ed*.
9. Write two NEW WORDS with the adjective-forming suffix *-al*.
10. In *back-formation*, a short word is derived from a longer one by removing an ending. Write the verbs derived from *editor* and *enthusiasm* by back-formation. (The second verb is informal.)

C.   SOUND, STRUCTURE, AND MEANING

1. a. Write the NEW WORD that has two /s/ sounds, spelled once with *c* and once with *ss*.
   b. Write the word in which one *c* spells /s/ and one *c* spells /k/.
2. Write a NEW WORD with the *ua* letter combination, which follows the same spelling pattern as in *guard*.
3. Write the NEW WORD that has /ē/ spelled *ei*.
4. Write the NEW WORDS that have /ch/ spelled *ti* or *tu*.
5. Which NEW WORD has /gz/ spelled *xh*?
6. Which has final /shən/ spelled *cion*?
7. One NEW WORD has a double consonant because the last letter of the prefix and the first letter of the root are the same. Write this word.
8. Write the same NEW WORD for both sentences. Label the part of speech for each answer.
   a. The editor rewrote his ____ seven times.
   b. George found his ____ duties easier than he had expected.
9. Write a NEW WORD for the second blank in the following sentence, and the first three letters of the same word for the first blank. Please get ____ of that ____ picture.
10. Write the doublet of *guarantee*. (See the Speller Dictionary.)
11. Write a spelling word for each meaning.
    a. Not limited by any outside influence.
    b. To give as a gift.
12. a. Write the root word of *ruined*.
    b. Use a form of that word for each blank. The ____ plans did not ____ the man's reputation as an excellent guide to the ____ of Babylon.
13. Use the same NEW WORD for both sentences.
    a. Mother used a ____ compress on the fevered child.
    b. The rich man built barns for his ____ goods.
14. Write one sentence with *abandon* as a verb and one sentence with *abandon* as a noun.

Notes on Part B

Exercise 1: Etymological meaning and common definition may be very dissimilar. A connection can often be made between the two, but it may be difficult to choose the answer. A good approach is to make a guess and check that word's etymology in the Speller Dictionary.

Exercise 5: These answers are not words from the spelling list. Such exercises broaden students' skill in using affixes. The aim of this course is not only to learn the words in the spelling list, but also to develop functional skill with the language.

Answer Key—Part B (19 points)

1. a. suspicion
    b. opinion
2. communion
3. companion
4. onion
5. a. discussion
    b. separation
    c. confusion
    d. completion
    e. resurrection
6. icicles, swamps
7. exhausted, ruined
8. wretched
9. (any two) celestial, editorial, temporal (*Mutual* does not have a suffix, and *editorial* may be a noun.)
10. edit, enthuse

Notes on Part C

Exercise 10: Doublets are words that stem from the same source but have developed into different words in modern English. The Semantic Study in *Language Lineage* of Lesson 17 explains the development of some doublets.

Exercise 14: Writing sentences can be difficult if the word is not a part of the student's fluent vocabulary. The examples of usage in the dictionary can help to familiarize the meaning, but students should avoid forming their sentences from these examples. A student having difficulty can be encouraged to use a synonym to compose his sentence and then to replace the synonym with the required word. Inflectional changes are acceptable, such as *abandons* for the given word *abandon*.

Answer Key—Part C (26 points)

1. a. necessity
    b. icicles
2. guarantee
3. leisure
4. celestial, mutual
5. exhausted
6. suspicion
7. underrate
8. a. editorial, noun
    b. editorial, adjective
9. rid, ridiculous
10. warranty
11. a. absolute
    b. bestow
12. a. ruin
    b. ruined, ruin, ruins
13. a. temporal
    b. temporal
14. (Sample sentences)
    v. We had to *abandon* the project.
    n. The children skipped with *abandon* down the meadow slope.

D.   LANGUAGE LINEAGE

INFLUENCE OF THE PRINTING PRESS

The English language of the 1400s was diversified in spelling and usage. Writers spelled words basically the way they spoke them. But pronunciation varied from one area to another, and so did vocabulary.

Every book that was written carried some spelling influence from the writer to the reader. But books were few and expensive because they all had to be copied by hand. Then in the 1450s, Johannes Gutenberg and his associates in Germany developed a printing press with moveable type. This invention made it possible to produce thousands of books that were exactly identical. The printing press soon came to England, where it helped to unify the English language by providing many printed examples of spelling and usage.

London was the center of printing in England. Thus, of all the varieties of English then prevalent, the form used in London became a widely familiar standard for the English language.

Spelling was in the hands of the printer. As he prepared the works of different writers, he could apply consistency of spelling according to his own preference. Often it was more convenient *not* to spell words consistently. A printer might take the liberty to double letters or to tack on a final *e* whenever it helped to fill out a line of type. One printer actually spelled *fellow* with all the following variations in the same book: felow, felowe, fellow, fallow, fallowe.

Even with these variations, the general effect of the printing press was to standardize English spelling. There was no dictionary to use as an authority, but people followed the examples that they saw in print. The influence of many identical copies helped to bring writers and printers to a certain degree of uniformity.

Exercises

1. What was the chief guide to spelling for Englishmen in the 1400s?
2. What other influence became a guide for spelling?
3. Why did the form of English that was used in London become the general standard for the language?

4. Why did early printers use various spellings for the same word?
5. Why was English spelling in 1500 more uniform than in 1400?

Notes on Part D

      The printing press came to England with William Caxton in 1476. An Englishman by birth, he had lived abroad for many years and learned printing in Germany in his older years. He then returned to London and set up a press in Westminster Abbey.

Answer Key—Part D (5 points)

(Italics represent the core of the answer.)

1. *Pronunciation* was the chief guide to spelling in the 1400's.
2. The *printing press* produced many standard copies which influenced spelling practices.
3. London was the *printing center* of England.
4. Each printer spelled as he preferred. Sometimes altered spellings helped to *fill lines of type evenly.*
5. The printing press made so many *identical examples* that people started copying what they saw.

LESSON 3

NEW WORDS

accommodation
adoration
amphibian
anticipation
biography
biology
cancellation
classification
conjunction
elaborate
fission
graduation
immortal
mortgage
omission
petition
precipitation
sympathy
vital
vitamins

REVIEW WORDS

admission
application
caution
diary
occasion

A. UNEARTHING THE ROOTS

ROOT	MEANING	EXAMPLE
Latin *vita*	= life	vitality
Greek *bio*	= life	biography
Latin *mort*	= death	mortal
Greek *patho*	= feeling, suffering	pathetic

1. List the lesson roots, and after each write one or more NEW WORDS that contain that root. Use eight NEW WORDS.
2. One NEW WORD is a root with only one letter added. Write the word and its etymological definition.
3. Which NEW WORD with *vita* names organic compounds necessary to life?
4. Which NEW WORD has the etymological definition "life on both sides"? In this word, the *o* of *bio* is replaced by the vowel __ of the suffix.
5. Write spelling words for these definitions.
   a. A written account about life.
   b. The science of plant and animal life.
6. a. The examination of a dead body to find the cause of death is (an autopsy, a biopsy).
   b. The examination of tissue from a living body is (an autopsy, a biopsy).
7. Records of birth, marriage, and death are ____* statistics.
8. Write a NEW WORD for the etymological meaning "no death."
9. A person who prepares dead bodies for burial is called an undertaker or a (mortgager, mortician, mortuary).
10. Write words from 1 Corinthians 15 that have the *mort* root: "This _(dying)_ must put on _(the undying)_ ."
11. One NEW WORD has the *mort* root because a borrower pledges certain property to be "dead" to his full ownership until a loan is repaid. Which word is this?
12. In Colossians 3:5, the Christian is commanded to (put to death, bring to life) the earthly members of his body.
13. We appreciate _path_* from others in a time of grief.
14. Write *apathy* or *antipathy* for each definition.
   a. Strongly opposed feeling; enmity.
   b. Lack of feeling; indifference.
15. The sight of the suffering children was __etic.
16. A (biologist, pathologist) is one who studies diseases.

*Remember that an asterisk directs you to use a spelling word.

Lesson 3

(Total points: 101)

Notes on Part A

Selected Words With Lesson Roots

L *vita:* **vital, vitamins,** viable, vitality

Gk. *bio:* **amphibian, biography, biology,** biodegradable, biohazard, biome, biopsy, biosphere

L *mort:* **immortal, mortgage,** mortal, mortality, mortician, mortify, mortuary

Gk. *patho:* **sympathy,** apathy, homeopath, pathetic, pathologist, pathos

Exercise 1: *Amphibian* will be harder to identify as a word with the *bio* root. Following exercises will bring it to light.

Exercises 10, 13, and 15: A word in parentheses on a blank is the root meaning of an answer. Plain letters on a blank are part of the answer, given as a clue.

Answer Key—Part A (33 points, including 1 point for each root given)

1. *vita:* vital, vitamins
   bio: biology, biography, amphibian
   mort: immortal, mortgage
   patho: sympathy

2. vital, life

3. vitamins

4. amphibian, *a*

5. a. biography
   b. biology

6. a. an autopsy
   b. a biopsy

7. vital

8. immortal

9. mortician

10. mortal, immortality

11. mortgage

12. put to death

13. sympathy

14. a. antipathy
    b. apathy

15. pathetic

16. pathologist

Lesson 3 Test Sentences

1. *conjunction* Use a *conjunction* in a compound sentence. *conjunction*
2. *omission* The *omission* of one word caused confusion. *omission*
3. *precipitation* A record amount of *precipitation* fell. *precipitation*
4. *accommodation* The dam's *accommodation* is adequate. *accommodation*
5. *cancellation* Icy roads led to *cancellation* of the meeting. *cancellation*
6. *caution* Everyone warned us to drive with *caution*. *caution*
7. *elaborate* Joseph gave Benjamin an *elaborate* meal. *elaborate*
8. *sympathy* He masked his *sympathy* upon finding the cup. *sympathy*
9. *adoration* Joseph really had *adoration* for his brother. *adoration*
10. *petition* Judah's *petition* freed Benjamin. *petition*
11. *biology* We examined insects in *biology* class. *biology*
12. *classification* Lewis knows detailed *classification* of bees. *classification*
13. *amphibian* The salamander is an *amphibian*. *amphibian*
14. *graduation* We saw the *graduation* from tadpole to frog. *graduation*
15. *vital* Exercise is *vital* to good health. *vital*
16. *vitamins* The best *vitamins* are in fresh food. *vitamins*
17. *mortgage* It does not pay to *mortgage* your health. *mortgage*
18. *application* Do you have your job *application*? *application*
19. *admission* What is the *admission* fee per person? *admission*
20. *fission* Nuclear *fission* is a result of nuclear reaction. *fission*
21. *biography* The Bible is a *biography* of Jesus. *biography*
22. *immortal* It is an *immortal* story. *immortal*
23. *occasion* The family sale was a special *occasion*. *occasion*
24. *anticipation* I could feel *anticipation* in the air. *anticipation*
25. *diary* The dusty old notebook was Grandmother's *diary*. *diary*

PUPIL

B.   AFFIXING AFFIXES

1. Variant forms of *-ion* are *-tion* and *-sion*.
   a. Write four NEW WORDS in which the root word ends with *-ate,* but the final *e* was dropped before adding *-ion.*
   b. Write four spelling words in which *-ation* or *-cation* was added to the root.
   c. Write two spelling words in which the final consonant was changed before adding *-sion.* What was the final consonant in both root words?
2. Write the NEW WORD that names a part of speech. Underline its prefix and suffix.
3. An ending like *-ion* is not always an English suffix. Write two spelling words ending with *-sion* and two ending with *-tion* in which no recognizable root is left if these endings are removed.
4. Add a noun-forming suffix to *elaborate.*

Noun-forming Suffixes

SUFFIX	MEANING	EXAMPLE
-tion	act, state, or	description
-sion	quality of	omission

5. Write the noun form of each word.
   a. explore   e. justify
   b. meditate   f. sanctify
   c. create   g. mortify
   d. dedicate   h. beautify
6. Write the NEW WORD that has an inflectional suffix.
7. Write the two NEW WORDS that end with *al.*
8. Write the plural form of each word.
   a. accommodation
   b. biography
   c. mortgage
   d. petition
   e. sympathy
   f. diary

C.   SOUND, STRUCTURE, AND MEANING

1. Write the REVIEW WORD that has the vowel digraph *au.*
2. Write the NEW WORD that has the letters *ua,* each letter being a long vowel that is a syllable by itself.
3. Write the NEW WORD that has a silent *t.*
4. Write the NEW WORD that has two double consonants.
5. Write eight spelling words that end with /ā shən/.
6. a. Write the spelling word that ends with /ā zhən/.
   b. How is this ending different from the endings in your answers to number 5?
7. Write spelling words that have these meanings.
   a. Request; plea.
   b. Division of atoms.
   c. Carefulness; watchfulness.
   d. Pledge of property to secure a debt.
   e. Act of leaving out.
8. Use the same NEW WORD for each blank. Mark the long *a* in the answer that is a verb.
   a. Despite our ____ directions, Peter lost his way.
   b. He would not ____ on his adventure in the city.
9. a. Write a definition for *diary* and one for *dairy.*
   b. Use both words in one sentence.
10. Write a sentence using the word *anticipation.*
11. Write the etymological meaning for *adoration.*

Notes on Part B

Exercise 5: The last four words have the intermediate syllable *ca* between the root word and suffix. Students will probably have little trouble because the forms are familiar.

Exercise 8: Review the rule for changing *y* to *i* when adding a suffix to a word that ends with *y*. When *y* follows a consonant, change it to *i* to add *es*.

Answer Key—Part B (34 points)

1. a. accommodation, anticipation, graduation, precipitation
   b. adoration, cancellation, classification, application
   c. omission, admission, *t*
2. <u>conjunction</u>
3. fission, occasion, petition, caution
4. elaboration
5. a. exploration
   b. meditation
   c. creation
   d. dedication
   e. justification
   f. sanctification
   g. mortification
   h. beautification
6. vitamins
7. immortal, vital
8. a. accommodations
   b. biographies
   c. mortgages
   d. petitions
   e. sympathies
   f. diaries

Answer Key—Part C (26 points)

1. caution
2. graduation
3. mortgage
4. accommodation
5. accommodation, adoration, anticipation, cancellation, classification, graduation, precipitation, application
6. a. occasion
   b. This word uses *s* instead of *t*.
7. a. petition
   b. fission
   c. caution
   d. mortgage
   e. omission
8. a. elaborate
   b. elaborāte
9. (Sample definitions)
   a. *diary*—a written record of daily happenings.
      dairy—a place where milk is produced, processed, or sold.
   b. (Sample sentence) Her diary vividly describes life on a dairy farm.
10. (Sample sentence) Anticipation of the evening brightened his whole day.
11. to pray to

D. LANGUAGE LINEAGE

THE GREAT VOWEL SHIFT

Language is a living, changing thing. If people of the same language are separated into different areas for several generations, each group will develop a distinct regional variation, or dialect, of the language. If they are separated long enough without interchange, their dialects will become so dissimilar that they are actually separate languages. Then the different groups can no longer understand each other at all.

The printing press in the Middle Ages brought increased communication that helped to arrest or reverse the divergence of English. Printed literature preserved the written form of many words. But it did not preserve spoken sounds. During the 1600s and 1700s, a gradual shift took place in the pronunciation of English vowels, and especially of the long vowels.

A word such as *bone* continued to be written with *o* even though the spoken sound changed. Today the *o* in that word represents /ō/ to us, but it spelled /ā/ in Old English. The letter *i* in *bite* says /ī/ to us; but in Old English it stood for /ē/, as it still does in Spanish and some other languages. In 1550, an Englishman's reading of the sentence "We will bide at the stone house" would have sounded like "Way will beed at the stane hoos."

This gradual change of long vowel sounds has been named The Great Vowel Shift. Sounds on the tongues of Englishmen changed, but they did not adjust their spelling to match their speech, because their words were set in black and white by the printing press. Our present letter–sound correspondence seems right to us because that is how we learned it, but it is actually a shift from the original English letter–sound correspondence.

Exercises

1. What causes the development of different dialects within a language?
2. When does a dialect become a new language?
3. What helped to unify the dialects of Middle English?
4. What happened in English speech after spelling was stabilized by the printing press?

5. Choose the probable Old English pronunciation for these words. Write the number of your choice.
   a. meat   (1) /mēt/   (2) /māt/
   b. fly   (1) /flē/   (2) /flō/
   c. wait   (1) /wīt/   (2) /wāt/
   d. blow   (1) /blō/   (2) /blü/

Notes on Part D

Exercise 5: Examination of the sample sentence at the end of paragraph 3 will show that a present-day long *e* word (we) and long *o* word (stone) were both said with /ā/ in Middle English. By comparing the words in the sample sentence, you can conclude the pronunciation for answers *a* and *b*. Items *c* and *d* will be guesswork, easily done if you choose a pronunciation different from Modern English.

Below are some other examples of pronunciation changes through the Great Vowel Shift.

Our word	*Old pronunciation*
bite	/bēt/
fly	/flē/
blood	/blōd/
love	/lüv/
meat	/māt/
wait	/wīt/
blow	/blü/

Answer Key—Part D (8 points)

(Italics represent the core of the answer.)

1. Different dialects develop when people who speak the same language are *separated long enough.*

2. When the differences are great enough that the two groups can *no longer understand each other at all,* the dialects are considered two different languages.

3. Increased communication by the *printing press* helped to unify the dialects of Middle English.

4. There was a gradual *change in the pronunciation of long vowels* after spelling was stabilized.

5. a. (2)
    b. (1)
    c. (1)
    d. (2)

LESSON 4

NEW WORDS

advisory

auditor

beggar

benign

commentator

counselor

customary

desirable

dictator

dormitory

evangelist

hangar

laboratory

malice

malicious

malignant

migratory

missionaries

pursue

summary

REVIEW WORDS

actor

auxiliary

benediction

beneficial

mandatory

A. UNEARTHING THE ROOTS

ROOT	MEANING	EXAMPLE
Latin *bene*	= well	benefit
Greek *eu*	= well, good	eulogy
Latin *mal*	= bad	malady
Greek *caco*	= bad	cacophony

1. Write REVIEW WORDS for these etymological meanings.
   a. To do well. b. To speak well.
2. Write the meaning of this line from a song: "He is the donor of mercies benign."
3. Choose the correct word for each sentence.
   benefactor   benevolent
   eucalyptus   eulogize   euphemism
   a. The _____ tree was named for the covering on its buds. The etymology means "well covered."
   b. God has a _____ nature.
   c. Onesiphorus was Paul's _____ (2 Timothy 1:16–18).
   d. Saying, "He was relieved of his duties" is a _____ for saying, "He was fired."
   e. To _____ someone is to speak well of him.
4. The English *u* and *v* both come from one Greek letter.
   a. Write the NEW WORD in which the Greek root *eu* is spelled *ev*.
   b. Write the original Greek spelling of this word.
5. a. Write three NEW WORDS with the *mal* root.
   b. Which one describes Diotrephes's words in 3 John 10?
   c. Which one is an evil listed in Ephesians 4:31?
6. If you are sick, you might say you have a <u>mal</u>.
7. In Luke 23:32, the two men crucified with Jesus are called <u>mal</u> because they had done something bad.
8. According to the etymology for *malaria,* people thought this sickness was caused by _____ air.
9. *Mal-* is also a prefix meaning "bad" or "badly," as in *malnourished* for "badly nourished." Write words with *mal-* for the following meanings.
   a. Badly formed.   c. Bad practice.
   b. Badly adjusted.   d. Bad function.
10. Write *antonyms* or *synonyms* for these word pairs.
    a. cacophony, euphony
    b. benediction, malediction

Lesson 4

(Total points: 77)

Notes on Part A

Selected Words With Lesson Roots

L *bene:* **benediction, beneficial, benign,** benefactor, benevolent

Gk. *eu:* **evangelist,** eucalyptus, eulogize, eulogy, euphemism, euphony, euthanasia

L *mal:* **malice, malicious, malignant,** malady, malaria, malefactor, malfunction, malnourished

Gk. *caco:* cacography, cacophony

There are no *caco* words in the spelling list. The root is included in the box and in exercise 10 to balance the Latin and Greek pairs of meaning.

Exercise 2: The quoted line is from the song "O Come, Let Us Worship," which may be found in the *Christian Hymnary,* number 18.

Answer Key—Part A (24 points)

1. a. beneficial
   b. benediction

2. He is the one who gives kind mercies.

3. a. eucalyptus
   b. benevolent
   c. benefactor
   d. euphemism
   e. eulogize

4. a. evangelist
   b. euangelos

5. a. malice, malicious, malignant
   b. malicious
   c. malice

6. malady

7. malefactors

8. bad

9. a. malformed
   b. maladjusted
   c. malpractice
   d. malfunction

10. a. antonyms
    b. antonyms

Lesson 4 Test Sentences

1. *hangar* A large jet rolled past the *hangar.* *hangar*
2. *missionaries* Ten *missionaries* boarded the plane. *missionaries*
3. *evangelist* One of the men was an *evangelist.* *evangelist*
4. *pursue* The Bible urges us to *pursue* holiness. *pursue*
5. *desirable* Meekness and humility are *desirable* traits. *desirable*
6. *malice* We must rid ourselves of *malice* and envy. *malice*
7. *counselor* Jesus is a faithful *counselor* and guide. *counselor*
8. *benediction* The minister pronounced the *benediction.* *benediction*
9. *auditor* A new *auditor* checked the records. *auditor*
10. *summary* He gave a *summary* at the business meeting. *summary*
11. *beneficial* The new tool proved to be *beneficial.* *beneficial*
12. *dictator* The *dictator* grew more and more violent. *dictator*
13. *advisory* He needed a new *advisory* committee. *advisory*
14. *malicious* Three *malicious* men killed many villagers. *malicious*
15. *mandatory* It was *mandatory* to enlist in the army. *mandatory*
16. *auxiliary* Fresh *auxiliary* troops were sent to the area. *auxiliary*
17. *dormitory* Monica lived in the *dormitory* three weeks. *dormitory*
18. *migratory* Robins are *migratory* birds. *migratory*
19. *customary* It is *customary* for them to return every spring. *customary*
20. *commentator* The *commentator* explained this verse. *commentator*
21. *actor* One little *actor* imitated the visitors. *actor*
22. *beggar* He pretended that he was a *beggar.* *beggar*
23. *laboratory* We waited tensely for the *laboratory* report. *laboratory*
24. *benign* The tumor was *benign.* *benign*
25. *malignant* Mr. Smith had a *malignant* disease. *malignant*

B.   AFFIXING AFFIXES

1. Write spelling words with the Latin suffix *-or* to match these definitions.
   a. One who audits.
   b. One who comments.
   c. One who counsels.
   d. One who dictates.
   e. One who acts.
2. Write words with the suffix *-ar* to match these definitions.
   a. One who begs*.
   b. One who tells lies.
   c. One who goes to school.
   d. Pertaining to a particle.
   e. Pertaining to a family.
3. In exercises 1 and 2, adding the suffixes changes verbs to ____ and nouns to ____.
4. Write words with the suffix *-ary* or *-ory* to match these definitions.
   a. Pertaining to custom*.

Noun- and Adjective-forming Suffixes

SUFFIX	MEANING	EXAMPLE
-or	one who	sailor
-ory	pertaining to	observatory
-ar	one who	familiar
-ary	pertaining to	customary

   b. Pertaining to a mandate*.
   c. Pertaining to migration*.
   d. A place to sleep*.
   e. A place for a certain kind of labor*.
   f. With authority to advise*.
   g. Pertaining to help*.
   h. Pertaining to respiration.
   i. Pertaining to literature.
   j. A building for observing the heavens.
   k. A report of the sum of a matter*.
5. In which NEW WORD is the suffix *-ary* altered by an inflectional suffix?

C.   SOUND, STRUCTURE, AND MEANING

1. Copy each word, and place a macron (ˉ) or a breve (˘) over the *i* to show whether it is long or short.
   a. malign
   b. malignant
   c. benign
   d. benignant
2. Write another word with /īn/ spelled *ign,* and two of its derivatives, for these blanks.
   a. Read the paper carefully before you ____ your name.
   b. There was no ____ on the note, but we recognized the handwriting.
   c. At the ____ to begin, the students began rapidly writing answers.
3. Write the singular form of *missionaries.*
4. Write the NEW WORD that is made from *desire* plus a suffix. What letter is dropped when the suffix is added?
5. a. Write *hangar* and *hanger,* along with the meaning of each word.
   b. According to the etymology of *hangar,* this word comes from the name of a building used for what purpose?
6. Write an antonym from the spelling list for each of these words.
   a. unusual
   b. optional
   c. flee
   d. contemptible
   e. affectionate
7. Look up *counselor* in the Speller Dictionary, and note its alternate spelling. Write both spellings, and underline the one given in the spelling list.

Answer Key—Part B (24 points)

1. a. auditor
   b. commentator
   c. counselor
   d. dictator
   e. actor
2. a. beggar
   b. liar
   c. scholar
   d. particular
   e. familiar
3. nouns, adjectives

4. a. customary
   b. mandatory
   c. migratory
   d. dormitory
   e. laboratory
   f. advisory
   g. auxiliary
   h. respiratory
   i. literary
   j. observatory
   k. summary
5. missionaries

Notes on Part C

Exercises 1 and 2 focus on the pronunciation shift that changes silent *g* to hard *g*.

Answer Key—Part C (22 points)

1. a. malīgn
   b. malĭgnant
   c. benīgn
   d. benĭgnant
2. a. sign
   b. signature
   c. signal
3. missionary
4. desirable, *e*
5. a. hangar—a building for housing or repairing airplanes
      hanger—a device on which to hang something
   b. for shoeing horses
6. a. customary
   b. mandatory
   c. pursue
   d. desirable
   e. malicious
7. <u>counselor</u>, counsellor

20   *Lesson 4*

D.   LANGUAGE LINEAGE

A SHIFTING LANGUAGE

During the Middle Ages, English was an informal language of the common people. The ruling class used French. The educated used Latin. The English of the common people was not restrained by official and formal use, and so it drifted through many changes.

Word forms changed. Many inflections were dropped, which simplified the language. For instance, our adjective *glad* has a single form whether it describes one person or several and whether the condition is past, present, or future. Old English had inflected adjective forms for all these different uses. Though we have some irregular verb forms today, such as *eat–ate–eaten,* the majority of Modern English verb inflections are formed with *-ed.* Old English had many more irregular verb forms; but with time, these were lost to the simpler, regular forms. Our adjective *molten* is a surviving example of an old inflection of the verb *melt.*

Pronunciation changed. The Great Vowel Shift was the greatest pronunciation change from Old English to Modern English. But a number of smaller changes also took place. Some of the spelling patterns in our language are remnants of bygone pronunciations. The silent consonants in *lamb, knife,* and *half* are there because they were formerly pronounced.

Old English had words like *hwæt* (what) and *hwenne* (when), in which *hw* was a typical consonant cluster. Other initial consonant clusters were *hl* and *hr,* in words such as *hlëapen* (leap), *hlūd* (loud), and *hrœfn* (raven). Today the *hr* and *hl* clusters have been lost; and in the *hw* cluster, the order of the two letters has been reversed.

A lingering evidence of shifting language is found in some modern variations of speech. Do you eat the /rüt/ or the /rùt/ of the carrot plant? Do you pronounce *either* as /ē ꟳHər/ or /ī ꟳHər/?

Exercises

1. Why was the English language so open to change in the Middle Ages?
2. What change of word forms took place?
3. What was The Great Vowel Shift? (See Lesson 3.)
4. What other pronunciation shift occurred, with the result that some words were not spelled as they sounded?
5. Write the modern spellings of the Old English words below. Their meanings are given in parentheses.
   a. *hlæne* (thin)
   b. *hring* (circle)
   c. *hwær* (at what place)

Notes on Part D

The ruling class used French because William the Conqueror placed Frenchmen in all the high government positions and declared French to be the official language of England. (See Lesson 31 *Language Lineage* in Grade 7 of this series.) While English was out of court, it underwent extensive leveling of inflections.

Adjective inflections: A complicated maze of number, gender, and case gave the adjective *old* eight different forms: *eald, ealda, ealde, ealdes, ealdum, ealdne, ealdre, ealdra.*

Middle English verb inflections had many more forms, including these standard endings: *-e, -est, -eth, -en, -ede, -edest, -ed, -ende, -inge.* Today English verb inflections are basically made with *-ed, -ing,* and *-s* or *-es.* Some *-est* and *-eth* words are familiar from the Bible. *Laden, shaven,* and *swollen* are a few more examples of old verb forms that survive as adjectives.

Noun inflections that changed for case as well as number include *man, men, mannes, manne, mennes.* The silent *e* on many of our words is a remnant of inflectional endings that ceased to be pronounced.

Lesson 21 of Grade 7 also gives some detail on Old English inflections.

Exercise 5: Think of synonyms for the given meanings. Look for words that have at least some of the same letters.

Answer Key—Part D (7 points)

1. English was the informal language of the common people, and it was *not restrained by formal and official use.*
2. Many *inflections were dropped.*
3. The Great Vowel Shift was a gradual *change in the pronunciation of long vowels.*
4. *Some letters were no longer sounded,* but they were still written.
5. a. lean
   b. ring
   c. where

A. UNEARTHING THE ROOTS

LESSON 5

ROOT	MEANING	EXAMPLE
Latin *ple*	= fill	plenty
Latin *verb*	= word	verbal
Greek *logos*	= word, study	dialogue

NEW WORDS

abstain
acquaintance
ample
amusement
apologize
bookkeeping
cease
chemical
controlling
countenance
Decalogue
extinct
geology
livelier
logical
luncheon
plenteous
preceding
vacuum
verbal

REVIEW WORDS

biology
compass
exorbitant
sacrilege
theology

1. Write the lesson roots, and beside each one write the spelling words containing that root. You should have nine words in all.
2. One NEW WORD with the *ple* root is related to the Latin word *plus,* which means "more." Write the NEW WORD. One meaning of the word could be "enough and ____."
3. We believe in the (plenary, plethoric) inspiration of the Bible because it is *fully* inspired by God.
4. The garden yielded a (fill) * harvest.
5. The words *complement* and *compliment* both contain the *ple* root with the thought of filling or completing. Complete each sentence with *complement* or *compliment.* The one spelled with *e* means a completing part. The one spelled with *i* is an expression of praise.
   a. That Scripture motto is a ____ to your room.
   b. The visitor's ____ renewed the students' enthusiasm.
   c. *Brilliant* is a ____ in the following sentence structure: The flowers are brilliant.
   d. Father gave Roy a ____ on the well-mowed lawn.
6. This map booklet is a <u>sup</u> to fill out our geography course.
7. Which lesson root can stand alone as a word? This word is an example of specialization. It formerly meant any word. Now it means ____.
8. Communication in (graphic, verbal) form is done by speaking.
9. If someone is <u>ose</u>, he uses too many words.
10. Write the NEW WORD with the *logos* root, which means "according to reason."
11. Which NEW WORD might be defined as "ten words"?
12. Write the three spelling words that refer to fields of study.

Lesson 5

(Total points: 88)

Notes on Part A

Selected Words With Lesson Roots

L *ple:* **ample, plenteous,** complement, completely, compliment (26), plethoric, supplement (31)

L *verb:* **verbal,** adverb, verb, verbalize, verbatim, verbose

Gk. *logos:* **apologize, biology, Decalogue, geology, logical, theology,** analogy,

Exercise 1: Find words with the *logos* root by looking for *log.*

Exercise 3: In the Mennonite Confession of Faith, Article 1 begins, "We believe in the plenary and verbal inspiration of the Bible as the Word of God." *Plethoric* also comes from the *ple* root, meaning "excessive in amount or style."

Exercises 4, 6, and 9: A word in parentheses on a blank is the root meaning of the answer. Plain letters on a blank are part of the answer, given as a clue. One of the Latin or Greek roots should be joined to the given letters as another part of the answer.

Exercise 5: Focus on the *i* and *e* that distinguish the spelling of the two words. *I* like a compli*-ment. E* makes comple*te.*

Exercise 7: The process of specialization is discussed in *Language Lineage* of Lesson 11 in Grade 7 in this series.

Answer Key—Part A (30 points)

1. *ple:* ample, plenteous
   verb: verbal
   logos: apologize, Decalogue, geology, logical, biology, theology

2. ample, more

3. plenary

4. plenteous

5. a. complement
   b. compliment
   c. complement
   d. compliment

6. supplement

7. verb, a word of action (being, ownership...)

8. verbal

9. verbose

10. logical

11. Decalogue

12. geology, biology, theology

Lesson 5 Test Sentences

1. *countenance* Sara's *countenance* was all sunshine. *countenance*
2. *amusement* Her *amusement* tickled her brother. *amusement*
3. *livelier* Soon they had *livelier* antics. *livelier*
4. *vacuum* The noise of the *vacuum* cleaner ended the frolic. *vacuum*
5. *acquaintance* It was special to renew the *acquaintance. acquaintance*
6. *extinct* We walked the rim of the *extinct* volcano. *extinct*
7. *chemical* A *chemical* explosion is dangerous. *chemical*
8. *biology* Planting seeds is a *biology* exercise. *biology*
9. *geology* Many rock samples came to *geology* class. *geology*
10. *bookkeeping* Who will fill the *bookkeeping* job? *bookkeeping*
11. *preceding* Try to condense the *preceding* paragraph. *preceding*
12. *logical* Tell the events in *logical* order. *logical*
13. *ample* We have *ample* time to rewrite the story. *ample*
14. *exorbitant* Joel paid an *exorbitant* price for the cheese. *exorbitant*
15. *luncheon* They wanted it for the *luncheon. luncheon*
16. *cease* Daniel did not *cease* to pray in captivity. *cease*
17. *sacrilege* Did he see the *sacrilege* of the temple vessels? *sacrilege*
18. *Decalogue* Israelites held the *Decalogue* in high esteem. *Decalogue*
19. *theology* Their *theology* came directly from God. *theology*
20. *apologize* It is honorable to *apologize* for your wrongs. *apologize*
21. *verbal* You need more than a *verbal* profession. *verbal*
22. *controlling* Who is *controlling* your thought life? *controlling*
23. *plenteous* There is *plenteous* grace for victory. *plenteous*
24. *abstain* Let us *abstain* from appearance of evil. *abstain*
25. *compass* Warm fellowship will *compass* the faithful. *compass*

B. AFFIXING AFFIXES

1. The Greek root *logos* in Part A is made into the suffix *-ology,* which means "study." Write words ending with *-ology* to match these definitions.

SUFFIX	MEANING	EXAMPLE
-ology	study or science of	meteorology

   a. Study of the earth*.
   b. Study of living things*.
   c. Study of God*.
   d. Study of animals and animal life: zo .
   e. Study of human society: soci .
   f. Study of the time order of events in history: chron .
   g. Study of the mind: psych .
   h. Study of the physical features of an area in relation to its history: top .
   i. Study of the stars to foretell the future, which is forbidden in the Bible: astr .
   j. Study of birds: ornith .
   k. Study of diseases: path .
   l. Study of the weather: meteor .
   m. Study of types: typ .

2. Write the NEW WORD with a suffix indicating that it is a form of comparison.

3. *Going* is a present participle. Write three NEW WORDS that are present participles.

C. SOUND, STRUCTURE, AND MEANING

1. Write the NEW WORD in which *ch* spells /k/.
2. Write the NEW WORD with /g/ spelled *gue.*
3. Write the NEW WORD that has a double *u.*
4. Write two NEW WORDS that have three vowels in a row.
5. Write the NEW WORD that is compound. Circle each set of double letters in this word.
6. a. Write the NEW WORD with the *ced* root, and also the form without *-ing.*
   b. Write words by attaching the following prefixes to *cede.*
      con-   inter-   re-   se-
   c. Only three English words have /sēd/ spelled *ceed,* and they begin with the prefixes shown below. Write those words.
      ex-   pro-   suc-
7. Write spelling words that are antonyms of these words.
   a. indulge
   b. cheap
   c. unspoken
   d. begin
   e. scanty
   f. following
   g. unreasonable
8. Write a single sentence in which you use *cease* and *extinct.*
9. Use *amusement* and *countenance* in the same sentence.
10. Write the spelling words that have these etymological meanings.
    a. Light snack, from *none* (noon) + *schench* (drink).
    b. To circle with steps, from *com-* (together) + *passus* (step).
    c. To go off track, from *ex-* (out of) + *orbita* (track).
    d. To hold away, from *ab-* (away) + *tenēre* (to hold).
    e. To steal sacred things, from *sacer* (sacred) + *legere* (to pick up).

Notes on Part B

Exercise 3: A participle is a form of a verb that is used as an adjective. It is part verb and part adjective. A present participle ends in -*ing*.

Answer Key—Part B (17 points)

1. a. geology
   b. biology
   c. theology
   d. zoology
   e. sociology
   f. chronology
   g. psychology
   h. topology
   i. astrology
   j. ornithology
   k. pathology
   l. meteorology
   m. typology

2. livelier

3. bookkeeping, controlling, preceding

Notes on Part C

Exercise 5: *Bookkeeping* is the only English word that has three consecutive sets of double letters.

Exercise 6c: These three words can be remembered with a sentence memory device. *Proceeds* must *exceed* cost to *succeed* in business.

Exercise 7: One tip for an exercise of this type is to especially consider the spelling words that have not yet been used in the exercises. All the words should be used in the lesson.

Answer Key—Part C (31 points)

1. chemical

2. Decalogue

3. vacuum

4. acquaintance, plenteous

5. bookkeeping

6. a. preceding, precede
   b. concede, intercede, recede, secede
   c. exceed, proceed, succeed

7. a. abstain
   b. exorbitant
   c. verbal
   d. cease

   e. ample *or* plenteous
   f. preceding
   g. logical

8. (Sample sentence) Day and night will not *cease* until the earth is *extinct*.

9. (Sample sentence) *Amusement* will show on your *countenance*.

10. a. luncheon
    b. compass
    c. exorbitant
    d. abstain
    e. sacrilege

D. LANGUAGE LINEAGE

SEMANTIC STUDY: FUNCTIONAL CHANGE

Semantics is the study of word meanings, and especially of how word meanings develop and change. One of these changes is in the way words are used. A word that originally functioned as a noun may become a verb. One that was at first a verb might become a noun or an adjective. An adjective may become a noun or verb.

Finger is a noun; it names one of the digits on your hand. But when you finger the finger food, the word becomes a verb and an adjective. *Pen* is a noun, yet you can pen a story under a pen name. *Desk* is a noun. Do you desk your books? All it would take is for a prominent writer or speaker to publicly use the word in that sense. If it is noticed and the usage becomes popular, its verb meaning would soon be registered in the dictionary.

Find is a verb. When the action is accomplished and the reward is outstanding, you have indeed made a find (noun). *Rise* is a verb, but you can also build a house on a rise. *Grow* is a verb. Would you say that a tall eighth grader has had a good grow? Functional change could make that logical terminology someday.

Color names are typically adjectives. But association has led to using some color names as nouns. We speak of the white of an egg, a business that is in the red, and a heavenly home beyond the blue. We use a color name as a verb when we black our shoes.

Plastic is an adjective meaning "pliable." It has also come to be the name of a chemically formed substance, including some types that are not pliable. And from that noun it has become an adjective that describes an object made of such a substance, pliable or not.

The following sentences illustrate the many ways in which some words can function.

We used yellow brick to brick the path between the brick houses.

Shall we light the light blue lamp for light at our light supper?

Exercises

1. Name the function of the italicized words with these parts of speech: *n., v., adj.,* or *adv.*
   a. yellow *brick*
   b. *brick* the path
   c. *brick* houses
   d. *light* the lamp
   e. *light* blue lamp
   f. for *light*
   g. *light* supper

2. For each italicized word below, write a sentence in which that word functions as a different part of speech.
   a. You may *package* the cookies by dozens.
   b. Jesus came not to call the *righteous.*
   c. Shawn painted the *block* wall white.

Answer Key—Part D (10 points)

1. a. n.
   b. v.
   c. adj.
   d. v.
   e. adv.
   f. n.
   g. adj.

2. (Sample sentences)
   a. *n.* The *package* was wrapped in a towel. *or*
      adj. They offer a *package* deal for new customers.
   b. *adj.* Gladly support a *righteous* cause.
   c. *v. Block* the hole with steel wool. *or*
      n. We walked around the *block.*

24

LESSON 6

1	2	3	4	5
abhor	abandon	accommodation	advisory	abstain
alloys	bestow	adoration	auditor	acquaintance
bumblebees	celestial	amphibian	beggar	ample
engagement	divinity	anticipation	benign	amusement
exploring	editorial	biography	commentator	apologize
fascinating	enthusiastic	biology	counselor	bookkeeping
infallible	exhausted	cancellation	customary	cease
initiation	guarantee	classification	desirable	chemical
inspiration	icicles	conjunction	dictator	controlling
justified	leisure	elaborate	dormitory	countenance
materially	mutual	fission	evangelist	Decalogue
overreactions	necessity	graduation	hangar	extinct
perished	ridiculous	immortal	laboratory	geology
precaution	ruined	mortgage	malice	livelier
process	suspicion	omission	malicious	logical
reconcile	swamps	petition	malignant	luncheon
recovered	temporal	precipitation	migratory	plenteous
representatives	theology	sympathy	missionaries	preceding
scheduled	underrate	vital	pursue	vacuum
unlikely	wretched	vitamins	summary	verbal

A.   UNEARTHING THE ROOTS

L *div*	= God		L *bene*	= well
Gk. *theo*	= God		Gk. *eu*	= well, good
			L *mal*	= bad
L *vita*	= life		Gk. *caco*	= bad
Gk. *bio*	= life			
L *mort*	= death		L *ple*	= fill
Gk. *patho*	= feeling, suffering		L *verb*	= word
			Gk. *logos*	= word, study

Lesson 6

(Total points: 75)

Lesson 6 Test Sentences

Notes on Parts A and B

Encourage students to review former lessons for help.

1. *precaution* Take special *precaution* with poisons. *precaution*
2. *fascinating* Chording of music is a *fascinating* study. *fascinating*
3. *abhor* Learn to *abhor* pride. *abhor*
4. *initiation* There was a short *initiation* assignment. *initiation*
5. *scheduled* The real work is *scheduled* to begin tomorrow. *scheduled*
6. *reconcile* Can you *reconcile* the checkbook figures? *reconcile*
7. *alloys* Many *alloys* are stronger than iron. *alloys*
8. *infallible* The conscience is not an *infallible* guide. *infallible*
9. *process* We will *process* your order immediately. *process*
10. *justified* Abraham was *justified* by faith. *justified*
11. *bestow* What can you *bestow* on the orphan? *bestow*
12. *guarantee* Do you *guarantee* your products? *guarantee*
13. *abandon* Cover the well if you *abandon* it. *abandon*
14. *underrate* People usually *underrate* the value of prayer. *underrate*
15. *leisure* All his *leisure* time is spent in gardening. *leisure*
16. *mutual* We bought the desk with *mutual* funds. *mutual*
17. *enthusiastic* Sandra is an *enthusiastic* baker. *enthusiastic*
18. *ruined* Grasshoppers *ruined* the crop. *ruined*
19. *ridiculous* This is *ridiculous* weather for sledding. *ridiculous*
20. *divinity* Demons recognized the *divinity* of Jesus. *divinity*
21. *graduation* Regular *graduation* was seen in postage rates. *graduation*
22. *mortgage* His *mortgage* was almost paid. *mortgage*
23. *amphibian* Put a little amphibian in your *terrarium*. *amphibian*
24. *precipitation* Those clouds promise *precipitation*. *precipitation*
25. *accommodation* Your *accommodation* was most helpful. *accommodation*
26. *immortal* We follow an *immortal* guide. *immortal*
27. *cancellation* The lunch *cancellation* was expected. *cancellation*
28. *omission* Do you mind the *omission* of a meal? *omission*
29. *petition* An angry *petition* is not quickly granted. *petition*
30. *vital* The victim's *vital* signs improved slightly. *vital*
31. *summary* John prepared a *summary* of his sales. *summary*
32. *pursue* It is vain to *pursue* happiness. *pursue*
33. *desirable* Contentment is a more *desirable* goal. *desirable*
34. *evangelist* The busy *evangelist* traveled widely. *evangelist*
35. *auditor* An *auditor* needs complete records. *auditor*
36. *malice* "In *malice* be ye children" (1 Corinthians 14:20). *malice*
37. *counselor* Choose a *counselor* who fears God. *counselor*
48. *benign* Our family cow is a *benign* creature. *benign*
39. *laboratory* Please clean the *laboratory* equipment. *laboratory*
40. *migratory* Can geese lose the *migratory* impulse? *migratory*
41. *abstain* You must *abstain* consistently. *abstain*
42. *countenance* Father's *countenance* told us his answer. *countenance*
43. *apologize* Be quick to *apologize* for an offense. *apologize*
44. *logical* The *logical* course is to repair the pump. *logical*
45. *luncheon* We held the *luncheon* on the lawn. *luncheon*
46. *extinct* Why is the passenger pigeon *extinct*? *extinct*
47. *amusement* A ripple of *amusement* passed over the class. *amusement*
48. *acquaintance* My *acquaintance* with him was brief. *acquaintance*
49. *cease* When did they *cease* minting one-dollar coins? *cease*
50. *vacuum* Can sound travel through a *vacuum*? *vacuum*

1. Choose words from Lesson 2 for these exercises.
   a. *en-* (in) + (God) = ____
   b. (God) + (study) = ____
   c. (God) + *-ity* = ____
2. Write words from Lesson 3 to match these etymologies.
   a. *sun* (together) + (feeling) = ____
   b. (life) + (study) = ____
   c. (life) + *graphia* (write) = ____
   d. *in-* (not) + (death) = ____
   e. (death) + *gage* (pledge) = ____
   f. (life) + *-al* = ____
3. Write the word that contains the prefix *amphi-* (on both sides) and the Greek root for *life.*
4. Write a plural word with a root meaning "life," which names some organic compounds.
5. Choose words from Lesson 4 for these exercises.
   a. (good) + *angelos* (messenger) = ____
   b. (bad) + *-ice* = ____
6. Write the Lesson 4 REVIEW WORDS that match these etymologies.
   a. (well) + *facere* (to do) = ____
   b. (well) + *dīcere* (to say) = ____
7. Answer with spelling words having the *bene* or *mal* root.
   a. Larry thanks his ____ uncle for supporting him at the orphanage.
   b. Balaam's love of money had a ____ effect on him.
   c. If you speak ____ words, you are revealing a bad attitude toward others.
8. Choose words from Lesson 5 for these exercises.
   a. *am-* + (fill) = ____
   b. *deka* (ten) + (word) = ____
9. Write words from Lesson 5 for these definitions.
   a. Speak words in regret or defense.
   b. Pertaining to sound, sensible words.
   c. Pertaining to spoken words.
10. Which two words in Lesson 5 are synonyms?

B. AFFIXING AFFIXES

1. Write words from Lesson 1 for these answers.
   a. Four words with an inflectional suffix that changes number.
   b. Four words with an inflectional suffix that changes tense.
   c. Three words with derivational suffixes that form nouns.
   d. Two words with the same derivational suffix. One forms an adverb, and the other an adjective.
2. a. Write a word from Lesson 2 that contains a suffix meaning "act, state, or quality of."

-ion	act, state, or quality of
-tion, sion	act, state, or quality of
-or, -ory	one who, pertaining to
-ar, ary	one who, pertaining to
-ology	study or science of

   b. Is the suffix in this word derivational or inflectional?
3. From the following words, choose the one in which *-ion* is *not* a suffix.
   action   corporation   onion
4. From Lesson 3, write the four *-ation* words derived from verbs ending with *-ate.*

Answer Key—Part A (25 points)

1. a. enthusiastic
   b. theology
   c. divinity

2. a. sympathy
   b. biology
   c. biography
   d. immortal
   e. mortgage
   f. vital

3. amphibian

4. vitamins

5. a. evangelist
   b. malice

6. a. beneficial
   b. benediction

7. a. benign
   b. malignant
   c. malicious

8. a. ample
   b. Decalogue

9. a. apologize
   b. logical
   c. verbal

10. ample, plenteous

Answer Key—Part B (40 points)

1. a. alloys, bumblebees, overreactions, representatives
   b. justified, perished, recovered, scheduled
   c. engagement, initiation, inspiration (Accept *overreactions.*)
   d. materially, unlikely

2. a. suspicion
   b. derivational

3. onion

4. accommodation, anticipation, graduation, precipitation

5. Write the Lesson 3 words that contain these adjustments.
   a. The final consonant of the root word was doubled before adding the suffix.
   b. The final consonant of the root word was changed to another letter before adding the suffix.
   c. Final *y* was changed to *i* before adding the suffix.

6. Write five words from Lesson 4 that have a suffix meaning "one who."
7. Write six words from Lesson 4 that have a suffix that means "pertaining to."
8. From any of the lists, write three words that have the Greek suffix for study. Also write the etymological meaning for each one.

D. LANGUAGE LINEAGE

REVIEW

1. a. What was the basis for the King James translation of the Bible?

   b. Who produced the King James translation?

2. a. When did Europeans begin to print with movable type?

   b. How did the printing press help to standardize English spelling?

3. Why did the form of English spoken in London become the general English standard?

4. What was the "Great Vowel Shift"?

5. Why was it easy for the English language to change during the Middle Ages?

6. How has changing pronunciation made spelling more complicated?

7. Write a sentence using a color word as a noun. Use the same word as an adjective.

5. a. cancellation
   b. omission
   c. classification

6. auditor, beggar, commentator, counselor, dictator

7. advisory, customary, dormitory, laboratory, migratory, summary

8. theology—God study
   biology—life study
   geology—earth study

Answer Key—Part D (10 points)

1. a. The King James Version was translated from the original *Hebrew and Greek* with other translations compared.
   b. A team of *about 50 scholars* wrote the translation at the direction of King James I.

2. a. Europeans began to print with moveable type in the *1450s*.
   b. Spelling became somewhat standardized because the printing press made so *many identical copies* that people had more consistent examples to follow.

3. Because London was the *printing center* of England, the English of that area appeared in print.

4. The "Great Vowel Shift" was a gradual *change in pronunciation of long vowel sounds* during the Middle English period.

5. English in the Middle Ages was an informal language of the common people, so it was *not restrained by formal, official use.*

6. Written *spellings stayed the same* when some pronunciations changed, so some words have letters for sounds we do not say.

7. (Sample sentences—any color.)
   n. The meeting was held on the town *green.*
   adj. Holly made a pie with *green* tomatoes.

LESSON 7

A. UNEARTHING THE ROOTS

ROOT	MEANING	EXAMPLE
Latin *bi*	= two, twice	biennial
Latin *cent*	= hundred(th)	century
Latin *oct*	= eight	octet
Latin *quart*	= fourth	quarter
Latin *uni*	= one	unity

NEW WORDS

abolish
abstinence
adolescence
binoculars
canvass
carton
cylinder
desirous
devotional
exhaust
grippe
instinct
obstacle
octagon
peril
procedure
sketch
substantial
support
uniform

REVIEW WORDS

biennial
centipede
deduct
quartet
unique

1. Write the lesson roots in the order of numerical value.
2. A bicuspid is so named because it has ____ cusps (points).
3. Glasses with <u>bi</u> lenses help one's eyes to focus on things at two distances (nearby and farther away).
4. Write spelling words for these etymological meanings.
   a. two eyes   c. four (people or things)
   b. two years
5. Write the name of a two-wheeled vehicle. Its etymology combines the Latin root for *two* with the Greek root for *wheel.*
6. Write words that have these meanings.
   a. one sound: <u>son</u>   d. one kind*
   b. one-sided: <u>lateral</u>   e. one form*
   c. one wheel: <u>cycle</u>
7. One fourth of a gallon is a ____.
8. A (biannual, quarterly) newsletter is published every three months or ____ times a year.
9. The United States was founded in 1776, and in 1976 its (centennial, bicentennial) was celebrated.
10. The Latin root for *quartet* passed through what other language before it became an English word?
11. *Quater* is a root similar to *quart* and means "four times."
    a. Which word in Acts 12:4 names a group of four soldiers?
    b. How many soldiers guarded Peter?
12. Matthew 8:5 tells about an officer who came to Jesus. How many soldiers were under his command?
13. A (centipede, crustacean, millipede) is a creature that is supposed to have one hundred feet.
14. An octogenarian is a person who has lived (sixty, seventy, eighty) years.
15. a. A figure having eight sides is an ____*.
    b. Write the etymology for this word.
    c. What language is the *oktō* root from?
16. Write the English word for this Greek etymology: *oktō + pous.* Also write the meaning of *oktō* and *pous.*

Lesson 7

(Total points: 86)

Notes on Part A

Selected Words With Lesson Roots

L *bi:* **biennial, binoculars,** ambidextrous, bicentennial, biceps, bicuspid, bicycle, bifocals, billion, biped

Ambidextrous is derived from Latin roots meaning "on both sides right-handed."

L *cent:* **centipede,** cent, centavo, centennial, centigrade, century

L *oct:* **octagon,** octane, octave, octet, October, octogenarian, octopus

Octane is a hydrocarbon with the formula C_8H_{18}.

L *quart:* **quartet,** quart, quarterly.   The Latin root *quat/quad* means "four." Derivatives are *quadrilateral, quadriplegic, quadruplet, quaternion.*

L *uni:* **uniform, unique,** triune, unanimous (23), unicycle, unilateral, union, unison, unit, unity, universe, university (31)

Exercise 5: *Bicycle* is a hybrid. The Latin number *bi* is joined with the Greek root *kuklos.* Part B of this lesson defines hybrids.

Exercise 15: Teach the students that "Write the etymology" means to copy everything in the brackets.

Exercise 16: The Latin root *oct* and the Greek root *okt* both mean "eight." In this exercise the word is a Greek combination. The Latin root for "foot" is *ped.*

Answer Key—Part A (32 points)

1. *uni, bi, quart, oct, cent* (Accept *quart* in first position, as a fraction of one.)

2. two

3. bifocal

4. a. binoculars   c. quartet
   b. biennial

5. bicycle

6. a. unison   d. unique
   b. unilateral   e. uniform
   c. unicycle

7. quart

8. quarterly, four

9. bicentennial

10. Italian

11. a. quaternion(s) b. sixteen

12. one hundred

13. centipede

14. eighty

15. a. octagon
    b. [< Gk. *oktā* eight + *gōnia* angle]
    c. Greek

16. octopus, eight, foot

Lesson 7 Test Sentences

1. *centipede* A long *centipede* scurried into the crack. *centipede*
2. *binoculars* Morris followed the eagle with *binoculars.* *binoculars*
3. *procedure* He dreamed of a *procedure* to capture the bird. *procedure*
4. *obstacle* An opportunity may look like an *obstacle.* *obstacle*
5. *carton* Each *carton* holds twelve dozen pencils. *carton*
6. *abolish* Abraham Lincoln meant to *abolish* slavery. *abolish*
7. *instinct* A robin's *instinct* tells it when to fly south. *instinct*
8. *sketch* This *sketch* shows the migratory pattern. *sketch*
9. *peril* Paul was in *peril* on the sea. *peril*
10. *abstinence* After days of *abstinence,* God spoke to Paul. *abstinence*
11. *substantial* There was *substantial* evidence of God's care. *substantial*
12. *canvass* Did they *canvass* the island for converts? *canvass*
13. *cylinder* A silo is a *cylinder.* *cylinder*
14. *biennial* Nobody wanted to miss the *biennial* reunion. *biennial*
15. *grippe* Grandmother had the *grippe.* *grippe*
16. *quartet* A *quartet* of boys sang for her. *quartet*
17. *devotional* Father led a *devotional* from Psalm 23. *devotional*
18. *desirous* We are *desirous* to walk with the Shepherd. *desirous*
19. *support* Thank God for the *support* of friends. *support*
20. *exhaust* We shall never *exhaust* God's mercies. *exhaust*
21. *adolescence* Skills learned in *adolescence* stick with you. *adolescence*
22. *deduct* You may *deduct* ten dollars from the bill. *deduct*
23. *unique* This quilt has a *unique* design. *unique*
24. *octagon* The darkest patches form an *octagon.* *octagon*
25. *uniform* All the curtains have a *uniform* pattern. *uniform*

28   *Lesson 7*

B.   AFFIXING AFFIXES

Suffixes are added to the end of root words to make inflected or derived forms. Prefixes are added to the beginning of words to modify meanings. A prefix can change a meaning to its opposite, as in *satisfied—dissatisfied;* or it can modify a meaning in some other way, as in *read—reread.* Sometimes the Latin roots for numbers are used as prefixes before English words. A word formed with elements from different languages is called a *hybrid.*

1. Form hybrids by using the Latin root for *two* as a prefix with these English words. Write the meaning of each hybrid.
   a. weekly
   b. metal
   c. plane
   d. valve

> ### Numerical Prefixes

2. Write three NEW WORDS with derivational suffixes that form adjectives. Also write the correct spelling of each word without those suffixes.

3. a.   Write the NEW WORD derived from *proceed.*
   b. What part of speech is formed by adding the suffix?
   c. These related words illustrate two spellings of the Latin root that is pronounced /sēd/. What are the two spellings?

4. Write two NEW WORDS that have the same noun-forming suffix.

C.   SOUND, STRUCTURE, AND MEANING

1. Write the NEW WORD in which final /ch/ after a short vowel is spelled *tch.*

2. Write two NEW WORDS in which *ti* spells /sh/.

3. Write the NEW WORD derived from *abstain.* How is the vowel changed in the second syllable?

4. Write spelling words for these etymologies.
   a. *in-* + *stinguere* (to prick)
   b. *kulindein* (to roll)
   c. *charta* (sheet of papyrus)
   d. *dē-* + *dūcere* (to lead)

5. Write the NEW WORDS that are antonyms of these words.
   a. promote
   b. safety
   c. replenish
   d. hinder
   e. benefit

6. a.   Write the NEW WORD that is a homonym of *grip,* and write its definition.
   b. Write the etymological definition, and explain how it fits the word.

7. Write the same spelling word or its homonym for each of these blanks.
   a. _____ is a coarse, heavy fabric woven of cotton, hemp, or flax.
   b. _____ is a thorough search or solicitation.
   c. Every year we _____ the hillside for mushrooms.
   d. His _____ of the want ads gave him five job possibilities to check.
   e. Let's frame the _____ that has a waterfall.
   f. Each family will _____ five city blocks with Bible school invitations.
   g. Here is _____ to patch the tent.
   h. They had to _____ the cornfield to find the lost child.

8. Find *quartet* in the Speller Dictionary. Write the alternate spelling of this word.

Notes on Part B

Exercise 3: This exercise can be a reminder of the trio of -*ceed* words: *proceed, exceed, succeed.* (See Lesson 5, "Notes on Part C," exercise 6.) The derivative—*procedure*—gives the illusion that a final *e* was dropped to add the suffix.

Answer Key—Part B (20 points)

1. a. biweekly—twice a week or once in two weeks
    b. bimetal—made of two kinds of metal
    c. biplane—an airplane with two sets of wings, one above the other
    d. bivalve—a mollusk with a shell that has two parts

2. desirous, desire
    devotional, devotion
    substantial, substance

3. a. procedure
    b. noun
    c. *ceed, cede*

4. abstinence, adolescence

Notes on Part C

Exercise 3: The spelling and pronunciation change from *abstain* to *abstinance* is similar to the change in *maintain—maintenance* and in *retain—retention.*

Answer Key—Part C (27 points)

1. sketch

2. devotional, substantial

3. abstinence, *ai* is changed to *i.*

4. a. instinct
    b. cylinder
    c. carton
    d. deduct

5. a. abolish
    b. peril
    c. exhaust
    d. support
    e. obstacle

6. a. grippe, a kind of influenza
    b. to seize
        Someone with grippe is seized by sickness.

7. a. Canvas
    b. Canvass
    c. canvass
    d. canvass
    e. canvas
    f. canvass
    g. canvas
    h. canvass

8. quartette

D. LANGUAGE LINEAGE

ENGLISH AND THE RENAISSANCE

The word *renaissance* comes from a Latin word that means "rebirth." After the Roman Empire fell in A.D. 476, the advances of the Greek and Roman civilizations were largely forgotten. People in Europe followed an unchanging and rather primitive pattern of life for hundreds of years. Then from the 1300s through the 1500s, there came a general awakening (rebirth) of education, inventions, and improvements in living and working. This period in history is called the Renaissance.

Because the printing press made literature so accessible, many common people learned to read and write. In England, the official language of court and society was English by this time, and Englishmen prided themselves in being able to express lofty ideas in their own language. The works of many ancient historians and philosophers, as well as the Bible, were translated into English. Such translations stimulated the vocabulary of Early Modern English, helping it to meet the growing needs of expression.

The Renaissance brought many new demands on the English vocabulary. New tools and products appeared. Transportation and communication increased contact with other cultures. Exploration of newly discovered lands in America expanded knowledge. New words were needed for the new ideas and products of the age.

To meet many of the new needs, words were adopted from other languages. New words also came from writers of this period. Sometimes these writers adapted older words of the language, sometimes they made dialectal words common, and sometimes they invented words.

The English language gained thousands of words during this time. Some outstanding writers have been called "makers of English" because of their effectiveness in adding new words to the language. John Skelton, a satire-writing clergyman, was probably the greatest contributor of new words. Sir Thomas Elyot made a deliberate effort to give English the capacity to serve all branches of learning. His works included treatises on education and medicine. Sir Thomas More was another writer noted for expanding English in his formal writing. A few of the words contributed by these three men are listed below.

Skelton: advantage, celebrate, economy, miserable, tolerate
Elyot: animate, encyclopedia, exhaust, irritate, modesty
More: exaggerate, monopoly, obstruction, paradox, utopia

Exercises

1. What was "reborn" in the Renaissance?
2. Why were new words needed during the Renaissance?
3. What were two means of adding words to the English language?
4. Name three men who were "makers of English."

Notes on Part D

The literature of the educated had long been locked in the classical languages of Latin and Greek. The Renaissance did not see the multitudes studying these languages, but a move to translate the old works into common languages.

It was a controversial thing to make theology, medicine, and philosophy available to the common public. Richard Mulcaster, headmaster of the Merchant Taylors' School, was a strong advocate of scholarly English. He wrote:

> "Is it not in dede a mervellous bondage, to becom servants to one tung for learning sake, the most of our time, with losse of most time, whereas we maie have the verie same treasur in our own tung, with the gain of most time?"

Not only was it a matter of the attitude toward the language, but it was a challenge for English vocabulary to have the capacity of expression for the lofty and abstract ideas of literature. To meet this challenge, scholars brought many words into English from Latin and other languages, as well as coining new words. This was also protested by some linguists of the time. John Cheke declared:

> "Our own tung shold be written cleane and pure, unmixt and unmangeled with borowing of other tunges, wherin if we take not heed by tijm, ever borowing and never payeng, she shall be fain to keep her house as bankrupt."

But Sir Thomas Elyot claimed in his writing that "there was no terme new made by me of a latine or frenche worde, but it is there declared so playnly by one mene or other to a diligent reder that no sentence is therby made derke or harde to be understande."

Functional change had its part in the expansion of English. Among the vocabulary credited to John Skelton is the use of *ram* and *people* as verbs, and *native* as an adjective.

Answer Key—Part D (7 points)

1. *Education, inventions,* and *improved methods* of labor and living were reborn in the Renaissance.
2. New words were needed because there were *new ideas and products* to name.
3. New words were brought to English from *other languages or made by writers.* (Accept details of how the writers made words.)
4. *John Skelton, Sir Thomas Elyot,* and *Sir Thomas More* were called "makers of English."

LESSON 8

NEW WORDS

aeronautics
Antarctic
anticipating
antiseptic
arguing
breadth
compromise
conveniently
duplex
elapsed
glacier
heresy
kimono
mathematics
peculiar
Pentateuch
protein
recognize
statistics
trivial

REVIEW WORDS

Decalogue
decimal
dual
enormous
triplet

A.   UNEARTHING THE ROOTS

ROOT	MEANING	EXAMPLE
Latin *du*	= two	duplicate
Latin *tri*	= three	tricycle
Greek *tetra*	= four	tetrarch
Greek *penta*	= five	pentagon
Greek *deca*	= ten	decade

1. List the lesson roots, and beside each one write the spelling word or words derived from it. (One root has no spelling word.)
2. We lived with Grandfather and Grandmother in a du__*.
3. A du__ of little girls sang "Jesus Loves Me."
4. This product has a du__* purpose. It fertilizes the soil and helps to keep it loose.
5. Write the names of three geometric figures by combining lesson roots with *angle* or *gon* (a Greek root that means "angle").
6. Complete the following series.
      twin, _____*, quadruplet, quintuplet, sextuplet
7. Write the spelling word that is a combination of *via* (road) and the root that means "three."
8. You are probably acquainted with bifocal lenses. To focus on things at *three* distances, some people wear glasses with tri__ lenses.
9. Some Roman provinces were divided into four parts, with a _____ ruling over each part. (See Luke 3:1.)
10. The word *tetrapod* refers to a class of animals having (two, three, four) limbs.
11. Moses wrote the five books of the _____*.
12. A variant spelling of the Greek root *penta* is *pente.* Use this spelling to write the name of a Jewish feast held fifty days after the Passover.
13. A number system based upon ten is a _____* system.
14. Write a spelling word with the etymological meaning "ten words."
15. The words *pentathlon* and *decathlon* name athletic contests. Which of the two would be more extensive?
16. Use the proper nouns in the spelling list for this sentence: The _____ can be found in the _____.

Lesson 8

(Total points: 84)

Notes on Part A

Selected Words With Lesson Roots

L *du:* **dual, duplex,** duplicate

L *tri:* **triplet, trivial,** triangle, tricycle, trifocal, trigonometry, trilingual, trillion, trinity, trio, triple, tripod, trivet

Trigonometry is literally "triangle measure."

Tripod and *trivet* have very close origins, but they are not quite doublets. *Tripod* comes from Greek [*tri* three + *pous* foot]; *trivet* from Latin [*tri* three + *ped* foot].

Gk. *tetra:* tetra, tetrachloride, tetrarch

The name *tetra* for a class of fish was derived from *Tetragonopterus* which literally translates to "four-cornered wing."

Gk. *penta:* **Pentateuch,** pentagon, pentathlon, Pentecost

Gk. *deca:* **Decalogue, decimal,** decade, decathlon, December, decimate, decimeter, decameter (*or* dekameter)

Exercise 10: *Tetrapod* has a Greek source [*tetra* four + *pous* foot]. A quadruped is the same thing, named with Latin roots [*quad* four + *ped* foot].

Answer Key—Part A (30 points)

1. *du:* duplex, dual
   tri: trivial, triplet
   tetra
   penta: Pentateuch
   deca: Decalogue, decimal
2. duplex
3. duet
4. dual
5. (any three) triangle, trigon, tetragon, pentagon, decagon
6. triplet
7. trivial
8. trifocal
9. tetrarch
10. four
11. Pentateuch
12. Pentecost
13. decimal
14. Decalogue
15. decathlon
16. Decalogue, Pentateuch

Lesson 8 Test Sentences

1. *Pentateuch* Moses wrote the *Pentateuch. Pentateuch*
2. *Decalogue* The *Decalogue* is in the book of Exodus. *Decalogue*
3. *elapsed* Forty years *elapsed* in the wilderness. *elapsed*
4. *peculiar* God formed a nation of *peculiar* people. *peculiar*
5. *breadth* They filled the length and *breadth* of Canaan. *breadth*
6. *compromise* Joshua made a *compromise* with Gibeon. *compromise*
7. *anticipating* All the tribes were *anticipating* conquest. *anticipating*
8. *arguing* God is not pleased when we are *arguing. arguing*
9. *triplet* This song has a *triplet* in the first score. *triplet*
10. *mathematics* The order in *mathematics* is very consistent. *mathematics*
11. *trivial* A *trivial* mistake can be crucial. *trivial*
12. *decimal* Do you remember your *decimal* points? *decimal*
13. *enormous* One small error caused *enormous* loss. *enormous*
14. *antiseptic* Mother poured *antiseptic* on the wound. *antiseptic*
15. *Antarctic* Does the *Antarctic* Circle cross any land? *Antarctic*
16. *glacier* A *glacier* moves very slowly. *glacier*
17. *protein* That tan sponge is a skeleton of *protein. protein*
18. *kimono* A flowing *kimono* dominated the Japanese exhibit. *kimono*
19. *recognize* God expects us to *recognize* truth and error. *recognize*
20. *heresy* We must be alert to avoid *heresy. heresy*
21. *dual* Emily travels freely with a *dual* citizenship. *dual*
22. *conveniently* She can *conveniently* cross the border. *conveniently*
23. *aeronautics* Each pilot took a course in *aeronautics. aeronautics*
24. *duplex* Our neighbors moved to a *duplex* in town. *duplex*
25. *statistics* Copy your *statistics* carefully. *statistics*

B. AFFIXING AFFIXES

1. Write words with the Greek prefix *anti-* to match these definitions.
   a. The area opposite the region of the North Pole*.
   b. A substance that fights germs*.
   c. A liquid that prevents freezing in an engine.
   d. A strong feeling (*-pathy*) against something.
   e. An enemy of Christ.
   f. Another word for *counterclockwise*.

2. Do not confuse *anti-* with the Latin prefix *ante-*, which means "before." Use the prefix *ante-* to write words for these sentences.
   a. The noun that "goes before" a pronoun is its ____.
   b. The ____ of a church building is a room that you enter before going into the main auditorium.
   c. A bird's wings are fastened to the _ior part of its body.
   d. A.M. means morning because the letters

PREFIX	MEANING	EXAMPLE
anti-	against or contrary to	antifreeze

stand for ____ *meridiem*, Latin words meaning "before noon".

3. Write the NEW WORD that appears to have the Greek prefix *anti-* but actually has the Latin prefix *ante-*. (It means "looking forward to.")

4. Form hybrids by using the Latin root for "three" as a prefix with these English words. Write the meaning of each hybrid.
   a. state
   b. color
   c. syllable

5. Write three NEW WORDS that look like plural forms, but are usually singular names for branches of study.

6. Write a NEW WORD with a derivational suffix that changes an adjective to an adverb.

C. SOUND, STRUCTURE, AND MEANING

1. Write the NEW WORDS that have these phonetic details.
   a. *ci* spells /sh/
   b. *ein* spells /ēn/ or /ē in/
   c. *ea* spells /e/
   d. *ch* spells /k/

2. Write the NEW WORD whose etymology has the idea of "air sailor." Underline the Greek spelling of *air* in this word.

3. Write the NEW WORD that has the etymological meaning "to promise together."

4. Write eight spelling words that are accented on the second syllable.

5. a. What part of speech is *trivial?*
   b. Remove the last letter to spell a plural noun meaning "unimportant details."

6. a. Write two NEW WORDS in which final *e* was dropped before *-ing* was added.
   b. Write the root word of each one.

7. a. Write the NEW WORD that means "unorthodox belief."
   b. Write the plural form of this word.

8. a. Write the NEW WORD that means "to know and remember upon seeing again."
   b. Write a doublet of this word, and give its definition.

9. a. Copy the two pronunciations of *kimono.*
   b. What language is the source of this word?

10. Write the alternate spelling of Decalogue.

Answer Key—Part B (21 points)

1. a. Antarctic
    b. antiseptic
    c. antifreeze
    d. antipathy
    e. antichrist
    f. anticlockwise

2. a. antecedent
    b. anteroom
    c. anterior
    d. *ante*

3. anticipating

4. a. tristate—of three states
    b. tricolor—having three colors
    c. trisyllable—a word with three syllables

5. aeronautics, mathematics, statistics

6. conveniently

Answer Key—Part C (29 points)

1. a. glacier
    b. protein
    c. breadth
    d. Pentateuch

2. <u>ae</u>ronautics

3. compromise

4. Antarctic, anticipating, conveniently, elapsed, kimono, peculiar, statistics, enormous

5. a. adjective
    b. trivia

6. a. anticipating, arguing
    b. anticipate, argue

7. a. heresy
    b. heresies

8. a. recognize
    b. reconnoiter—to examine on ahead

9. a. (kə mō′ nə) (kə mō′ nō)
    b. Japanese

10. Decalog

D.   LANGUAGE LINEAGE

ENGLISH AND THE REFORMATION

The Renaissance was a general awakening to literature and art. One aspect of the Renaissance was also a religious awakening. Certain priests began studying the Scriptures seriously, and they challenged the corruption of the formal church system. "Should we not be living and teaching according to the Word of God?" they asked. Efforts to reform the apostate church led to the start of Protestant churches. This phase of the Renaissance is called the Reformation.

In the 1530s, King Henry VIII steered England into Protestantism. Because of a personal dispute with the pope, he renounced Catholicism and established the Church of England with himself as the head. Though his motive was political, this action opened the way for religious reform in his country. That was the time in which translation of the Scriptures into English was legalized and became prosperous.

Effects of the Reformation were not confined to officials of the church and government. No longer were the Scriptures in the exclusive possession of the pope and priests. Some had leaked into the English language in Wycliffe's time 150 years earlier, and now the printing press released a flood that spread over the land. Even the plowboy could study God's Word for himself.

Spiritual hunger was a tremendous incentive to literacy. Because the Bible was available, people learned to read. After 1611, the King James Version became widely accepted as the best English translation ever produced. Its universal reading helped to guide Englishmen into a common, familiar standard for their language.

Literacy in turn accelerated the Renaissance. Because people could read, they had access to an ever-widening range of knowledge. Great ideas could travel far and fast. The momentum of the Renaissance continued as education and progress spread among the common people.

Exercises

1. How is the Reformation related to the Renaissance?
2. What move triggered the Reformation in England?
3. What motivated many people to learn to read?
4. What happened because people could read?

Notes on Part D

Martin Luther in Germany and Ulrich Zwingli in Switzerland were priests who studied the Scriptures and worked for reformation of the Roman Catholic Church, to bring it back to a Biblical doctrine and practice.

It was not for reasons of Scriptural purity that King Henry VIII of England renounced Catholicism. He wanted to end his marriage to Catherine of Aragon so that he could marry another woman, who would hopefully provide him with a male heir. The pope refused his case, and King Henry proceeded to get his own way by changing the church system of England.

God uses the moves of kings to work out His purposes. Among the English populace were persecuted Lollards since the time of Wycliffe and his poor priests. Many of the common people were eager to know spiritual truth, and the Reformation put the Bible into their hands.

A daughter of King Henry's rejected first wife became the queen called Bloody Mary. She married King Philip of Spain and reinstated Catholicism in England, executing many Protestant officials. Mary was succeeded by Elizabeth, daughter of King Henry VIII's second wife, Anne Boleyn. Queen Elizabeth reverted to Protestantism. During Elizabeth's reign, the Spanish Armada was defeated by the small English navy and by God's control of the weather. England now became a major world power, and the English language assumed greater significance.

Answer Key—Part D (4 points)

1. The Reformation was the religious awakening that was *part of* the Renaissance.
2. *King Henry VIII renounced Catholicism,* and that started the Reformation in England.
3. People learned to read so that they could *read the Bible.*
4. Because they could read, people *gained knowledge* in many different areas.

LESSON 9

A. UNEARTHING THE ROOTS

ROOT	MEANING	EXAMPLE
Latin *magn*	= great	magnificent
Greek *macro*	= large	macron
Latin *mini*	= small	minimum
Greek *micro*	= small	microscope
Latin *quant*	= how great	quantity
Latin *qual*	= what sort	qualify

NEW WORDS

access
asphalt
atheist
attorney
disqualify
immense
magnificence
magnify
maximum
microfilm
microphone
miniature
minister
quantity
security
subtle
symbol
sympathetic
symptom
synthetic

REVIEW WORDS

quality
sympathy
synagogue
transferred
vaccine

1. Complete the acrostic below with words that have lesson roots for *great* or *small*. Choose from the following list for answers that are not spelling words.

   magnitude Magna Carta magnate minimal microwave

   a. To enlarge the real size.*
   b. The great charter that guaranteed liberties to the people of England.
   c. A person of great power or importance.
   d. Splendor; grandeur.*
   e. Greatness of size, importance, or brightness.
   f. A servant.*
   g. A device that converts sound into an electric current.*
   h. An electromagnetic wave that produces heat.
   i. Very small in amount or degree.
   j. A greatly reduced photographic copy.*

```
              a. - - G - - - -
      b. - - - - - - R - -
        c. - - - - - - E
                  d. - A - - - - - - - - - -
        e. - - - - - T - - -
          f. - - - - S - - -
                g. M - - - - - - - -
      h. - - - - - - A - -
      i. - - - - - - L -
    j. - - - - - - - L -
```

2. Which NEW WORD has another form of the *magn* root?
3. The root *mini* has been combined with a number of English words to form hybrids like *minivan*. Write another modern hybrid that contains *mini*.
4. Write a word that means "of less importance, smaller." It can also mean "under the age of eighteen or twenty-one."
5. Write the two spelling words with the same root meaning "what sort."
6. Isaiah 22:24 mentions vessels of small (how much)*.

Lesson 9

(Total points: 65)

Notes on Part A

Selected Words With Lesson Roots

L *magn:* **magnificence, magnify, maximum,** Magna Carta, magnate, magnitude

Gk. *macro:* macro, macrobiotic, macrograph, macron, macroscopic

Macro is short for *macroinstruction,* a sequence of computer commands linked together. *Macrobiotic* describes something long-lived, as a seed. A *macrograph* is a representation of an object as large as or larger than normal.

L *mini:* **minister,** diminish, minimal, minimize, minimum, minor, minority

Mini, as we use it for something miniature, fits well with the meaning of the Latin root *mini,* but it is actually a back-formation. *Miniature* comes from *miniāre*—to color with red lead (*minium*), as was done to illustrate handwritten manuscripts. Objects drawn in such illumination were very small-scale drawings.

Gk. *micro:* **microfilm, microphone,** microbe, micrometer, microscope, microwave

A microwave is a short radio wave useful in radar, communication, and cooking.

L *quant:* **quantity,** quantify, quantum

L *qual:* **disqualify, quality,** qualification

Answer Key—Part A (16 points)

1.
   a. maGnify
   b. Magna CaRta
   c. magnatE
   d. mAgnificence
   e. magniTude

   f. miniSter
   g. Microphone
   h. microwAve
   i. minimaL
   j. microfiLm

2. maximum

3. (Sample answers—only one required) minibike, minibus, minicar, minimart, minitrack

4. minor

5. disqualify, quality

6. quantity

Lesson 9 Test Sentences

1. *synagogue* Paul taught in the *synagogue. synagogue*
2. *magnify* He sought to *magnify* Jesus as the Messiah. *magnify*
3. *minister* He could also *minister* to the sick. *minister*
4. *access* Jesus is our *access* to God. *access*
5. *security* No insurance can grant *security* as Jesus does. *security*
6. *atheist* The *atheist* has a hopeless future. *atheist*
7. *symptom* Prolonged fever is a *symptom* of hepatitis. *symptom*
8. *transferred* A helicopter *transferred* the sick child. *transferred*
9. *asphalt* New *asphalt* was spread on the drive. *asphalt*
10. *disqualify* Bits of chaff *disqualify* the flour. *disqualify*
11. *vaccine* Is there a *vaccine* for malaria? *vaccine*
12. *quantity* The temple contained a large *quantity* of gold. *quantity*
13. *immense* The pillars were *immense. immense*
14. *quality* Everything showed good *quality* workmanship. *quality*
15. *magnificence* The queen was awed by its *magnificence. magnificence*
16. *synthetic* Do shoes made of *synthetic* material last as long? *synthetic*
17. *subtle* Satan devises *subtle* temptations. *subtle*
18. *microphone* Is the *microphone* switched on? *microphone*
19. *attorney* Father asked an *attorney* about the deed. *attorney*
20. *microfilm* He located some *microfilm* documents. *microfilm*
21. *miniature* We pored over the *miniature* pictures. *miniature*
22. *maximum* What is the *maximum* rainfall record for May? *maximum*
23. *symbol* Print the information beside the rainfall *symbol. symbol*
24. *sympathetic* Jesus is *sympathetic* to our human feelings. *sympathetic*
25. *sympathy* We should show the same *sympathy* to others. *sympathy*

68

PUPIL

34   *Lesson 9*

B.   AFFIXING AFFIXES

Sometimes a prefix is affected by the first letter of the root word. The pronunciation of words with initial *m, b,* or *p* begins with closed lips. This affects the pronunciation of a prefix to make it similar to the beginning sound of the word. Thus *syn-* is changed to *sym-* when used with root words that begin with *m, b,* or *p.* That change is called *assimilation.*

PREFIX	MEANING	EXAMPLE
syn-, sym-	together	synthetic
		symptom
a-, an-	without	atheist
		anarchy

1. Write the spelling words with these etymological meanings; the Greek roots are given in italics. If the word is an assimilated form, write *A* after it.
   a. *pathos* (feel together) (2)
   b. *ballein* (throw together)
   c. *tithenai* (put together)
   d. *piptein* (fall or happen together)
   e. *agein* (bring together)
2. When the prefix *a-* comes before a root that begins with a vowel, use *an-*. Write words for the following etymological meanings. Use one spelling word and these three words:
       apathy   anarchy   anonymous

   a. without *arkhos* (a ruler)
   b. without *onoma* (a name)
   c. without *theos* (God)
   d. without *pathos* (feeling)
3. a. Choosing between apple pie and cherry pie has no moral significance. It is an (amoral, antimoral) choice.
   b. People who do not believe in a literal thousand-year reign of Christ at the end of the world hold the (premillennial, amillennial) view.
4. a. Write two NEW WORDS with the suffix *-ity.*
   b. Write the adjective ending with *e* from which one of the words is derived.
5. Write the REVIEW WORD that has an inflectional suffix. Also write its root word.

C.   SOUND, STRUCTURE, AND MEANING

1. Write the spelling words that have these phonetic features.
   a. double *c* spells /ks/ (2)
   b. *ph* spells /f/ (2)
   c. silent *b*
2. Write the NEW WORD that may be pronounced with three syllables or four. The four-syllable pronunciation can help you to spell it correctly.
3. Write four other NEW WORDS that are pronounced with four syllables.
4. Write the plural form of each word.
   a. attorney
   b. quantity
   c. security
   d. sympathy
5. Write spelling words that are synonyms of these words.
   a. huge
   b. small
   c. conveyed
   d. unbeliever
   e. crafty
   f. stability
6. Write a sentence using *attorney* and *sympathetic.*
7. Write the two plural forms of *maximum.*
8. Write the alternate spelling of *synagogue.*

Notes on Part B

The word *assimilation* itself illustrates the principle. In its etymology (*ad-* to + *similis* like) the prefix *ad-* changes to join the /s/ sound of the root. Complete assimilation is a change that matches the sound. Partial assimilation makes connecting sounds more compatible, such as the closed-lips /m/ sound adjacent to *b* or *p*.

Exercise 1: Additional examples

symmetry = together + measure

symphony = together + sound

Answer Key—Part B (20 points)

1. a. sympathetic, sympathy, A
   b. symbol, A
   c. synthetic
   d. symptom, A
   e. synagogue
2. a. anarchy
   b. anonymous
   c. atheist
   d. apathy
3. a. amoral
   b. amillennial
4. a. quantity, security
   b. secure
5. transferred, transfer

Answer Key—Part C (25 points)

1. a. access, vaccine
   b. asphalt, microphone
   c. subtle
2. miniature
3. disqualify, magnificence, security, sympathetic
4. a. attorneys
   b. quantities
   c. securities
   d. sympathies
5. a. immense
   b. miniature
   c. transferred
   d. atheist
   e. subtle
   f. security
6. (Sample sentence) The *attorney* was very *sympathetic* about our loss.
7. maximums, maxima
8. synagog

D. LANGUAGE LINEAGE

WILLIAM TYNDALE'S TRANSLATION

William Tyndale was not the first man to translate the Scriptures into English, but his work was distinctive and influential. Renaissance English with its unregulated spelling and its multitudes of new words presented a challenging task. Tyndale met the challenge, and his work made a great contribution toward refining Early Modern English.

William Tyndale was highly educated and was familiar with eight languages, including Hebrew, Greek, and Latin. But he did not despise the uneducated. He possessed a remarkable skill in communicating with simple but dignified language, and he was consumed with a passion to provide the Scriptures for the common people. Tyndale sacrificed his life to give the Bible to his countrymen.

With his excellent command of scholarly language, William Tyndale composed his translation in a natural, conversational style. He wrote in the spoken vocabulary of the people, avoiding abstract and stilted phraseology. The result was a work of simple grandeur, free from exaggerated or pretentious wordiness. So excellent was his translation that later versions used much of the same wording. A large percentage of the King James Bible is in Tyndale's language.

Because of persecution, Tyndale was compelled to flee from England. He found shelter in Germany, where he continued his translation and had his work published. Completed New Testaments were smuggled into England and distributed in secret. Ironically, at the very dawning of official approval for the Bible in English, Tyndale was arrested. His work on the Old Testament ended when Catholic officials executed him as a heretic near Brussels, Belgium. But his work could not be undone. By skillfully translating the supreme work of literature with such effective words, Tyndale had accomplished as much as any man to promote Bible reading and to refine his maturing language.

Exercises

1. Why was it a special challenge to translate the Bible into English in William Tyndale's day?

2. Why was Tyndale's knowledge of Hebrew, Greek, and Latin especially valuable to him?

3. What made Tyndale's translation so effective?

4. Why did Tyndale not finish translating the Old Testament?

Notes on Part D

Tyndale lived in 1492–1536 just prior to the scenes described in Lesson 8. He was contemporary with Sir Thomas More (1478–1535), one of the "makers of English" named in Lesson 7. In the theological controversy between them, More contended for supreme authority of the church, and Tyndale argued that the ultimate standard was the Scriptures. In his zeal for the Scriptures, Tyndale once told a high-ranking church official, "If God spares my life, ere many years I will take care that a plowboy shall know more of the Scriptures than you do." The Reformation made possible the fulfillment of that prediction.

God spared his life long enough to see the New Testament translated and spread among his countrymen. But his work on the Old Testament was cut off by his death. In 1534 Tyndale was arrested and imprisoned in the Netherlands. For a year and a half, he continued his translating in prison, and manuscripts were completed through 2 Chronicles. On October 6 in 1536 Tyndale was publically strangled and then burned. His last words were, "Lord! Open the King of England's eyes."

Within a year the Bible was legally published in England. Tyndale's Old Testament work was not wasted. It was used in the Matthews Bible, published in 1537.

Answer Key—Part D (4 points)

1. The English language of William Tyndale's day had *inconsistent spelling, and a rapidly expanding vocabulary.*

2. Knowing Hebrew, Greek, and Latin let him read the Scriptures in the *original languages and earliest translations.*

3. He used *simple language* that communicated to common people.

4. He was arrested and *executed* before he finished his Old Testament translation.

LESSON 10

NEW WORDS

accommodate
advisable
apology
apostasy
apostrophe
candidate
catalog
cataract
category
ceremony
chronicles
curse
diameter
employment
evident
flammable
manufacturers
modest
significant
speedometer

REVIEW WORDS

address
bananas
believable
circulation
moderate

A.   UNEARTHING THE ROOTS

ROOT	MEANING	EXAMPLE
Latin *mod*	= measure, manner	moderate
Greek *metron*	= measure	meter
Greek *chron*	= time	chronic

1. List the lesson roots and the spelling words derived from each one. There are six words in all.
2. Write the NEW WORD that has the *mod* root and the etymological meaning "to make suitable."
3. First Timothy 2:9 mentions ____* apparel, which is clothing of sufficient measure.
4. Use these words for the following blanks.
   meter   mode   model   modern
   a. A ____ device is made in the manner of the present day.
   b. Walking is still a common ____ (manner) of travel in many countries.
   c. Take as your ____ (person to measure yourself by) someone who lives Bible truth.
   d. This ____ measures the electricity we use.
5. Geometry and trigonometry are studies that deal mainly with (computation, measurement).
6. Write a NEW WORD for this etymology: *dia* (through) + (measure). Draw a diagram to illustrate its meaning.
7. Which NEW WORD is a hybrid with these word elements? OE *spēd* (success) + Gk. (measure)
8. Would a chronometer be used to record your expenses or to adjust your clock?
9. The study of the time order of historical events is (chronology, metrology).
10. ____* is the name of two books of the Bible. Why do they have this name?
11. Events written in the order of time are given in <u>chron</u> order.
12. An illness that lasts a long time is (an acute, a chronic) illness.
13. The word ____* could mean "measured just right; not extreme."
14. The Greek root *therm* means "heat." A ____ measures heat.

Lesson 10

(Total points: 86)

Notes on Part A

Selected Words With Lesson Roots
L *mod:* **accommodate, modest,** mode, model, moderate, modern, modify, modular, modulate, module

Gk. *metron:* **diameter, speedometer,** geometry (22), meter (29), thermometer (15), trigonometry

Gk. *chron:* **chronicles,** chronic, chronological, chronology, chronometer

Exercises 2 and 7: These items encourage use of the Speller Dictionary.

Answer Key—Part A (27 points)

1. *mod:* accommodate, modest, moderate
   metron: diameter, speedometer
   chron: chronicles

2. accommodate

3. modest

4. a. modern
   b. mode
   c. model
   d. meter

5. measurement

6. diameter (Diagram should show a circle with a line through the center.)

7. speedometer

8. to adjust your clock

9. chronology

10. Chronicles
    The books of Chronicles tell about events in the order they happened.

11. chronological

12. a chronic

13. moderate

14. thermometer

Lesson 10 Test Sentences

1. *chronicles* Scribes recorded *chronicles* of the kingdom. *chronicles*
2. *curse* Prophets declared God's *curse* on disobedience. *curse*
3. *apostasy* His people had gone into *apostasy. apostasy*
4. *catalog* I will share my *catalog* with you. *catalog*
5. *manufacturers* Both *manufacturers* offer similar products. *manufacturers*
6. *circulation* What is the *circulation* of the report? *circulation*
7. *accommodate* How many guests can you *accommodate? accommodate*
8. *category* Divide each *category* into three types. *category*
9. *apostrophe* Use an *apostrophe* in a possessive noun. *apostrophe*
10. *diameter* Sam can accurately judge the *diameter* of a tree. *diameter*
11. *employment* He has *employment* at the sawmill. *employment*
12. *believable* The beggar told a very *believable* story. *believable*
13. *bananas* We found some cheap *bananas* at market. *bananas*
14. *evident* It is *evident* that they need to be used very soon. *evident*
15. *cataract* My uncle had *cataract* surgery. *cataract*
16. *significant* Now he views *significant* stars clearly. *significant*
17. *apology* We make no *apology* for living Biblically. *apology*
18. *modest* A humble manner must go with *modest* apparel. *modest*
19. *moderate* Keep the furnishings *moderate* and practical. *moderate*
20. *ceremony* The baptism *ceremony* drew extra visitors. *ceremony*
21. *speedometer* The truck *speedometer* is no longer accurate. *speedometer*
22. *advisable* It is *advisable* to get that fixed. *advisable*
23. *candidate* Each *candidate* will give a speech. *candidate*
24. *address* They usually *address* current issues. *address*
25. *flammable* We discarded the *flammable* drapes. *flammable*

B. AFFIXING AFFIXES

1. Write spelling words for these definitions, using the Greek prefixes given in the box.
   a. A symbol to indicate that letters are taken away.
   b. A statement made to take away offense.
   c. A falling down of water.
2. Use *apo-* or *cata-* to form words with the following definitions. (One contains a slightly altered form.)
   a. A systematic list*: __log
   b. A messenger sent away with the Gospel: __stle
   c. A downward turn of events; disaster: __strophe
   d. A violent change in the earth's crust: __clysm

PREFIX	MEANING	EXAMPLE
apo-	away	apostasy
cata-	down	catastrophe

   e. A moving away from one's stand of faith*: __stasy
   f. A specifically defined division*: __gory
3. a. Form two words by adding *in-* and *non-* to *flammable.*
   b. Are they synonyms or antonyms?
4. Write three spelling words in which a final *e* was dropped before a suffix was added that begins with a vowel.
5. Write the spelling words that are plural.

C. SOUND, STRUCTURE, AND MEANING

1. Write three spelling words that have double consonants. Circle the double letters.
2. Write one spelling word with /ər/ spelled *ir* and one with /ər/ spelled *ur.*
3. The letter *c* spells /s/ when followed by *e* or *i.* Write two spelling words that illustrate this pattern.
4. Write *curse,* its past form, and its variant past form.
5. Write the alternate spelling of *catalog.*
6. Write the NEW WORDS that have these definitions.
   a. Of noticeable importance.
   b. Easy to see or understand.
   c. Occupation; activity.
   d. Group; classification.
   e. High waterfall.
7. The Latin word *candidus* means "white."
   a. Write the NEW WORD that comes from this Latin word.
   b. Write the definition.
   c. Explain the link between *white* and today's meaning of the word. (See the etymology.)
8. Write the same NEW WORD for both of these sentences. After each answer, write the appropriate definition from the Speller Dictionary.
   a. Have you read Justin Martyr's ____ of Christian doctrines?
   b. Walter made his ____ for using the wrong paint.
9. Write the same NEW WORD for both sentences. This word has separate dictionary entries because it came into the English language by two different routes. Write the definition after each answer.
   a. Do not use an ____ to write the possessive form of *it.*
   b. His ____ told us how much he missed the children.
10. One of your NEW WORDS, with an apostrophe included, will spell four words that could finish this sentence: "My hands may be sticky when the delivery man wants a signature, so you ———."
   a. Write the four words.
   b. Write the four words as one.

Notes on Part B

Exercise 3: *Flammable* and *inflammable* are identical in meaning. Safety authorities have adopted *flammable* because too many people understood *inflammable* to mean "not flammable."

Answer Key—Part B (18 points)

1. a. apostrophe
   b. apology
   c. cataract
2. a. catalog
   b. apostle
   c. catastrophe
   d. cataclysm
   e. apostasy
   f. category

3. a. inflammable, nonflammable
   b. antonyms
4. advisable, believable, circulation (Accept *flammable, itemized, manufacturers*. The last two might appear to retain the *e* because the suffix begins with *e*.)
5. chronicles, manufacturers, bananas

Notes on Part C

Exercise 1: A spelling tip for *accommodate:* This word has all the *c*'s and all the *m*'s it can accommodate.

Answer Key—Part C (29 points)

1. accommodate, flammable, address
2. circulation, manufacturers (Accept *curse.*)
3. ceremony, circulation
4. curse, cursed, curst
5. catalogue
6. a. significant
   b. evident
   c. employment
   d. category
   e. cataract
7. a. candidate
   b. Someone who seeks or is suggested by others to fill a position or office.
   c. Romans seeking office wore white togas.
8. a. apology—The defense of an idea or a belief by reasoning.
   b. apology—The expression of regret or sorrow for a wrong action.
9. a. apostrophe—The mark used to make possessive forms.
   b. apostrophe—A comment made aside to an absent or imaginary person.
10. a. sign if I can't
    b. significant

D.   LANGUAGE LINEAGE

THE INFLUENCE OF SHAKESPEARE

William Shakespeare was a poet and play writer who lived around 1600, in the same period when the King James Bible was produced. Shakespeare had an outstanding mastery of the English language, and he wrote with keen understanding about the nature and experiences of people. Of course, since Shakespeare wrote from a secular viewpoint, his works contain many things that Christians find unprofitable. But as people recognized the skill and power of his writing, it brought increased respect for the English language.

Shakespeare was especially capable in creating new and unique ways of saying things. It did not matter to him that a word was a noun; if he wanted to use it as a verb, he did. If he wanted to coin a new word, he did not consider whether it was in the dictionary, for there was no dictionary. His figurative language stimulated the minds of his readers.

Shakespeare was a master at using the sounds of words for literary effect. His poetry abounds with alliteration, repetition, and other devices that make the lines pleasing to the ear. Skillful use of rhythm also enhanced his works. As Tyndale refined English in his day, so Shakespeare adorned the language of his day.

What the King James Version did for the quality of the Bible, Shakespeare did for the quality of secular literature. His creative writing made a deep impression on English in its formative years, when it had a wealth of new words but no rules restricting usage. Though most of Shakespeare's work displays carnal human nature with its violence and lust, his style did serve as a strong influence in shaping the English language.

Exercises   Use these lines from Shakespeare's writing to do the exercises below.

> Good name in man or woman, dear my lord,
> Is the immediate jewel of their souls:
> Who steals my purse steals trash; 'tis something, nothing;
> 'Twas mine, 'tis his, and has been slave to thousands;
> But he that filches from me my good name
> Robs me of that which not enriches him,
> And makes me poor indeed.

1. Because language changes, some expressions of Shakespeare's time sound strange to us.
   a. Rearrange the last three words of the first line, as they would be expressed today.
   b. Reword this phrase in the way we would say it today: *not enriches him.*
2. What figure of speech is used to describe the value of a good name?

3. Alliteration is the repetition of beginning consonant sounds. Write examples of alliteration from the following lines.
   a. line 3 (two sets)
   b. line 4 (two sets)
   c. line 5 (two sets)
   d. line 7
4. Copy lines 3 and 4, and show the rhythm by placing accent marks above the accented syllables.

Notes on Part D

William Shakespeare was already famous by the time he was thirty. He gained most of his fame by writing plays. Instead of concerning himself with rules and correctness, Shakespeare developed his skill with an instinct for human communication. Scholars can trace the increase of his skill through the works of his career. He was very popular in his life, but greater fame developed after his death. Here is another sample of his work, rich in alliteration and imagery.

Sonnet 73

That time of year thou may'st in me behold

When yellow leaves, or none, or few, do hang

Upon those boughs which shake against the cold,

Bare ruined choirs, where late the sweet birds sang.

In me thou see'st the twilight of such day

As after sunset fadeth in the west,

Which by and by black night doth take away,

Death's second self, that seals up all in rest.

In me thou see'st the glowing of such fire,

That on the ashes of his youth doth lie

As the deathbed whereon it must expire,

Consumed with that which it was nourished by.

This thou perceiv'st, which makes thy love more strong,

To love that well which thou must leave ere long.

Answer Key—Part D (12 points)

1. a. my dear lord
    b. does not enrich him

2. jewel of their souls

3. line 3: steals, steals, something;   trash, 'tis
    line 4: 'Twas, 'tis; his, has
    line 5: filches, from; me, my
    line 7: makes, me

4. Who steals my purse steals trash; 'tis something, nothing;

    'Twas mine, 'tis his, and has been slave to thousands;

A. UNEARTHING THE ROOTS

ROOT	MEANING	EXAMPLE
Latin *forma*	= shape	form
Greek *schema*	= shape, form	scheme
Latin *speci*	= kind, appearance	special
Latin *struct*	= arrange	structure
Greek *typos*	= impression	type

LESSON 11

NEW WORDS

capacity
cranberries
deform
destructive
detergent
deterrent
diagram
eligible
formula
metaphor
meteor
resign
scheme
souvenir
specific
specifically
specifications
structure
target
typical

REVIEW WORDS

arising
construction
diameter
formal
specified

1. Choose a word in the second column for each etymological definition. (Synonyms are in parentheses.)
   a. Arrange against. (hinder)   deform
   b. Shape to. (match)   transform
   c. Shape again. (improve)   conform
   d. Arrange together. (build)   reform
   e. Shape across. (change)   construct
   f. Shape off. (disfigure)   obstruct

2. Use a derivative of *forma* for each blank. After each answer, write a definition based on exercise 1.
   a. "And if ye will not be ____ by me by these things,... then will I... punish you" (Leviticus 26:23, 24).
   b. "And be not ____ to this world: but be ye ____" (Romans 12:2).

3. Which NEW WORD names a rule of a fixed "shape" that is used to solve math problems?

4. In the Bible, the Greek word *schema* means "the external condition." According to Philippians 2:8, Jesus was found in *schema,* or ____, as a man.

5. A color ____* is an orderly, effective use of colors.

6. Which spelling word is a lesson root and one more letter added?

7. It is impossible for a creature of one (kind) to evolve into another.

8. Use spelling words derived from the *speci* root for these answers.
   a. Mother had exact ____ marked on the pattern. (noun)
   b. She even ____ how many to cut. (verb)
   c. Do you have a ____ verse in mind? (adjective)
   d. Father ____ mentioned the publican to get us thinking. (adverb)

9. Walking was a ____* way of travel in Jesus' day.

Lesson 11

(Total points: 70)

Notes on Part A

Selected Words With Lesson Roots

L *forma:* **deform, formal, formula,** format, former, reform(ation), transform(ation), uniform (7)

Gk. *schema:* **scheme,** schematic

L *speci:* **specific, specifically, specifications, specified,** special, species

L *struct:* **construction, destructive, structure,** instruction, instrument, obstruction, restructure

Gk. *typos:* **typical,** antitype, type, typist (25), typographical

Answer Key—Part A (22 points)

1. a. obstruct
   b. conform
   c. reform
   d. construct
   e. transform
   f. deform

2. a. reformed—shaped again
   b. conformed—shaped to
      transformed—shaped across

3. formula

4. fashion

5. scheme

6. formal

7. species

8. a. specifications
   b. specified
   c. specific
   d. specifically

9. typical

Lesson 11 Test Sentences

1. *specific* Father's *specific* directions helped us. *specific*
2. *cranberries* Indians used *cranberries* for medicine. *cranberries*
3. *capacity* The freezer is filled to *capacity. capacity*
4. *formula* What is the *formula* for mixing this spray? *formula*
5. *specifications* Find the *specifications* on the can. *specifications*
6. *specified* Do we have the *specified* ingredients? *specified*
7. *detergent* Use *detergent* when you wash up. *detergent*
8. *typical* Jason was not a *typical* guide. *typical*
9. *meteor* His fame was like a *meteor,* bright and brief. *meteor*
10. *arising* Soon he saw complications *arising. arising*
11. *resign* He chose to *resign* his position. *resign*
12. *eligible* Is anyone *eligible* to take his place? *eligible*
13. *specifically* The manager *specifically* wants a young man. *specifically*
14. *scheme* Did your *scheme* work? *scheme*
15. *deterrent* Laziness is a *deterrent* to success. *deterrent*
16. *formal* There will be a *formal* meeting. *formal*
17. *destructive* Carelessness is *destructive* to friendships. *destructive*
18. *deform* Don't let it *deform* your life. *deform*
19. *structure* Sentence *structure* affects the message. *structure*
20. *diagram* Sometimes a *diagram* improves clarity. *diagram*
21. *metaphor* Find a *metaphor* in the first paragraph. *metaphor*
22. *target* A writer's *target* is the reader's opinion. *target*
23. *diameter* A path runs through the *diameter* of the park. *diameter*
24. *souvenir* A small *souvenir* stand sits at the center. *souvenir*
25. *construction* Road *construction* delayed our arrival. *construction*

B. AFFIXING AFFIXES

1. Use the *dia-* prefix with these endings to write words for the etymologies and definitions below.

   -dem   -gonal   -gram   -lect
   -logue   -meter   -gnosis

   a. Write through*.

   b. Measure through*.

   c. Bind across.

   d. Angle across.

   e. Conversation; discourse.
   f. A variation of speech within a language.
   g. Identification of a disease through examination.

2. Write words that begin with *meta-* to match the following descriptions. Use one

PREFIX	MEANING	EXAMPLE
dia-	through, across, apart	dialect
meta-	between, after	metamorphosis

spelling word and these words:

   metabolism
   metamorphosis
   metaphysical

   a. A figure of speech that calls one thing by another name, as "The LORD is my shepherd."
   b. The sum of all processes by which life is maintained in a living creature.
   c. Pertaining to things outside the natural realm, such as spirits.
   d. The process by which some insects and amphibians go through great changes in form as they develop.

C. SOUND, STRUCTURE, AND MEANING

1. Write the NEW WORDS that have these phonetic details.
   a. /īn/ spelled *ign*
   b. /sk/ spelled *sch*
   c. /chər/ spelled *ture*
   d. /sü/ spelled *sou*
2. The letter *g* followed by *e, i,* or *y* usually has the soft sound /j/.
   a. Write two NEW WORDS that have soft *g*.
   b. Write the NEW WORD that is an exception to this rule.
3. Match these etymological definitions with two NEW WORDS that are spelled alike except for one letter.
   a. To wipe off, from *de-* + *tergēre* (to wipe)

   b. to frighten away, from *de-* + *terrēre* (to frighten)
4. Write the three principal parts of *arise*. Also write its *-ing* form.
5. Find two plural spelling words, and write their singular forms.
6. Write two plural spellings of *formula*.
7. Complete these analogies with spelling words.
   a. helpful : harmful :: constructive : ____
   b. meter : length :: liter : ____
   c. kindness : attraction :: rudeness : ____
   d. slow : comet :: fast : ____
   e. deterioration : improvement :: demolition : ____
8. Write a sentence using *eligible* and *resign*.

Answer Key—Part B (11 points)

1. a. diagram
   b. diameter
   c. diadem
   d. diagonal
   e. dialogue
   f. dialect
   g. diagnosis
2. a. metaphor
   b. metabolism
   c. metaphysical
   d. metamorphosis

Notes on Part C

Exercise 7: The analogy *helpful : harmful :: constructive : ____* is read "Helpful is to harmful as constructive is to ———." Teach students to verbalize the word relationships if they need help in completing the analogy.

Helpful is the opposite of *harmful,* as *constructive* is the opposite of ____.
Meter is a measure of *length,* as *liter* is a measure of ____.
Kindness produces *attraction,* as *rudeness* produces ____.
Slow describes *comet,* as *fast* describes ____.
Deterioration is the opposite of *improvement,* as *demolition* is the opposite of ____.

Answer Key—Part C (24 points)

1. a. resign
   b. scheme
   c. structure
   d. souvenir
2. a. detergent, eligible
   b. target
3. a. detergent
   b. deterrent
4. arise, arose, arisen, arising
5. cranberry, specification
6. formulas, formulae
7. a. destructive
   b. capacity
   c. deterrent
   d. meteor
   e. construction
8. (Sample sentence) When you find another *eligible* clerk, I will *resign* my duties.

D.   LANGUAGE LINEAGE

SEMANTIC STUDY: WEAKENING WORDS

Words can be overused to the extent that they lose the strength of their meanings. This semantic change is called weakening. Word meanings become less vivid and forceful, probably through attempts to make things impressive when they really should be expressed more mildly.

In the first line of the song "How Great Thou Art!" *awesome wonder* is a vivid expression of deep reverence and marveling admiration. But how forceful are the words *awful* and *wonderful?* Even the phrase *awfully wonderful* hardly expresses the emotion originally felt in one of these words alone. They have undergone the semantic change of weakening.

Terrible formerly meant "causing fear and reverence." Today the word can be used in a much milder sense. Can you imagine a terrible pile of food in the pantry?

Presently once meant "at the present time and place." To answer a letter presently was to answer it immediately. Now *presently* gives you leisure to do it next week or maybe even next month. And have you ever waited "just a minute" for something that took ten or fifteen?

When there is no doubt about a certain matter, it is better to use a stronger term than *doubtless,* or your hearers will think you only mean "probably."

You may have a lovely walk in the lovely meadow on a lovely day, since *lovely* now describes anything with pleasing or attractive qualities. But originally it was used in a more personal sense, meaning "worthy to be loved."

Great originally meant "large in size," but now it describes something outstanding in any respect. For example, you might say that a fastidious person is given to "great triviality."

Such changes are not necessarily bad. We need not restore original meanings to be correct. Semantic weakening is gradual enough to cause no confusion in today's communication. But recognizing the process sheds helpful light on literature from the past. Various passages in the King James Bible become richer and clearer when we understand the older meanings.

Exercises

1. Write *original* or *weakened* to tell which meaning the italicized words have in these sentences.
   a. The travelers gave exclamations of wonder as they gazed on the *awful* mountains.
   b. The doctor will *presently* examine the eight patients who are waiting.
   c. We found a *lovely* pool nestled in the glen and fringed with violets.
   d. The commander tried to gain a *terrible* reputation among his soldiers.
   e. Haman was a *great* man in Shushan.
2. Read each Bible verse, and copy a word that has gone through semantic weakening. Then write a phrase or sentence that shows good understanding of the statement.
   a. Judges 13:6
   b. 2 Samuel 5:19
   c. Jeremiah 5:30
   d. Matthew 26:53

Notes on Part D

Exercise 2: Students may find it difficult to express the phrases with original meanings. Class discussion can strengthen this exercise; draw student contribution, and help them to word a good interpretation.

Answer Key—Part D (13 points)

1. a. original
   b. weakened
   c. weakened
   d. original
   e. weakened
2. (Sample explanations)
   a. terrible—The angel's face inspired fear and reverence.
   b. doubtless—I will definitely deliver the Philistines into your hand.
   c. wonderful—An amazing and horrible thing has happened.
   d. presently—God would send angels immediately if Jesus asked.

42

LESSON 12

7	8	9	10	11
abolish	aeronautics	access	accommodate	capacity
abstinence	Antarctic	asphalt	advisable	cranberries
adolescence	anticipating	atheist	apology	deform
binoculars	antiseptic	attorney	apostasy	destructive
canvass	arguing	disqualify	apostrophe	detergent
carton	breadth	immense	candidate	deterrent
cylinder	compromise	magnificence	catalog	diagram
desirous	conveniently	magnify	cataract	eligible
devotional	duplex	maximum	category	formula
exhaust	elapsed	microfilm	ceremony	metaphor
grippe	glacier	microphone	chronicles	meteor
instinct	heresy	miniature	curse	resign
obstacle	kimono	minister	diameter	scheme
octagon	mathematics	quantity	employment	souvenir
peril	peculiar	security	evident	specific
procedure	Pentateuch	subtle	flammable	specifically
sketch	protein	symbol	manufacturers	specifications
substantial	recognize	sympathetic	modest	structure
support	statistics	symptom	significant	target
uniform	trivial	synthetic	speedometer	typical

A.   UNEARTHING THE ROOTS

L *bi*	= two, twice	L *magn*	= great			
L *cent*	= hundred(th)	Gk. *macro*	= large	L *forma*	= shape	
L *oct*	= eight	L *mini*	= small	Gk. *schema*	= shape, form	
L *quart*	= fourth	Gk. *micro*	= small	L *speci*	= kind,	
L *uni*	= one	L *quant*	= how great		appearance	
		L *qual*	= what sort	L *struct*	= arrange	
L *du*	= two			Gk. *typos*	= impression	
L *tri*	= three	L *mod*	= measure, manner			
Gk. *tetra*	= four					
Gk. *penta*	= five	Gk. *metron*	= measure			
Gk. *deca*	= ten	Gk. *chron*	= time			

Lesson 12

(Total points: 61)

Lesson 12 Test Sentences

1. *devotional* The short *devotional* was very inspiring. *devotional*
2. *obstacle* The biggest *obstacle* is nothing to God. *obstacle*
3. *substantial* A slate roof must have *substantial* rafters. *substantial*
4. *abolish* Can the law *abolish* crime? *abolish*
5. *binoculars* Focus your *binoculars* on the cliff. *binoculars*
6. *procedure* Study the building *procedure* of the swallows. *procedure*
7. *cylinder* The *cylinder* is a common form in the kitchen. *cylinder*
8. *adolescence* Important choices are made in *adolescence*. *adolescence*
9. *peril* Beware the *peril* of wealth. *peril*
10. *exhaust* We never *exhaust* Aunt Ida's stories. *exhaust*
11. *anticipating* We are *anticipating* a long visit. *anticipating*
12. *elapsed* Two years have *elapsed* since we were together. *elapsed*
13. *trivial* Be alert to *trivial* signs of trouble. *trivial*
14. *statistics* Joan keeps careful *statistics* on her garden. *statistics*
15. *peculiar* Can you identify that *peculiar* odor? *peculiar*
16. *arguing* Don't try *arguing* with the weather. *arguing*
17. *breadth* The *breadth* of God's love is unmeasurable. *breadth*
18. *heresy* A self-centered man is prone to *heresy*. *heresy*
19. *protein* Nuts and beans are *protein* foods. *protein*
20. *mathematics* You must be awake for *mathematics* class. *mathematics*
21. *sympathetic* Her *sympathetic* smile encouraged me. *sympathetic*
22. *disqualify* Dirty hands *disqualify* you for making bread. *disqualify*
23. *miniature* The birdhouse is a *miniature* barn. *miniature*
24. *access* Faith gives us *access* to the grace of God. *access*
25. *immense* Solomon gathered *immense* stores of wealth. *immense*
26. *symptom* Failing vision is a *symptom* of old age. *symptom*
27. *asphalt* Utah has natural *asphalt* deposits. *asphalt*
28. *maximum* What is the *maximum* yield per acre of corn? *maximum*
29. *security* There is no *security* in money. *security*
30. *subtle* Praise of men is a *subtle* snare. *subtle*
31. *category* This poem fits in the narrative *category*. *category*
32. *employment* Many lost *employment* in the Depression. *employment*
33. *accommodate* Would that hole *accommodate* a fox? *accommodate*
34. *apostrophe* Place your *apostrophe* high enough to be clear. *apostrophe*
35. *manufacturers* Why do *manufacturers* advertise? *manufacturers*
36. *modest* One good advertisement is *modest* pricing. *modest*
37. *apology* Accept my *apology* for the mistake. *apology*
38. *advisable* When is it *advisable* to prune the trees? *advisable*
39. *catalog* A card *catalog* lists each book three ways. *catalog*
40. *significant* Each way has a *significant* purpose. *significant*
41. *capacity* Sorrow increases your *capacity* for joy. *capacity*
42. *detergent* This *detergent* gives me a rash. *detergent*
43. *formula* What is your *formula* for friendship? *formula*
44. *resign* A true friend will *resign* some preferences. *resign*
45. *specifically* David *specifically* requested direction. *specifically*
46. *meteor* We enjoyed the *meteor* shower in August. *meteor*
47. *target* The Christian is a *target* for ridicule. *target*
48. *destructive* Worry is as *destructive* as cancer. *destructive*
49. *souvenir* Leon's scar is a *souvenir* of his camel ride. *souvenir*
50. *eligible* No one was *eligible* for typing class. *eligible*

1. Write words from Lesson 7 for these exercises.
   a. (two at a time) + *oculus* (eyes) = ____
   b. (eight) + *gōnia* (angle) = ____
   c. (one) + (shape) = ____
   d. (hundred) + *pes* (foot) = ____ (REVIEW WORD)
   e. Four people form a ____ (REVIEW WORD)
   f. Adam was ____; there was no other creature like him. (REVIEW WORD)

2. Write words from Lesson 8.
   a. (two) + *plicāre* (fold) = ____
   b. (three) + *via* (road) = ____
   c. (five) + *teukhos* (scroll) = ____
   d. (ten) + *logos* (word) = ____ (REVIEW WORD)
   e. A set of three alike is a ____. (REVIEW WORD)

3. Write words from Lesson 9.
   a. Which word speaks of making an object great?
   b. Which word that means "greatest" has the lesson root slightly changed?
   c. Both the (what sort) and the (how much) of your work are important. (One answer is a REVIEW WORD.)
   d. (small) + *phōno* (sound) = ____
   e. Which word first referred to a small picture but now means anything smaller than normal?
   f. Which word has the original meaning "a lesser servant"?

4. Write words from Lesson 10.
   a. (to make suitable) = ____
   b. (through) + (measure) = ____
   c. *spēd* (success) + (measure) = ____
   d. Suitable clothes for Christians are "of sufficient measure" or ____.
   e. Which word has the Greek root *khronos?*

5. Write words from Lesson 11.
   a. *de-* + (shape) = ____
   b. *de-* + (arrange) + *-ive* = ____
   c. Which three words have the *speci* root?
   d. The log cabin was a (arrange) that was (impression) of pioneer days.
   e. Three carpenters worked out a (form) for rebuilding.

B. AFFIXING AFFIXES

1. Answer with spelling words that contain elements relating to numbers. Some of the answers are REVIEW WORDS.
   a. The standard shape of a stop sign is an ____.
   b. A policeman in ____ was directing traffic.
   c. Could you count the feet of a ____ as it scurries across the floor?
   d. A ____ sang "Heavenly Sunlight."
   e. Aunt Mary's quilt is ____. It is the only one of its kind.

2. Write words from Lesson 8 that contain

anti-	against or contrary to
syn-, sym-	together
a-, an-	without
apo-	away
cata-	down
dia-	through, across, apart
meta-	between, after

elements with these meanings.
   a. (contrary to) + *arktikos* (northern) = ____
   b. (against) + *sēptikos* (rotting) = ____

Answer Key—Part A (31 points)

1. a. binoculars
    b. octagon
    c. uniform
    d. centipede
    e. quartet
    f. unique

2. a. duplex
    b. trivial
    c. Pentateuch
    d. Decalogue
    e. triplet

3. a. magnify
    b. maximum
    c. quality, quantity
    d. microphone
    e. miniature
    f. minister

4. a. accommodate
    b. diameter
    c. speedometer
    d. modest
    e. chronicles

5. a. deform
    b. destructive
    c. specific, specifically, specifications
    d. structure, typical
    e. scheme

Answer Key—Part B (23 points)

1. a. octagon
    b. uniform
    c. centipede
    d. quartet
    e. unique

2. a. Antarctic
    b. antiseptic

44 *Lesson 12*

3. Write other words with the prefix *anti-* to match these definitions.
   a. (against) + bacteria + *-al* = ____
   b. (against) + poverty = ____
   c. (against) + slavery = ____
4. Write words using assimilated forms of *syn-* and *a-* for these definitions. Use words from Lesson 9 for *a–c*.
   a. A sign or object that represents something else.
   b. Having a feeling of kind compassion.
   c. An indication of a condition.
   d. Written without the author's name.
5. Write words from Lesson 10 for these etymologies.

   a. (away) + *logos* (speech) = ____
   b. (away) + *histanai* (standing) = ____
   c. (away) + *strephein* (turn) = ____
   d. (down) + *legein* (count) = ____
   e. (down) + *rassein* (striking) = ____
   f. (down) + *agora* (assembly) = ____
6. Write words from Lesson 11 for these descriptions.
   a. A "falling star," from (after) + *aoros* (lift).
   b. A drawing that explains, from (through) + *graphein* (write).
   c. A figure of speech, from (between) + *pherein* (carry).

D.   LANGUAGE LINEAGE

REVIEW

1. a. What was the Renaissance?
   b. Why were new words needed in the Renaissance?
2. a. What was the Reformation?
   b. How did the Reformation add momentum to the Renaissance?
3. How did William Tyndale influence the English language?
4. How did Shakespeare influence English?
5. What is semantic weakening?

3. a. antibacterial
   b. antipoverty
   c. antislavery

4. a. symbol
   b. sympathetic
   c. symptom
   d. anonymous

5. a. apology
   b. apostasy
   c. apostrophe
   d. catalog
   e. cataract
   f. category

6. a. meteor
   b. diagram
   c. metaphor

Answer Key—Part D (7 points)

1. a. The Renaissance was the general *awakening of education, inventions, and progress* in the Middle Ages.
   b. Words were needed to name new *tools, products, and things discovered* in other cultures.

2. a. The Reformation was a *religious awakening* that was part of the Renaissance.
   b. People *learned to read* so they could read the Bible, and then they learned many more things.

3. Tyndale *translated the Bible* with skillful use of the language, and it was spread to all the English-speaking world.

4. Shakespeare used *new words and new ways of saying things* that people liked.

5. Semantic weakening is a change in word meanings that makes them *less vivid and forceful*.

LESSON 13

A. UNEARTHING THE ROOTS

ROOT	MEANING	EXAMPLE
Greek *not, gnos*	= know	diagnosis
Latin *cert*	= sure	certain

NEW WORDS

acknowledgment

apostolic

artistic

ascertain

assurance

athletic

cardiac

certify

characteristic

colonel

consultation

cosmic

crisis

discord

dramatic

element

financial

heroic

intestine

noticeable

REVIEW WORDS

approximately

certificate

jealous

musical

potatoes

1. From each verse, copy one word with a lesson root.
   a. Colossians 2:2*   e. 2 Corinthians 1:14
   b. Deuteronomy 13:14   f. Acts 2:20
   c. Exodus 3:12   g. Proverbs 3:6
   d. Ezra 4:14   h. Ezra 5:10*

2. Write the word that Abimelech and his men used in Genesis 26:28 when they told Isaac they were sure the Lord was with him.

3. When you want to be sure that a letter reaches its destination, you can send it by <u>cert</u> mail.

4. You should ____* the truth of that report before you repeat it.

5. A birth ____* serves as a sure sign to prove the date of someone's birth.

6. The Greek word *gnōstos* means "to be known." The prefix *a-* can mean "not." A person who thinks that nothing can be known about God is an ____.

7. Choose the best word to complete the analogy below.
        (confusion, exaltation, sureness)
           great : large :: certitude : ____

8. The black splotch was so ____* that many visitors asked about it.

9. Someone who is well known for his wickedness is (annotated, notable, notorious).

10. The word *diagnosis* means (a guess at, known and stated facts about) something. Write the root that helps you understand the meaning of the word.

11. These words also have the *not* or *gnos* root. Write the correct one to fit each blank.
        incognito   cognition   recognize
    a. The professor refused to ____ the error he had made.
    b. We enjoyed the baby's rapidly developing ____.
    c. Menno Simons often traveled ____ to escape arrest.

Lesson 13

(Total points: 75)

Notes on Part A

Selected Words With Lesson Roots

Gk. *not, gnos:* **acknowledgment, noticeable,** agnostic, cognitive, connoisseur, diagnosis, incognito, notorious, prognosis, recognize (8)

L *cert:* **ascertain, certificate, certify,** certain, certitude, disconcerting

Exercise 1a: *Acknowledgment* may appear with an alternate spelling in most KJV Bibles. Note the retained *e* before the suffix *ment,* but emphasize the spelling given in the word list. (There could be two reasons in favor of retaining the *e:* the suffix does not begin with a vowel, and the *g* is to have its soft sound.)

Answer Key—Part A (21 points)

1. a. acknowledgment
   b. certain
   c. certainly
   d. certified
   e. acknowledged
   f. notable
   g. acknowledge
   h. certify
2. certainly
3. certified
4. ascertain
5. certificate
6. agnostic
7. sureness
8. noticeable
9. notorious
10. known and stated facts about, *gnos*
11. a. recognize
    b. cognition
    c. incognito

Lesson 13 Test Sentences

1. *apostolic* Peter was one of the *apostolic* leaders. *apostolic*
2. *characteristic* His impulsive *characteristic* led to grief. *characteristic*
3. *acknowledgment* His *acknowledgment* of error was clear. *acknowledgment*
4. *jealous* God is *jealous* over us. *jealous*
5. *assurance* We have *assurance* of His protection. *assurance*
6. *heroic* Joseph is a *heroic* example of faithfulness. *heroic*
7. *certify* You must *certify* ownership to cross the border. *certify*
8. *consultation* An officer held a *consultation* with the men. *consultation*
9. *financial* Some *financial* needs were evident. *financial*
10. *approximately* They paid *approximately* twenty dollars. *approximately*
11. *ascertain* Can you *ascertain* the flavor in this cookie? *ascertain*
12. *dramatic* There was *dramatic* improvement overnight. *dramatic*
13. *athletic* Studies come ahead of *athletic* events. *athletic*
14. *artistic* Practice develops *artistic* skill. *artistic*
15. *element* C is the symbol for the *element* carbon. *element*
16. *cosmic* Scientists measured *cosmic* rays. *cosmic*
17. *certificate* Gayle's *certificate* rewards perfect attendance. *certificate*
18. *musical* Howard talks in *musical* tones. *musical*
19. *noticeable* A *noticeable* tiredness came over him. *noticeable*
20. *crisis* A health *crisis* was evident. *crisis*
21. *intestine* Blockage of the *intestine* could be fatal. *intestine*
22. *cardiac* The *cardiac* muscle pumps a gallon a minute. *cardiac*
23. *discord* Do not sow *discord* among brethren. *discord*
24. *potatoes* Dwayne likes *potatoes* with gravy. *potatoes*
25. *colonel* A young *colonel* examined the draftees. *colonel*

46 *Lesson 13*

B. AFFIXING AFFIXES

1. Use the adjective-forming suffix -*ac* in these exercises.
   a. A _____* arrest is a heart attack.
   b. Jesus cast demons out of many <u>de__</u> people.
2. Use the suffix -*ic* to form adjectives descriptive of these people.
   a. artist*   d. athlete*
   b. hero*   e. apostle*
   c. prophet
3. Write the NEW WORD that is derived from *drama*. What letter is inserted before the suffix?
4. Write forms of the italicized word to fill the blanks in each sentence. Use lesson suffixes for the adjectives.
   a. The *criticism* of the (noun) seemed unnecessarily (adj.).
   b. After inspecting the *mechanism*, the (noun) corrected our (adj.) trouble.
   c. Some people live in a world of *fantasy* in which they (verb) about (adj.) events.
   d. The loyal *character* that (verb) Norman is also (adj.)* of his brothers.

Adjective-forming Suffixes

SUFFIX	MEANING	EXAMPLE
-ac	affected by, like	maniac
-ic	affected by, like	heroic
-ical	affected by, like	alphabetical

5. The cosmos is the orderly universe that God created. Write the NEW WORD that means "pertaining to the universe."
6. Write the REVIEW WORD that has a lesson suffix.
7. For each of the following derivational suffixes, write a NEW WORD and name its part of speech. Then write the root word, and name its part of speech.
   Example: -*able*
   Answer: noticeable—adj.
              notice—v.
   a. -*ment*
   b. -*ance*
   c. -*ial*
8. Write two spelling words in which the final *e* was not dropped when a derivational suffix was added.

C. SOUND, STRUCTURE, AND MEANING

1. Write the spelling words that have these phonetic features.
   a. A word that ends with /shən/.
   b. A word with /e/ spelled *ea*.
2. Write the REVIEW WORD that is plural. Also write its singular form.
3. Write the plural form of these words.
   a. hero   c. buffalo
   b. tomato   d. volcano
4. Write the spelling word that means "a situation that demands a prompt decision." Also write its plural form.
5. Use the same spelling word for these sentences, adding -*s* or -*ary* where needed.
   a. A chemical compound contains more than one _____.
   b. The first six grades of school are _____.
   c. Wood decays when exposed to the _____.
6. Write spelling words that are antonyms for these words.
   a. harmony
   b. cowardly
7. Write the NEW WORD that names a body part and comes from the Latin word *intus,* which means "internal."
8. Write the NEW WORD that is a homonym of *kernel*. This pronunciation survived a spelling change from a French form that contained the letter *r.*

Notes on Part B

Exercise 8: Maintaining the final *e* of *notice* helps to preserve the soft *c* sound. There could be the tendency to give it the /k/ sound if followed by the *a* of the suffix.

Answer Key—Part B (33 points)

1. a. cardiac
   b. demoniac

2. a. artistic
   b. heroic
   c. prophetic
   d. athletic
   e. apostolic

3. dramatic, *t*

4. a. critic, critical
   b. mechanic, mechanical
   c. fantasize, fantastic
   d. characterizes, characteristic

5. cosmic

6. musical

7. a. acknowledgment—n.
      acknowledge—v.
   b. assurance—n.
      assure—v.
   c. financial—adj.
      finance—v.

8. noticeable, approximately

Notes on Part C

Exercise 8: *Colonel* is a vivid example of language shifts such as described in *Language Lineage* of Lessons 3 and 4.

Answer Key—Part C (17 points)

1. a. consultation
   b. jealous

2. potatoes, potato

3. a. heroes
   b. tomatoes
   c. buffalo *or* buffaloes *or* buffalos
   d. volcanoes *or* volcanos

4. crisis, crises

5. a. element
   b. elementary
   c. elements

6. a. discord
   b. heroic

7. intestine

8. colonel

D.   LANGUAGE LINEAGE

STANDARDIZATION OF THE ENGLISH LANGUAGE

Language is a living, changing thing. The English language expanded in the Renaissance and bloomed under the influence of Shakespeare. But if all writers created and changed words as they pleased, what confusion would result! The language could change so much that the masterpieces of one era would be meaningless to people a few centuries later.

Englishmen recognized that ongoing change would soon render their current literature obsolete. With the large number of speakers and writers who used English, the language was becoming widely varied. The result was that no one could be sure about proper usage. How could a person know whether he was writing correctly if there were no fixed standards? Some thought that order should be established by developing a set of permanent rules for the language.

France and Italy had associations called academies for the preservation and improvement of their languages. These were groups of authorities who considered language questions and then published guides to inform the public about acceptable or unacceptable usage. Englishmen considered appointing such a group for their own language.

Several members of England's Royal Society had keen interest in language regulation and improvement. In 1664 this society established a committee for improving the English language. The members met several times to consider spelling reform and grammar standards; but little came out of their ambitions, and the committee faded away.

In 1712, Jonathan Swift made an influential appeal to the Earl of Oxford, lamenting the great imperfections in English. He urged that a group be appointed to formulate rules of grammar, to establish the acceptability of words, and then to keep the perfected language from changing. The earl listed a number of qualified men and prepared to see the queen for financial support. But the death of the queen and disagreement among court officials put an end to the work before it even started.

As years went by, people changed their minds about having authorities dictate how they should speak and write. Even though France and Italy had language academies, they could not keep their languages from changing. England never did establish a committee to dictate what is correct use of the language. That function was gradually and unofficially filled by the arrival of the dictionary.

Exercises

1. Why was it desirable to standardize the English language?
2. What was the purpose of the language academies in France and Italy?
3. What matters were considered by the language committee of the Royal Society?
4. What eventually became an authority for correct English usage?

Notes on Part D

Students today are not very far into their schooling before they are studying the structure and correct usage of English. In the time described in this article, there were no English books and no language rules. Men recognized the instability this permitted, which fed the concern for standardizing English. To save his writings from becoming obsolete, Francis Bacon translated his works into Latin at the end of his life. A poet named Waller wrote:

But who can hope his lines should long

Last, in a daily changing tongue?

While they are new, Envy prevails;

And as that dies, our language fails....

Poets that Lasting Marble seek,

Must carve in Latin or in Greek;

We write in Sand...

Thomas Sheridan made this plea to the earl of Chesterfield:

Suffer not our Shakespear, and our Milton, to become two or three centuries hence what Chaucer is at present, the study only of a few poring antiquarians, and in an age or two more the victims of bookworms.

In 1697 Daniel Defoe proposed an academy consisting of twelve nobles, twelve private gentlemen, and twelve men chosen by merit of their study. No man should then coin new words without the approval of this society.

Jonathan Swift's letter protested several aspects of change in the language. Besides the coining of new words, he objected to contractions and the shortening of polysyllables, such as *rep* for *reputation, ult* for *ultimate,* and *extra* for *extraordinary.* Some shortened polysyllables that we use are *phone, bus, hyper,* and *ad.*

Although no academy was formed to do the preserving these men sought, the English language did stabilize. Their concern was expressed for the work of the poets, but of far greater value is the Word of God. The King James Version still communicates to us in the language of several centuries ago.

Answer Key—Part D (4 points)

1. With a standardized language, the literary masterpieces of one generation can be enjoyed by many *later generations.*

2. Language academies established rules and standards *to preserve and improve the language.*

3. The language committee of the Royal Society considered *spelling reform and grammar standards.*

4. *The dictionary* eventually became the English language authority.

48

LESSON 14

A. UNEARTHING THE ROOTS

ROOT	MEANING	EXAMPLE
Latin *audi*	= hear	audience
Greek *phono*	= sound	phonograph
Latin *lumin*	= light	illuminate
Greek *photo*	= light	photograph

NEW WORDS

allegiance
amuse
ascension
brilliancy
ceased
constellation
correspondence
decorations
discrepancy
efficient
evidently
hatred
illuminate
iniquities
intelligence
leisurely
photograph
remembrance
resistance
violence

REVIEW WORDS

audience
auditor
emergency
microphone
residence

1. Write the five spelling words that contain lesson roots. After each word, write its etymological meaning.
2. Use words in this list for answers to the acrostic puzzle below.

audible	audiovisual
auditory	illumination
luminous	telephone
telephoto	phonics
phonograph	photography
photosensitive	photosynthesis

a. Study of letters and the sounds they represent.
b. Device for carrying sound afar.
c. Loud enough to be heard.
d. Device that produces sound from a disc.
e. Nerve that carries sound impulses to the brain.
f. Emitting light.
g. Affected by light.
h. Cameraman's occupation.
i. Process by which plants produce food by light energy.
j. Lens that brings far-off objects into near focus.

```
    a. - - - - - S
    b. - - - - - - O - -
         c. - U - - - - -
    d. - - - N - - - - - -
       e. - - D - - - - -
            f. L - - - - -
g. - - - - - - - - I - - -
     h. - - - - - G - - - -
i. - - - - - - - - H - - -
   j. - - - - - - - T -
```

Lesson 14

(Total points: 95)

Notes on Part A

Selected Words With Lesson Roots
L *audi:* **audience, auditor,** audible, audiovisual, audition, auditorium, auditory

Gk. *phono:* **microphone,** earphone, phoneme, phonics, phonograph, telephone

L *lumin:* **illuminate,** lumens, luminous

Gk. *photo:* **photograph,** photocopy, photometer, photon, photosensitive, photosynthesis, telephoto

Where do manufacturers look for pleasing and meaningful names for car models? Do your students recognize *Audi* and *Lumina?*

Answer Key—Part A (20 points)

1. audience, to hear
microphone, small sound
photograph, to write with light
illuminate, to light up
auditor, to hear

2. a. phonicS
   b. telephOne
   c. aUdible
   d. phoNograph
   e. auDitory

   f. Luminous
   g. photosensItive
   h. photoGraphy
   i. photosyntHesis
   j. telephoTo

Lesson 14 Test Sentences

1. *photograph* I have a *photograph* of Great-grandfather. *photograph*
2. *residence* It shows the *residence* where he lived. *residence*
3. *remembrance* A picture is a special *remembrance.* *remembrance*
4. *ascension* That was before their *ascension* to the hill farm. *ascension*
5. *decorations* Donna did the *decorations* on the cake. *decorations*
6. *leisurely* A *leisurely* walk refreshed us. *leisurely*
7. *brilliancy* The *brilliancy* of the stars was glorious! *brilliancy*
8. *constellation* Do you know the *constellation* above Orion?
   constellation
9. *intelligence* Man's *intelligence* is puny. *intelligence*
10. *microphone* The *microphone* stopped working. *microphone*
11. *audience* Half the *audience* could not hear. *audience*
12. *amuse* A mean joke does not *amuse* a gentleman. *amuse*
13. *illuminate* God can *illuminate* the darkest heart. *illuminate*
14. *hatred* He changed Saul's *hatred* to love. *hatred*
15. *resistance* Saul's program of *resistance* stopped. *resistance*
16. *allegiance* He switched his *allegiance* to Christ. *allegiance*
17. *iniquities* All his *iniquities* were washed away. *iniquities*
18. *ceased* Persecution *ceased* in Jerusalem. *ceased*
19. *correspondence* The girls' *correspondence* was inspiring.
    correspondence
20. *evidently* They were *evidently* good friends. *evidently*
21. *violence* Someone threatened *violence* on the plane. *violence*
22. *emergency* The pilot made an *emergency* landing. *emergency*
23. *auditor* The records are ready for the *auditor.* *auditor*
24. *efficient* We appreciate *efficient* bookkeeping. *efficient*
25. *discrepancy* A small *discrepancy* appeared in the figures. *discrepancy*

B.   AFFIXING AFFIXES

1. Copy each word, and label its part of speech. Then write the noun in the spelling list that is derived from it.

    Example: agent
    Answer: agent, n.—agency

    a. brilliant
    b. correspond
    c. discrepant
    d. emergent
    e. intelligent
    f. remember
    g. resist
    h. reside
    i. violent

2. Write other words with this lesson's noun-forming suffixes for these definitions.

    a. The act of being arrogant.
    b. The state of being vacant.
    c. The quality of being sufficient.

Noun-forming Suffixes

SUFFIX	MEANING	EXAMPLE
-ance	act, state, or	tolerance
-ancy	quality of	hesitancy
-ence	act, state, or	subsistence
-ency	quality of	consistency

    d. The quality of being efficient.

3. Write spelling words with other noun-forming suffixes for these.

    a. The act of going up.
    b. Things to make attractive.
    c. The condition of enmity.
    d. One who examines records.

4. Write two NEW WORDS that have adverb-forming suffixes.

5. Write the NEW WORDS that have suffixes for these inflections.

    a. past tense
    b. plural (2)

C.   SOUND, STRUCTURE, AND MEANING

1. Write the NEW WORDS that have these spellings of /s/.

    a. *sc*
    b. both *c* and *s* (4)

2. Write the spelling words that have double letters.

3. Write the NEW WORD in which *ie* comes after *c*. This happens because *-cient* spells /shənt/.

4. Write the NEW WORD that has the letters *ei*.

5. Write NEW WORDS that are antonyms of these words.

    a. hastily
    b. disloyalty
    c. annoy
    d. wasteful

6. *Ascension* means "the act of going up." It is capitalized when referring to Christ's ascent into heaven after the resurrection. Write the word correctly for each sentence.

    a. The balloonist asked the crowd to move back before his ____.
    b. The Holy Spirit was poured out ten days after the ____.

7. Use NEW WORDS to finish the analogies.

    a. love : tenderness :: hatred : ____
    b. correspondence : information :: souvenir : ____

8. Two of your NEW WORDS are variant forms, acceptable with the suffix *-ance* or *-ancy*. Write both forms of each word.

9. Write the NEW WORDS that have these etymologies.

    a. *in-* (not) + *aequus* (equal)
    b. *com-* (together) + *stēlla* (star)
    c. *dis-* (apart) + *crepāre* (to rattle)

Notes on Part B

Exercises 1 and 5: The directions use the words *derived* and *inflections*. Can the students easily distinguish derivational and inflectional suffixes? If not, have them return to the hint in Lesson 1.

Answer Key—Part B (40 points)

1. a. brilliant, adj.—brilliancy
    b. correspond, v.—correspondence
    c. discrepant, adj.—discrepancy
    d. emergent, adj.—emergency
    e. intelligent, adj.—intelligence
    f. remember, v.—remembrance
    g. resist, v.—resistance
    h. reside, v.—residence
    i. violent, adj.—violence
2. a. arrogance
    b. vacancy

    c. sufficiency
    d. efficiency
3. a. ascension
    b. decorations
    c. hatred
    d. auditor
4. evidently, leisurely
5. a. ceased
    b. decorations, iniquities

Notes on Part C

Exercise 3: The word *efficient* appears to break the rule "*I* before *e* except after *c*." But *ci* is the spelling for /sh/ in words like *sufficient* and *concience*.

Exercise 4: *Leisurely* does break the "*I* before *e*" rule.

Exercise 7: *Love* is expressed by *tenderness,* as *hatred* is expressed by ____.

    Correspondence gives one *information,* as *souvenir* gives one ____.

Answer Key—Part C (29 points)

1. a. ascension
    b. ceased, correspondence, discrepancy, resistance
2. allegiance, brilliancy, constellation, correspondence, efficient, illuminate, intelligence
3. efficient
4. leisurely
5. a. leisurely
    b. allegiance
    c. amuse
    d. efficient

6. a. ascension
    b. Ascension
7. a. violence
    b. remembrance
8. brilliancy, brilliance
    discrepancy, discrepance
9. a. iniquities
    b. constellation
    c. discrepancy

D. LANGUAGE LINEAGE

JOHNSON'S DICTIONARY

Samuel Johnson single-handedly became the "academy" for the English language by publishing a dictionary in 1755. Eight years of labor went into the preparation of his big two-volume *Dictionary of the English Language*. His desire was to fix pronunciation and usage so that the language would not continue to suffer change.

Johnson's was not the first English dictionary. Thirty-four years earlier, Nathaniel Bailey had published a smaller dictionary featuring pronunciations, syllable divisions, etymologies, and illustrative quotations. Earlier dictionaries were simply listings of hard words or words new to the language, with explanations of their meanings.

Bailey and Johnson both attempted to include every word in the language, but Johnson's work was more exhaustive. His etymologies were more comprehensive than those in Bailey's dictionary. Besides giving definitions, Johnson included thousands of examples of usage by other writers, which helped to distinguish subtle shades of meaning. Spelling was largely standardized by this time, but Johnson's dictionary helped to establish it even more firmly.

So thorough and systematic was Johnson's work that it was hailed as the authority for a hundred years. The age of adoption and change was largely concluded, and Englishmen were ready for the security of an authoritative standard.

Being the work of one man, however, Johnson's dictionary was subject to bias and prejudice. By today's standards, his writing style was ponderous and elaborate. Following are a few examples of his definitions that amuse modern scholars.

Cough: A convulsion of the lungs, vellicated by some sharp serosity.

Network: Anything reticulated or decussated, at equal distances, with interstices between the intersections.

Oats: A grain, which in England is generally given to horses, but in Scotland supports the people.

Exercises

1. What was Samuel Johnson's purpose in publishing a dictionary?
2. Tell how Johnson's and Bailey's dictionaries surpassed previous works in these aspects.
   a. Entry characteristics.
   b. Language coverage.
3. How was Johnson's dictionary different from Bailey's?
4. What effect did Johnson's dictionary have on English spelling?
5. What was one reason for weaknesses in Johnson's dictionary?

Notes on Part D

Some of the first English dictionaries appeared because of additions to the language, and they helped to secure those words in general use.

1604: *A Table Alphabeticall of Hard Wordes,* published by Robert Cawdrey. It defined words that had been adopted from other languages.

1658: *Glossographia,* published by Thomas Blount. It had some etymologies.

1708: *Dictionarium Anglo-Brittanicum,* published by Thomas Kersey. This work indentified legal, dialectal, and archaic terms, making a more useful literary tool.

1721: *Universal Etymological Dictionary of the English Language* by Nathan Bailey. It was an attempt to include all English words, not just the hard ones.

1755: *Dictionary of the English Language* by Samuel Johnson. Johnson's hope in preparing his dictionary was "to fix pronunciation, to preserve the purity of the language, to ascertain its usage, and to lengthen its duration." It did indeed have the effect of an academy. Many people were pleased to have an authority and willingly surrendered their language to Johnson's dictatorship. Especially in the matter of pronunciation, correctness was sought as social status, and many pronunciation dictionaries flourished in the late eighteenth century.

1769: *New English Dictionary* by James Buchanan.

1773: *New Dictionary of the English Language* by William Kenrick.

1780: *General Dictionary of the English Language* by Thomas Sheridan.

1791: *Critical and Pronouncing Dictionary and Expositor of the English Language* by John Walker.

Answer Key—Part D (6 points)

1. He wanted to *fix pronunciation and usage* so that it would not change.

2. a. Theirs had *pronunciations, syllable divisions, etymologies, and illustrative quotations,* whereas earlier dictionaries were merely lists of hard or new words.
   b. Both Johnson's and Bailey's dictionaries were attempts to include *every word* in the language.

3. Johnson's dictionary was *more complete and thorough.*

4. It helped to *fix spelling standards* more firmly.

5. It was the work of *one man* alone.

LESSON 15

NEW WORDS

armor
behavior
buyer
calorie
challenge
contrite
convenient
dedicate
exceedingly
indefinite
Israelite
meteorite
nonsense
refrigerator
regretting
satellite
surgeon
surplus
thermometer
thermostat

REVIEW WORDS

appetite
beggar
faithfully
favorite
infinite

A.   UNEARTHING THE ROOTS

ROOT	MEANING	EXAMPLE
Latin *cal*	= heat	calorie
Greek *therm*	= heat	thermal
Latin *frig*	= cold	frigid

1. Write the lesson roots and the spelling words derived from each one.
2. When digested food reaches the cells of the body, it is used to produce heat and other forms of energy. Which NEW WORD names a unit used to measure the heat energy of food?
3. Write the word found in 1 Samuel 2:14 that names a cooking vessel and has one of the lesson roots.
4. Unscramble the letters *d-a-c-s-l* to form a word that can mean "to dip in boiling water." Underline the lesson root in the word.
5. Write the spelling word with this etymology: (heat) + *metron* (measure).
6. A <u>therm</u> blanket is designed to help retain body heat.
7. The purpose of a _____* is to provide "heat that stands" at a constant temperature.
8. If you want a hot drink for lunch at school, you can put it into a _____ bottle in the morning. (Capitalize this word because it is a trademark.)
9. The element *geo* means "earth." Choose one of these meanings for *geothermal*.
   (a) Pertaining to warm air moving over the earth.
   (b) Pertaining to heat from inside the earth.
10. Without consulting a dictionary, choose the word that best fits this definition: "pertaining to the combining of atoms at a very high temperature."
    fusillade   metencephalon   thermonuclear
11. Complete this analogy with a NEW WORD.
    reaper : combine :: icebox : _____
12. The coldest climate zone on earth is the <u>frig</u> zone.
13. Add a suffix to your answer for number 12 to form a noun for the blank in this sentence: The _____ of her manner made me feel unwelcome.

Lesson 15

(Total points: 69)

Notes on Part A

Selected Words With Lesson Roots
L *cal:* **calorie,** caldron, caliduct, scald

Gk. *therm:* **thermometer, thermostat,** geothermal, thermal, thermonuclear, Thermos

L *frig:* **refrigerator,** frigid, frigidity

Exercise 1: Do the students need a reminder to guess and then check the Speller Dictionary for identifying words with lesson roots?

Exercise 10: For the connoisseur of words who may wish to pursue the meaning of the other two choices:

fusillade—multiple firearms shot simultaneously or in rapid succession

metencephalon—early formative part of the brain that develops into the cerebellum

Exercise 11: *Reaper* was forerunner of *combine,* as *icebox* was forerunner of ____.

Answer Key—Part A (19 points)

1. *cal:* calorie
   therm: thermometer, thermostat
   frig: refrigerator
2. calorie
3. caldron
4. scald
5. thermometer
6. thermal
7. thermostat
8. Thermos
9. b. Pertaining to the heat from inside the earth.
10. thermonuclear
11. refrigerator
12. frigid
13. frigidity *or* frigidness

Lesson 15 Test Sentences

1. *satellite* The moon is a *satellite* of the earth. *satellite*
2. *meteorite* Could this odd pebble be a *meteorite?* *meteorite*
3. *calorie* Figure the *calorie* content of that dessert. *calorie*
4. *contrite* God honors a *contrite* spirit. *contrite*
5. *infinite* His *infinite* view sees the heart. *infinite*
6. *behavior* We see the fruits of *behavior.* *behavior*
7. *faithfully* Let us serve Him *faithfully. faithfully*
8. *thermostat* The *thermostat* was bumped to 85 degrees. *thermostat*
9. *dedicate* We could *dedicate* our recess to cleaning. *dedicate*
10. *nonsense* Goliath's threat was no *nonsense. nonsense*
11. *armor* David rejected the *armor* of Saul. *armor*
12. *challenge* His *challenge* angered the giant. *challenge*
13. *surplus* David had four *surplus* stones. *surplus*
14. *Israelite* The *Israelite* army sprang to action. *Israelite*
15. *favorite* That is Eric's *favorite* Bible story. *favorite*
16. *indefinite* We can use an *indefinite* number of volunteers. *indefinite*
17. *convenient* Choose a *convenient* spot to meet. *convenient*
18. *appetite* Larry has a big *appetite* after school. *appetite*
19. *refrigerator* It often leads him to the *refrigerator. refrigerator*
20. *beggar* We met a *beggar* on the street corner. *beggar*
21. *regretting* He was *regretting* his choice. *regretting*
22. *buyer* Along came a *buyer* for his labor. *buyer*
23. *exceedingly* He was *exceedingly* grateful for the work. *exceedingly*
24. *thermometer* The *thermometer* showed a record cold. *thermometer*
25. *surgeon* The *surgeon* was as relieved as anyone. *surgeon*

B. AFFIXING AFFIXES

1. Write words with the *-ite* suffix for these definitions.
    a. That which comes from a meteor*.
    b. That which is favored*.
    c. That which writes. (The Greek root *graphein* means "to write.")
    d. That which is opposed.
    e. That which is composed of various parts.
    f. One who is a descendant of Israel*.
    g. One who follows the teachings of Menno Simons.
    h. One who follows the teachings of Jacob Hutter.
    i. One who is a descendant of Benjamin (1 Samuel 9:21).

2. For these definitions, write spelling words that end with *-ite*.
    a. Desire for something.
    b. Repentant.
    c. An orbiting body.

Noun-forming Suffix

SUFFIX	MEANING	EXAMPLE
-ite	that which, one who	Canaanite

3. Write two spelling words that have two suffixes. After each one, write the root word with both suffixes removed.

4. Write two spelling words with suffixes other than *-ite* that mean "a person who."

5. The Latin root *finis* means "end; limit." Choose the correct word from this list to match the definitions that follow.

    define   finite
    definite   infinite
    indefinite

    a. Existing for a limited time.
    b. Uncertain; lacking precise limits.
    c. To limit with precise meaning.
    d. Having no boundaries or limits.
    e. Having distinct limits.

C. SOUND, STRUCTURE, AND MEANING

1. Write three NEW WORDS that have the soft *g* sound.

2. Write the NEW WORD in which a consonant was doubled to add *-ing*. Also write the root word.

3. In a two-syllable word, double the final consonant to add *-ing* if the second syllable is accented. Follow this rule as you write the *-ing* forms of these words.
    a. defer
    b. tutor
    c. begin
    d. gallop
    e. forbid
    f. forget
    g. market

4. Write the NEW WORDS that have the following roots.
    a. convene
    b. define
    c. sense
    d. plus

5. Find a NEW WORD ending with /ər/ in each of these verses. Many Bibles use the British spelling of these words. Write each word in both forms.
    a. Ephesians 6:11
    b. Titus 2:3

6. Write the NEW WORD that has this etymology: *dē-* (apart) + *dicāre* (proclaim).

7. The plural noun *regrets* has a special meaning. Write a sentence using the word in this way.

Notes on Part B

Exercise 1: Every answer uses a form of one word in the definition.

Answer Key—Part B (23 points)

1. a. meteorite
   b. favorite
   c. graphite
   d. opposite
   e. composite
   f. Israelite
   g. Mennonite
   h. Hutterite
   i. Benjamite

2. a. appetite
   b. contrite
   c. satellite

3. exceedingly, exceed
   faithfully, faith

4. buyer, beggar

5. a. finite
   b. indefinite
   c. define
   d. infinite
   e. definite

Notes on Part C

Exercise 5: If students' Bibles do not have the British spelling, it can be found in the Speller Dictionary.

Answer Key—Part C (22 points)

1. challenge, refrigerator, surgeon

2. regretting, regret

3. a. deferring
   b. tutoring
   c. beginning
   d. galloping
   e. forbidding
   f. forgetting
   g. marketing

4. a. convenient
   b. indefinite
   c. nonsense
   d. surplus

5. a. armor, armour
   b. behavior, behaviour

6. dedicate

7. (Sample sentence) We received your *regrets* the day before the program.

D. LANGUAGE LINEAGE

WEBSTER'S DICTIONARY

Young Noah Webster was a schoolteacher in colonial America. The English schoolbooks of his day were from England and failed to reflect American culture; and besides, they were always in short supply. When the American Revolution made them even scarcer, Noah Webster set out to write his own. He prepared a three-part series titled *Grammatical Institute of the English Language*. His spelling book was published in 1783, a grammar book the following year, and a reader one year later.

Webster became a strong advocate of a distinctively American education. He thought spelling unity would help to join the colonies into one stable nation. He also recognized the developing independence of American vocabulary. Some words no longer held the same meanings to the colonists that they did to the British, and new words came into use because of new scenes and experiences foreign to England. He thought Americans needed a dictionary of their own.

Noah Webster published a small school dictionary in 1806. He considered it a preliminary book and spent the next twenty years writing a more comprehensive work for broader use. He studied foreign languages and traveled to France and England in search of helpful information.

In 1828, when Noah Webster was seventy years old, he finally was able to publish his *American Dictionary of the English Language*. The 70,000 entries filled two volumes. This was by far the most extensive English dictionary yet. It included many scientific and technical terms as well as more extensive and accurate etymologies. Webster's was the first dictionary with tables of money, weights, and measures, and with other generally helpful information.

Sold in England and America, Webster's dictionary drew criticism for increasing the differences between American English and British English; but all the copies were sold in little more than a year. With academic weapons, Noah Webster was helping to mold young America into an independent and unified nation.

Exercises

1. For what two reasons did Noah Webster write his own schoolbooks?
2. How many years did Webster work on his big dictionary?
3. What new features did he include in his dictionary?
4. What political influence did Webster's dictionary have?

Notes on Part D

"A national language is a band of national union," Noah Webster wrote in 1789. He held many public offices and supported various causes, but his ultimate project was the dictionary.

In the field of etymologies, he found an especially large task. "In searching for the original of English words, I soon found the field of etymology had been very imperfectly explored: and one discovery succeeding another, my curiosity was excited to persevere in the pursuit. At length finding no safe clue to conduct me through the labyrinth, I adopted a new plan of investigation, that of examining and comparing the primary elements, articulations or consonants of words in 20 different languages or dialects." Webster spent about ten years pursuing this synopsis.

In 1807, he had mastered twelve languages. By 1813 he knew twenty, of which were Chaldaic, Syriac, Arabic, Samaritan, Hebrew, Ethiopic, Persian, Irish, Amoritic, Anglo-Saxon, German, Dutch, Swedish, Danish, Greek, Latin, Italian, Spanish, French, and Russian. He later added Portuguese, Welsh, Gothic, and the early dialects of English and German.

Near the end of his project, Webster traveled to Europe to visit the libraries of France and England. It was a momentous hour when he wrote the last entry in his manuscript at his lodging in Cambridge, England. The sixty-seven-year-old man found his hand trembling so much that he could hardly hold his pen steady to write.

Answer Key—Part D (5 points)

1. English schoolbooks were in *short supply,* and they *did not reflect American culture.*
2. Noah Webster worked *twenty years* on his big dictionary. (Accept twenty-two years, as the time from 1806 to 1828.)
3. Webster's dictionary included *tables of money, weights, and measures,* and other helpful general information.
4. It helped Americans to become *independent and unified.*

LESSON 16

NEW WORDS

abstract
anointing
appendicitis
arthritis
autograph
bored
civilized
competent
conferred
deeply
delinquent
enlighten
esteemed
exceptional
literary
literature
manuscript
prescribe
subscription
transcribe

REVIEW WORDS

additional
authority
photograph
Sabbath
telegraph

A.   UNEARTHING THE ROOTS

ROOT	MEANING	EXAMPLE
Greek *graph*	= write	autograph
Latin *scrib, script*	= write	inscribe
Latin *littera*	= letter	literate

1. Write two lesson roots that can stand alone as words.
2. Write the REVIEW WORD with the etymological definition "written with light."
3. For each etymological definition, write the correct word from the list at the right.
    a. life writing   autograph
    b. self writing   biography
    c. earth writing   calligraphy
    d. shake writing   geography
    e. beautiful writing   phonograph
    f. sound writing   seismograph
4. Use words with the Latin root for *write* in these blanks. Dedicated (writers) carefully copied the Holy (writings). It would have been disrespectful for them to (write sloppily).
5. Write spelling words for these etymologies.
    a. *manus* (hand) + (write)   d. (letter) + *-ary*
    b. *tēle* (distant) + (write)   e. (letter) + *-ture*
    c. *trans* (across) + (write)
6. Which word in Acts 17:23 refers to "something written" on the altar?
7. Find the NEW WORD that has the etymological definition "under writing," and write a form of that word for each sentence.
    a. Mr. Rud asked two witnesses to _____ the document.
    b. We paid for a three-year magazine _____.
    c. In the chemical formula for water (H_2O), the 2 is a _____.
8. Some medicines can only be obtained if a doctor will (write before)* that you need them.
9. According to John 7:15, some Jews thought Jesus was (literate, illiterate).
10. Those who obey John 13:14 to the letter will (literally, literacy) wash one another's feet.

Lesson 16

(Total points: 78)

Notes on Part A

Selected Words With Lesson Roots

Gk. *graph:* **autograph, photograph,** biography (3), calligraphy, digraph, geography, graph, graphite, orthography, paragraph, phonograph, seismograph

Orthography (spelling) is the art or study of writing letters in correct sequence.

L *scrib, script:* **manuscript, prescribe, subscription, transcribe,** inscribe, scribble, scribe, Scripture, subscript

L *littera:* **literary, literature,** illiterate, literacy, literal, obliterate

To obliterate is to erase [*ob* against + *littera* letter].

Answer Key—Part A (24 points)

1. graph, script

2. photograph

3. a. biography
   b. autograph
   c. geography
   d. seismograph
   e. calligraphy
   f. phonograph

4. scribes, Scripture(s), scribble

5. a. manuscript
   b. telegraph
   c. transcribe
   d. literary
   e. literature

6. inscription

7. a. subscribe
   b. subscription
   c. subscript

8. prescribe

9. illiterate

10. literally

Lesson 16 Test Sentences

1. *appendicitis* Carol had *appendicitis* last month. *appendicitis*
2. *arthritis* Grandfather suffers from *arthritis. arthritis*
3. *prescribe* What did the doctor *prescribe* for pain? *prescribe*
4. *competent* We are glad for *competent* doctors. *competent*
5. *anointing* The sick may call for *anointing* with oil. *anointing*
6. *authority* God has final *authority* on healing. *authority*
7. *conferred* Three men *conferred* about the damage. *conferred*
8. *abstract* The wallpaper has an *abstract* pattern. *abstract*
9. *Sabbath* The *Sabbath* ended at sundown. *Sabbath*
10. *delinquent* A *delinquent* payment damaged his credit. *delinquent*
11. *transcribe* Can you *transcribe* the message on tape? *transcribe*
12. *additional* We need four *additional* copies. *additional*
13. *civilized* Most people in a *civilized* culture can read. *civilized*
14. *literature* It is important to choose good *literature. literature*
15. *literary* What are your *literary* interests? *literary*
16. *subscription* Renew your *subscription* before it expires. *subscription*
17. *bored* Children get *bored* if they play all the time. *bored*
18. *autograph* Harlan let his friends *autograph* his cast. *autograph*
19. *exceptional* Dr. Mason did *exceptional* lettering. *exceptional*
20. *manuscript* Joel used tall *manuscript* characters. *manuscript*
21. *telegraph* News of the disaster came by *telegraph. telegraph*
22. *photograph* A large *photograph* was on the front page. *photograph*
23. *esteemed* Saints have always *esteemed* the psalms highly. *esteemed*
24. *deeply* Drink *deeply* of their inspiration. *deeply*
25. *enlighten* God will *enlighten* your understanding. *enlighten*

B. AFFIXING AFFIXES

1. Write words with the *-itis* suffix to name the following conditions.
   a. Inflammation of the appendix*.
   b. Inflammation of the *arthron* (joints)*.
   c. Inflammation of the tonsils.
   d. Inflammation of the larynx.
   e. Inflammation of the bronchial tubes.
   f. Inflammation of the meninges.
   g. Inflammation of *phlebos* (blood vessels).
2. Words with the suffixes *-ed* and *-ing* can function as verbs or adjectives. Use spelling words with these suffixes, and label each answer with *v.* or *adj.*
   a. Samuel brought the ____ oil with him.
   b. The prophet was ____ David according to God's direction.
   c. The natives preferred their primitive culture over that of the ____ foreigners.
   d. In just a few years the foreigners had

Noun-forming Suffix

SUFFIX	MEANING	EXAMPLE
-itis	disease or inflamation of	laryngitis

   ____ the natives.
   e. The electrician ____ three holes and passed wires through them.
   f. Six ____ patients sat in the dentist's waiting room.
   g. The doctors ____ at length about the boy's mangled foot.
   h. Everyone was very respectful to the ____ visitor.
3. Write the NEW WORD with a prefix and a suffix both spelled the same way. Also write the *-ed* and *-ing* forms of this word.
4. One NEW WORD has two suffixes and means "uncommon." Write this word, and also write its adverb form by adding *-ly.*

C. SOUND, STRUCTURE, AND MEANING

1. Write the two spelling words that begin with *au.*
2. How many syllables are in *arthritis?* Be sure not to insert an extra syllable when saying or writing this word.
3. Write the correct number of syllables for each of these words.
   a. athlete
   b. lightning
   c. afghan
   d. mathematics
   e. translate
4. Write the NEW WORD in which the final consonant was doubled before adding *-ed.* Which syllable of the root word is accented?
5. Write spelling words that are synonyms

of these words.
   a. capable
   b. negligent
   c. extra
   d. excellent
6. Write spelling words that are antonyms of these words.
   a. slightly
   b. concrete
   c. despised
   d. primitive
7. The word *bore* has four entries in the Speller Dictionary. Write a sentence using the noun.
8. Write a sentence using *Sabbath* and *esteemed.*

Notes on Part B

      Exercise 2: The words used as adjectives are participles. Sentences *a–f* are in pairs that use the same word. Sentences *g* and *h* use separate words.

Answer Key—Part B (28 points)

1. a. appendicitis
   b. arthritis
   c. tonsillitis
   d. laryngitis
   e. bronchitis
   f. meningitis
   g. phlebitis
2. a. anointing, adj.
   b. anointing, v.

   c. civilized, adj.
   d. civilized, v.
   e. bored, v.
   f. bored, adj.
   g. conferred, v.
   h. esteemed, adj.
3. enlighten, enlightened, elightening
4. exceptional, exceptionally

Notes on Part C

      Exercises 2 and 3: Practice correct pronunciation of these words, which are commonly said with an extra syllable.

      Exercise 4: The "Double the consonant" rule applies to two-syllable words that are accented on the second syllable.

      Double the ending consonant for these: occur, prefer, omit, repel, corral.

      Do not double the ending consonant for these: cover, armor, vomit, open, label.

Answer Key—Part C (21 points)

1. autograph, authority
2. three
3. a. two
   b. two
   c. two
   d. four *or* three
   e. two
4. conferred, second
5. a. competent
   b. delinquent
   c. additional

   d. exceptional
6. a. deeply
   b. abstract
   c. esteemed
   d. civilized
7. (Sample sentence—either one)
   A log of driftwood tumbled along with the *bore*.
   A mockingbird is not a *bore*.
8. (Sample sentence) The Pharisees *esteemed* the *Sabbath* more highly than the Lord.

D.   LANGUAGE LINEAGE

THE OXFORD DICTIONARY

By the mid 1800s, Johnson's dictionary was no longer sufficient for the scholars of England, and Webster's was too Americanized. In 1857, England's Philological Society appointed a committee to compile a list of words that were not in the dictionary. Perhaps a supplement could be published to fill in the lack. The committee prepared a set of principles for a good dictionary, and these convinced the Philological Society that a supplement would not meet the need. It would be better to start over and publish the ultimate dictionary.

In 1858 the society laid plans for this new dictionary. It was to record every word used in the English language since the year 1000. It would show the various forms and spellings of each word through history, record its uses, and define all its meanings. To find all the meanings and uses of every word required a systematic reading of practically everything published in the language. A call for volunteers was issued, and thousands of readers responded, submitting quotations of word usage from literature.

The original editor was a member of the committee that inspired the project. On his sudden death, another committee member took his place. But his increasing involvement in other interests led to the appointment of a third editor, under whose hand the project progressed through the printing of the first installment. When the first volume appeared in 1884, covering part of the "A" section, it was instantly recognized as a top authority. By 1900, four and one-half volumes were finished, extending through the letter H. Three additional editors were appointed along the way, providing a team of four to finish the work.

The project was financed by the Oxford University Press and printed there. The tenth and final volume appeared in 1928, seventy years after plans were begun for the dictionary. The Oxford Dictionary included 240,165 main entries containing a vast store of historical information and other exact details about the language. This was not a common desk dictionary, but a valuable resource for language study and research. It has greatly helped to increase the understanding of language and language changes.

Exercises

1. a. How many years passed from the time plans were laid until the first volume of the Oxford Dictionary was published?

   b. How much time elapsed between the printing of the first and last volumes?

2. What goals did the society have for this dictionary?

3. How many different editors served on the project?

4. In what way was the Oxford Dictionary a top authority?

Notes on Part D

Philological [< Gk *philologos* loving learning < *philos* loving + *logos* reason, speech]

Johnson's dictionary had taken one man eight years (with a crew of helpers who wrote down quotations he chose from literature). It had 43,500 entries in two volumes.

Webster worked on his dictionary for twenty years. It had 70,000 entries in two volumes.

The Oxford Dictionary was a seventy-year project, engaging a team of editors and many contributors. Ten volumes held the 240,165 original entries. The following were editors of the work.

1859	Herbert Coleridge
1861	F. J. Furnivall, replaced Coleridge on his death
1879	James A. H. Murry, replaced Furnivall when the project lagged
1888	Henry Bradley, coeditor
1901	William A. Craigie, coeditor
1914	Charles T. Onions, coeditor

The official title of the Oxford Dictionary was *A New English Dictionary on Historical Principles.* Its definitions are given in historical order, and dated quotations show how each word has been used through its history. This dictionary has influenced people's view of language. The history laid out so orderly helps them to see language in a more scientific way.

Answer Key—Part D (5 points)

1. a. The first volume appeared *twenty-six years* after the plans were laid.
   b. *Forty-four years* passed from the time the first volume was printed, until the last one was finished.

2. The dictionary was to record *every word in the language,* and show its various *forms, uses, and meanings*.

3. *Six* men served as editors of the Oxford Dictionary.

4. It contained a vast store of *historical information* and *exact details* about language.

A. UNEARTHING THE ROOTS

ROOT	MEANING	EXAMPLE
Latin *popul*	= people	populace
Greek *demos*	= people	democratic
Latin *urb*	= city	suburb
Greek *polis*	= city	metropolis
Latin *civi*	= citizen	civilize

LESSON 17

NEW WORDS

atone

civilian

convey

democracy

diagnosis

diphtheria

drowned

epidemic

helicopter

hypnotic

inconvenience

interval

label

melancholy

metropolis

politician

population

suburb

suspicious

tuberculosis

REVIEW WORDS

all right

humility

icicles

measles

possession

1. The NEW WORDS for these exercises contain slightly altered forms of lesson roots.
   a. Rule by the people.
   b. Spreading rapidly over the people.
   c. One involved in government.
2. Write the four NEW WORDS in which the lesson roots did not change when affixes were added.
3. A _popul_ person is in favor with many people.
4. Jesus preached to the (populace, populism).
5. The word *public* is derived from the Latin root *popul.* In the Bible we read of people whose work was to collect taxes from the public. Who were they?
6. The ____* of China is over a billion people.
7. Complete this analogy with a NEW WORD.
   monarch : kingdom :: people : ____
8. Without consulting a dictionary, choose the correct phrase. A demographer studies (government spending, radar control, human statistics).
9. Write a NEW WORD for this etymology:
   epi (over) + (people).
10. The traffic slowed as it passed through the _urb_ area.
11. In Numbers 35, the Levites received cities to dwell in, along with _urb_ * (surrounding lands) for their cattle.
12. Find a name in Romans 16:9 that is derived from a lesson root.
13. Write a NEW WORD that combines the Greek elements *mētēr* and *polis,* meaning "mother city."
14. Answer with words containing variant spellings of the italicized roots.
    a. The _polis_ were summoned to disperse the rioters.
    b. A Christian is a _cīvi_ of the heavenly kingdom.
15. Write the name of the district in Matthew 4:25 that means "ten cities."
16. War brings destruction of ____* property and military loss.

Lesson 17

(Total points: 84)

Notes on Part A

Selected Words With Lesson Roots

L *popul:* **population,** populace, popular, public(an) republic

Gk. *demos:* **democracy, epidemic,** democratic, demography

Demography is the study of human population statistics.

L *urb:* **suburb,** urban, urbane, urbanize

Gk. *polis:* **metropolis, politician,** Decapolis, Minneapolis, police, policy

Minneapolis is a hybrid of the Indian word *minne* (water) and Greek *polis*—the water city.

L *civi:* **civilian,** civics, civil(ize), civilization

Exercise 1: If pupils have difficulty recognizing roots in the spelling list, they should choose a spelling word that might be a possibility and look up its etymology.

Exercise 7: A *monarch* rules a *kingdom,* as *people* rule a _____.

Answer Key—Part A (22 points)

1. a. democracy
   b. epidemic
   c. politician

2. civilian, metropolis, population, suburb

3. popular

4. populace

5. publicans

6. population

7. democracy

8. human statistics

9. epidemic

10. urban

11. suburb(s)

12. Urbane

13. metropolis

14. a. police
    b. citizen

15. Decapolis

16. civilian

Lesson 17 Test Sentences

1. *tuberculosis* Is *tuberculosis* very serious? *tuberculosis*
2. *diphtheria* It is not as critical as *diphtheria. diphtheria*
3. *diagnosis* We heard the *diagnosis* on Anthony today. *diagnosis*
4. *measles* He has *measles* the second time. *measles*
5. *epidemic* Could there be an *epidemic? epidemic*
6. *hypnotic* Some doctors use *hypnotic* methods. *hypnotic*
7. *melancholy* Did that cause his *melancholy* moods? *melancholy*
8. *label* Read the *label* carefully. *label*
9. *helicopter* The tail rotor keeps a *helicopter* from spinning. *helicopter*
10. *drowned* Heavy rains *drowned* our first planting of peas. *drowned*
11. *all right* The later crop looks *all right. all right*
12. *convey* A small ditch will *convey* irrigation water. *convey*
13. *metropolis* Joel moved away from the *metropolis. metropolis*
14. *population* The *population* increased rapidly. *population*
15. *suburb* Soon his country village was a *suburb* of the city. *suburb*
16. *democracy* God does not rule the church by *democracy. democracy*
17. *politician* Every *politician* protects his reputation. *politician*
18. *civilian* The president wears *civilian* clothes. *civilian*
19. *interval* Can you sing the musical *interval* correctly? *interval*
20. *atone* Jesus came to *atone* for all man's sin. *atone*
21. *possession* He gives the priceless *possession* of peace. *possession*
22. *humility* Christ's *humility* is a pattern for us. *humility*
23. *suspicious* It pays to be *suspicious* of your own pride. *suspicious*
24. *icicles* A row of *icicles* sparkled in the sun. *icicles*
25. *inconvenience* Service does not measure *inconvenience. inconvenience*

B.   AFFIXING AFFIXES

1.   Write a word with the *-osis* suffix to match each definition below. Choose from these words or the spelling word list.

> cirrhosis   hypnosis
> prognosis   metamorphosis

   a.   A process of transformation.
   b.   The process of identifying a disease.
   c.   A prediction of the course of a disease.
   d.   An infectious disease involving the lungs.
   e.   A sleeplike condition of subjection to another.
   f.   A degenerating condition of liver cells.

2.   Two of the answers for number 1 have the root *gnos* (know). Write them for these etymological meanings.
   a.   To know through or thoroughly.
   b.   To know before.

3.   Write a word with the *-otic* suffix to match each definition. Choose from these words or the spelling word list.

> narcotic   chaotic   psychotic

   a.   Characterized by disorder and confusion.
   b.   Pertaining to severe mental disorder.
   c.   Producing sleep.

Noun- and Adjective-forming Suffixes

SUFFIX	MEANING	EXAMPLE
-osis	condition, process	osmosis
-otic	producing, characterized by	antibiotic

   d.   Producing numbness or stupor.

4.   Copy each word, and write what part of speech it is. Then write the spelling word derived from it, and name its part of speech.
   a.   humble
   b.   possess
   c.   suspect

5.   Write the NEW WORD that has a negative prefix and a noun-forming suffix.

6.   Write spelling words with inflectional suffixes for these changes.
   a.   A verb changed from present tense to past tense.
   b.   A noun changed from singular to plural.

7.   Write the REVIEW WORD that looks like a plural form but is usually considered singular.

C.   SOUND, STRUCTURE, AND MEANING

1.   Write the NEW WORDS that have these phonetic features.
   a.   /ā/ spelled *ey*
   b.   /f/ spelled *ph*
   c.   /k/ spelled *ch*

2.   Write the NEW WORD that ends with *el.* Also write the preferred *-ed* and *-ing* forms of this word (without doubling the final consonant, since the last syllable is unaccented).

3.   Write the NEW WORDS that have these etymologies.
   a.   *helix* (spiral) + *pteron* (wing)

   b.   *inter* (between) + *vallum* (wall)

4.   One entry in your spelling list is a two-word expression that is often incorrectly written as one word. Write a sentence using this expression.

5.   One NEW WORD was once a two-word expression, but now it is a single word that means "to make satisfactory payment for wrong." Write this word, and then write the two words of which it is composed.

6.   Write the word that is a doublet of *convey.* Write a sentence using *convey* and its doublet.

Answer Key—Part B (28 points)

1. a. metamorphosis
   b. diagnosis
   c. prognosis
   d. tuberculosis
   e. hypnosis
   f. cirrhosis

2. a. diagnosis
   b. prognosis

3. a. chaotic
   b. psychotic
   c. hypnotic
   d. narcotic

4. a. humble—adj., humility—n.
   b. possess—v., possession—n.
   c. suspect—v. *or* n., suspicious—adj.

5. inconvenience

6. a. drowned
   b. icicles

7. measles

Answer Key—Part C (14 points)

1. a. convey
   b. diphtheria
   c. melancholy

2. label, labeled, labeling

3. a. helicopter
   b. interval

4. (Sample sentence) It is *all right* to double the consonant on some two-syllable words.

5. atone, at one

6. convoy (Sample sentence) A *convoy* of soldiers and horsemen was charged to *convey* Paul away from Jerusalem.

D.   LANGUAGE LINEAGE

SEMANTIC STUDY: DOUBLETS

Words are frequently borrowed from another language. The Latin word *discus,* meaning "flat ring used in pitching games," entered the English language in the 500s or 600s as the word *disc* (for "plate or platter"). It has become our modern word *dish*. The same word *discus* developed into the Italian word *desco,* meaning "a flat top." English borrowed this from Italian and obtained *desk*. In the 1800s, English borrowed the word *discus* directly from Latin as the name of a heavy, circular object used in distance-throwing contests. And a few years later, the same Latin word became the source of English *disk* (for "flat circular plate"), which can refer to farming equipment, a device used in computers, a platelike structure in the spine, or a piece of candy. Because all these English words came from the same Latin source, they are doublets of one another.

Coffee and *cafe* are doublets stemming from the Italian word *caffè.* This word was received into the Dutch language as *koffie,* which English changed to *coffee* and used as the name of a beverage. The Italian word was also received into French as *café,* and from there it passed into English as the name of a coffeehouse or restaurant.

In some doublets it is easy to see the similarity of meaning. *Compute* comes from a Latin word meaning "to reckon together." Its doublet *count* became a French word before entering English. *Regal* and *royal* stem from the same Latin word, which became two different French words and then passed into English.

Some doublets have meanings so diverse that it is hard to imagine how they are related. *Cross* and *cruise* both come from Latin *crux,* meaning "cross." The word developed into *cross* as it passed through Irish and Norse and then into English. *Cruise* passed through the Dutch language. It is related to *cross* in that a leisurely cruise will "cross" back and forth over the most direct line of travel. *Chamber* and *camera* both stem from Latin *camera,* which means "a room." *Chamber* passed through the French language, bringing along its original meaning. The English word *camera* developed from *camera obscura,* a "dark chamber" that was the forerunner of the modern camera. This was a box large enough for a person to enter and trace the image projected on an inside wall from a hole in the opposite wall.

Exercises

1. a. List four doublets that originated from the Latin word *discus.*
   b. Which three of those words came directly to English from Latin?
   c. What other language was involved in the transmission of the fourth word?
2. a. What language provided the link between Italian *caffe* and English *coffee?*
   b. What language provided the link between Italian *caffe* and English *café?*
3. a. Write two pairs of doublets with similar meanings.
   b. Write two pairs of doublets with very different meanings.
4. Look up *plenty, please,* and *placid* in the Speller Dictionary. Write the two that are doublets.

Notes on Part D

Exercise 4: The Speller Dictionary does not label the words as doublets. Students must compare the word origins to recognize them.

Additional doublet examples:

cap [< ME *cappe* < OE *caeppe* < L *cappa* head covering, cloak]

cape [< Sp *capa* cloak < L *cappa*]

chapel [< ME *chapele* < OF < L *capella* < *cappa*] (from a shrine containing the cape of St. Martin of Tours)

chaperon [< F *chaperon* hood < *chape* covering < L *cappa*]

history [< L *historia*]

story [< ME *storie* < F *estorie* < L *historia*]

inch [< OE *ynce* < L *uncia* twelfth part < *unus* one]

ounce [< ME *unce* < F < L *uncia* < *unus*]

legible [< ME < L *legibilis* < *legere* to read]

legend [< ME < F *legende* < L *legenda* < *legere*]

lecture [< ME < F *lectura* < *legere*]

lectern [< ME *lectorn* < F *lettrun* < L *lecternum* < *legere*]

mint [< ME *mynt* < OE *mynet* < L *moneta*]

money [< ME *moneye* < F *moneie* < L *moneta*]

pattern [< ME *patron* < F < L *patrōnus* < *pater* father]

patron [< ME < F < L *patrōnus* < *pater*]

pawn [< ME < F *paon* < L *pedō* foot soldier < *pēs* foot]

pioneer [< F *pionier* foot soldier < *pion* < L *pedō*]

saint [< L *sanctus* holy]

sanction [< L *sanctio* an ordaining < *sanctus*]

Answer Key—Part D (20 points)

1. a. dish, desk, discus, disk
   b. dish, discus, disk
   c. Italian
2. a. Dutch
   b. French
3. a. compute, count; regal, royal
   b. cross, cruise; chamber, camera
4. placid, please

LESSON 18

13	14	15	16	17
acknowledgment	allegiance	armor	abstract	atone
apostolic	amuse	behavior	anointing	civilian
artistic	ascension	buyer	appendicitis	convey
ascertain	brilliancy	calorie	arthritis	democracy
assurance	ceased	challenge	autograph	diagnosis
athletic	constellation	contrite	bored	diphtheria
cardiac	correspondence	convenient	civilized	drowned
certify	decorations	dedicate	competent	epidemic
characteristic	discrepancy	exceedingly	conferred	helicopter
colonel	efficient	indefinite	deeply	hypnotic
consultation	evidently	Israelite	delinquent	inconvenience
cosmic	hatred	meteorite	enlighten	interval
crisis	illuminate	nonsense	esteemed	label
discord	iniquities	refrigerator	exceptional	melancholy
dramatic	intelligence	regretting	literary	metropolis
element	leisurely	satellite	literature	politician
financial	photograph	surgeon	manuscript	population
heroic	remembrance	surplus	prescribe	suburb
intestine	resistance	thermometer	subscription	suspicious
noticeable	violence	thermostat	transcribe	tuberculosis

A. UNEARTHING THE ROOTS

Gk. *not, gnos*	= know		Gk. *graph*	= write
L *cert*	= sure		L *scrib, script*	= write
			L *littera*	= letter
L *audi*	= hear			
Gk. *phono*	= sound		L *popul*	= people
L *lumin*	= light		Gk. *demos*	= people
Gk. *photo*	= light		L *urb*	= city
			Gk. *polis*	= city
L *cal*	= heat		L *civi*	= citizen
Gk. *therm*	= heat			
L *frig*	= cold			

Lesson 18

(Total points: 53)

Lesson 18 Test Sentences

1. *cosmic* The meteor shower was caused by *cosmic* dust. *cosmic*
2. *heroic* Many early Christians were *heroic* martyrs. *heroic*
3. *assurance* Strong *assurance* shone in their lives. *assurance*
4. *apostolic* Were people braver in *apostolic* times? *apostolic*
5. *noticeable* True character is *noticeable* in any age. *noticeable*
6. *crisis* It is especially clear in times of *crisis*. *crisis*
7. *colonel* A stern *colonel* interviewed the boys. *colonel*
8. *acknowledgment* He gave no *acknowledgment* of God. *acknowledgment*
9. *cardiac* Could you help someone with *cardiac* problems? *cardiac*
10. *athletic* An *athletic* lifestyle helps maintain a sound heart. *athletic*
11. *evidently* Stress and worry *evidently* bring health risks. *evidently*
12. *ceased* The winds *ceased* early in the morning. ceased
13. *violence* Broken trees revealed the *violence* of the storm. *violence*
14. *efficient* We had an *efficient* cleanup crew. *efficient*
15. *amuse* The birds at the feeder *amuse* Grandfather. *amuse*
16. *leisurely* He adjusted well to a *leisurely* life. *leisurely*
17. *correspondence* Letters are one type of *correspondence*. *correspondence*
18. *intelligence* Instinct, not *intelligence,* guides animals. *intelligence*
19. *discrepancy* Nancy found a *discrepancy* in the price list. *discrepancy*
20. *allegiance* Your uniform declares your *allegiance*. *allegiance*
21. *armor* Put on the whole *armor* of God. *armor*
22. *nonsense* There is no *nonsense* about a fire drill. *nonsense*
23. *thermometer* Does the *thermometer* register accurately? *thermometer*
24. *surgeon* A *surgeon* needs a steady hand. *surgeon*
25. *convenient* Tell the truth even when it is not *convenient*. *convenient*
26. *behavior* Tony's *behavior* confirms his testimony. *behavior*
27. *calorie* Like a snowflake, just one *calorie* hardly counts. *calorie*
28. *satellite* The mosquito attended me like a *satellite*. *satellite*
29. *indefinite* I'll lend the book for an *indefinite* time. *indefinite*
30. *contrite* God dwells with the *contrite* heart. *contrite*
31. *autograph* Boone carved his *autograph* on the door. *autograph*
32. *bored* He *bored* three holes to peg the leather hinge. *bored*
33. *literature* Sue found some new *literature* about pioneers. *literature*
34. *exceptional* She has *exceptional* interest in history. *exceptional*
35. *appendicitis* Are there home remedies for *appendicitis*? *appendicitis*
36. *conferred* We *conferred* a pompous name on the rooster. *conferred*
37. *subscription* Be sure to renew your *subscription* in time. *subscription*
38. *arthritis* Uncle Roy's *arthritis* makes him our weather man. *arthritis*
39. *competent* His *competent* service is free. *competent*
40. *delinquent* The *delinquent* assignment was finally done. *delinquent*
41. *civilian* Police officers sometimes dress in *civilian* clothes. *civilian*
42. *suspicious* Strange noises made us *suspicious* of visitors. *suspicious*
43. *diagnosis* The final *diagnosis* was squirrel activity. *diagnosis*
44. *convey* What else would *convey* acorns to the attic? *convey*
45. *atone* This gift is to *atone* for my forgetfulness. *atone*
46. *interval* There was a long *interval* between appointments. *interval*
47. *helicopter* The *helicopter* picked up shipwreck victims. *helicopter*
48. *drowned* Some of the crew *drowned* while helping others. *drowned*
49. *politician* A clever *politician* glamorized the rescue. *politician*
50. *label* He wanted to *label* the event for his credit. *label*

1. Write words from Lesson 13 for these exercises.
   a. Which word with a Greek root for *know* is used to describe things that can easily be known?
   b. Which word with a Greek root for *know* means "an indication of knowing"?
   c. Which word has the meaning "to make sure"?
2. Write words from Lesson 14.
   a. *in-* (in) + (light) = _____
   b. Which word is derived from the Greek root for *light?*
3. Write words from Lesson 15.
   a. Which word names the "heat energy" in food?
   b. Which word names a device used to "make heat stand"?

c. Which word names a device for making things cold?
4. Write words from Lesson 16.
   a. *sub-* (under) + (write)
   b. Which words contain the Latin word for *letter?*
5. Write words from Lesson 17.
   a. (people) + *kratos* (rule) = _____
   b. *epi-* (on) + (people) = _____
   c. *mētēr-* (mother) + (city) = _____
   d. *sub-* (below) + (city) = _____
   e. Which word is derived from the Latin root meaning "the people"?
   f. Which word names someone involved in government?
   g. Which word with a Latin root refers to a person not involved in government or military affairs?

B. AFFIXING AFFIXES

1. Write words from Lesson 13 to match these definitions.
   a. Pertaining to the apostles.
   b. Pertaining to art.
   c. Pertaining to an athlete.
   d. Pertaining to character.
   e. Pertaining to the cosmos.
   f. Pertaining to finances.
   g. Like a hero.
   h. Like music. (REVIEW WORD)
2. Write words from Lesson 14.
   a. The quality of being violent.
   b. The act of remembering.
   c. The condition of being brilliant.
   d. The act of corresponding.
   e. The state of being discrepant.
   f. A situation calling for prompt action. (REVIEW WORD)
   g. The state of being intelligent.
   h. The act of resisting.
3. Write words from Lesson 15.
   a. Remorseful.

-ac, -ic, -ical	affected by, like
-ance, -ancy	act, state, or quality of
-ence, -ency	act, state, or quality of
-ite	that which, one who
-itis	disease or inflammation of
-osis	condition, process
-otic	producing, characterized by

   b. Uncertain; without precise limits.
   c. Having no boundaries or limits. (REVIEW WORD)
   d. Orbiting heavenly body.
   e. Desire for something. (REVIEW WORD)
   f. Write two words in which *-ite* is a suffix meaning "one who" or "that which."
4. Write words from Lesson 16.
   a. Inflammation of the appendix.
   b. Inflammation of the joints.
5. Write words from Lesson 17.
   a. Tending to produce sleep.
   b. Conclusion of an examination.
   c. Disease affecting the lungs.

Answer Key—Part A (18 points)

1. a. noticeable
   b. acknowledgment
   c. ascertain
2. a. illuminate
   b. photograph
3. a. calorie
   b. thermostat
   c. refrigerator
4. a. subscription
   b. literary, literature
5. a. democracy
   b. epidemic
   c. metropolis
   d. suburb
   e. population
   f. politician
   g. civilian

Answer Key—Part B (28 points)

1. a. apostolic
   b. artistic
   c. athletic
   d. characteristic
   e. cosmic
   f. financial
   g. heroic
   h. musical
2. a. violence
   b. remembrance
   c. brilliancy
   d. correspondence
   e. discrepancy
   f. emergency
   g. intelligence
   h. resistance

3. a. contrite *or* regretting
   b. indefinite
   c. infinite
   d. satellite
   e. appetite
   f. Israelite, meteorite
4. a. appendicitis
   b. arthritis
5. a. hypnotic
   b. diagnosis
   c. tuberculosis

D. LANGUAGE LINEAGE

REVIEW

1. a. Why was standardization of English important?

   b. What body was formed in 1664 to regulate and improve the English language?

2. What was Samuel Johnson's intention in publishing his dictionary?

3. Why did Noah Webster think there should be an American dictionary?

4. a. Why was the Oxford Dictionary prepared?

   b. What has been the most valuable aspect of the Oxford Dictionary?

5. What makes one word a doublet of another?

Answer Key—Part D (7 points)

1. a. A standardized language can *communicate to many generations.*
    b. England's Royal Society formed a *committee.*
2. Johnson *wanted to fix pronunciation and usage.*
3. Some American *vocabulary and meanings were different* from the British.
4. a. Johnson's dictionary was *no longer sufficient,* and Webster's was *too Americanized* to suit the British.
    b. The Oxford Dictionary is a valuable resource on *language history.*
5. Words are doublets when they come from the *same source.*

LESSON 19

NEW WORDS

anticipate
ascend
carbohydrates
courier
discourse
dissatisfied
eclipse
embroider
emphasis
endure
energy
exclaim
excursion
exile
Exodus
extraordinary
incense
installation
occurred
transcend

REVIEW WORDS

encounter
encourage
example
ordinary
surrender

A. UNEARTHING THE ROOTS

ROOT	MEANING	EXAMPLE
Latin *scend*	= climb	ascend
Latin *curr*, *curs*	= run	current

1. Write the lesson roots and the NEW WORDS derived from them.
2. Use these words or words from the spelling list for the etymological definitions.

    crescendo   descend   transcend
  a. climb down   c. increase
  b. climb beyond   d. climb up

3. Which word in number 2 fits Paul's experience as described in 2 Corinthians 12:4?
4. Copy a word from Romans 12:16 that means "climb down together."
5. Write a NEW WORD to finish this analogy.
    adore : despise :: descend : ____
6. Write the noun form of *descend*. (Change just one letter.)
7. Each generation of Grandfather's <u>*scend*</u> is a step later or farther away from him.
8. According to 2 Samuel 18:19–28, Ahimaaz was a ____*.
9. Use these words to match the descriptions below.
    concur   current   cursive   cursory   incur
  a. "Running" handwriting.
  b. Brief and hasty.
  c. A running of water, air, or electricity.
  d. Run into (something unpleasant).
  e. Run together; agree.
10. The problem <u>(ran in the way)</u>* when we were least expecting it.
11. Copy a word from Hebrews 2:18 meaning "run to help."
12. Write answers to fill these blanks by using words in which Latin *curs* took the French form *cours*.
  a. A <u>dis</u>_* is a long, unhurried speech or writing.
  b. The river follows a winding ____.
  c. David's <u>re</u>_ in trouble was the Lord.
  d. In Acts 19:40, the rioters were told that they had no good reason for their <u>(running together)</u>.

Lesson 19

(Total points: 78)

Notes on Part A

Selected Words With Lesson Roots

L *scend:* **ascend, transcend,** condescend, descend(ant)

L *curr, curs:* **courier, discourse, excursion, occurred,** concourse, concur, course, current, cursive, cursory, incur, recourse, recur, succor

Succor is the American spelling for *succour* [<L *succurrere* run to help < *sub-* + *currere*]. A number of *course* words (*concourse, discourse, recourse*) received the *ou* spelling through the French language.

Exercise 1: Two of the spelling words have the *curr/curs* root spelled *cour.* You may want to clue the students on the altered spelling and tell them how many words to find. The REVIEW WORD *encourage* is not one of them. It has the *cor* (heart) root.

Exercise 5: *Adore* is the opposite of *despise,* as *descend* is the opposite of _____.

Exercise 8: The Bible passage does not use the spelling word, but it describes the activity of a courier.

Answer Key—Part A (30 points)

1. *scend:* ascend, transcend
   curr, curs: courier, discourse, excursion, occurred
2. a. descend   c. crescendo
   b. transcend   d. ascend
3. transcend
4. condescend
5. ascend
6. descent
7. descendants
8. courier
9. a. cursive
   b. cursory
   c. current
   d. incur
   e. concur
10. occurred
11. succour *or* succor
12. a. discourse
    b. course
    c. recourse
    e. concourse

Lesson 19 Test Sentences

1. *Exodus* Moses is the main character in *Exodus. Exodus*
2. *occurred* Signs and wonders *occurred* before Pharaoh. *occurred*
3. *surrender* He had many chances to *surrender* to God. *surrender*
4. *extraordinary* His army came to an *extraordinary* end. *extraordinary*
5. *incense* Israel's praise was a sweet *incense* to God. *incense*
6. *dissatisfied* The people were *dissatisfied* with manna. *dissatisfied*
7. *carbohydrates* Carbohydrates provide fuel for the body. *carbohydrates*
8. *energy* Sugar is a fast *energy* food. *energy*
9. *courier* A faithful *courier* will be prompt. *courier*
10. *discourse* His *discourse* was short but meaningful. *discourse*
11. *emphasis* The main *emphasis* was on safety. *emphasis*
12. *ordinary* Expression makes an *ordinary* story special. *ordinary*
13. *eclipse* A lunar *eclipse* happens only at full moon. *eclipse*
14. *excursion* We enjoyed an *excursion* to the creek. *excursion*
15. *encounter* Sam expected to *encounter* a snake. *encounter*
16. *exclaim* We heard him *exclaim* something to Noah. *exclaim*
17. *embroider* Use blue floss to *embroider* the bird. *embroider*
18. *example* John is a good *example* of steadfastness. *example*
19. *exile* He did not waste his time in *exile. exile*
20. *endure* Those who *endure* will be saved. *endure*
21. *ascend* Many prayers *ascend* for strength. *ascend*
22. *anticipate* We *anticipate* great joy in heaven. *anticipate*
23. *transcend* It will *transcend* any earthly pleasure. *transcend*
24. *installation* Are you ready for *installation* as captain? *installation*
25. *encourage* Let us *encourage* one another. *encourage*

64   *Lesson 19*

B.   AFFIXING AFFIXES

1. Write spelling words with *en-* or *em-* for these definitions.
   a. To put courage in.
   b. To bear hardship.
   c. To meet.
   d. To stitch designs in cloth.
   e. Power to work.
   f. Stress to show importance.

2. *Em-* is an assimilated form of *en-*, used to make pronunciation easier. Write the answers from number 1 in which *en-* is assimilated.

3. Write spelling words with *ex-* or *ec-* to complete these sentences.
   a. A total ____ will block out all the sunlight for a short while.
   b. We'll "run out" to the zoo for a family ____.
   c. The ____ was the going out from Egypt.
   d. Daniel remained faithful to God even in ____ far away from Jerusalem.

PREFIX	MEANING	EXAMPLE
en-, em-	on, in	empower
ex-, ec-	out	exit

   e. The sight of Jesus walking on the water made His disciples ____, "It is a spirit!"
   f. The ____ harvest yielded twice as much as normal.
   g. Take out some of the apples to display as an ____.

4. *Ec-* is an assimilated form of *ex-* that occurs before some consonants. Use these words with the assimilated prefix for the definitions below.
      eccentric   ecstatic   eczema
   a. Outbreak of skin sores.
   b. Out of center.
   c. Out of control through intense delight.

5. Write the NEW WORD that has a double letter because the prefix ends with the same letter that begins the root word.

C.   SOUND, STRUCTURE, AND MEANING

1. Write the NEW WORDS that have these phonetic details.
   a. /ī/ spelled *y*
   b. /s/ spelled *c* and /s/ spelled *s*
   c. /s/ spelled *sc* (2)
   d. /f/ spelled *ph*

2. One of the NEW WORDS is derived from a REVIEW WORD. Write both words.

3. Write the spelling words derived from these root words.
   a. install
   b. satisfy
   c. courage

4. Write the spelling words that are synonyms of these words.
   a. messenger
   b. yield
   c. perfume
   d. banishment
   e. expect
   f. rise
   g. common

5. When is *Exodus* written with a small *e?*

6. Write two pronunciations for *courier.*

7. Write the spelling word that may be pronounced with five or six syllables.

8. *Incense* has two entries in the Speller Dictionary. Both meanings relate to fire. Write the number of each entry, and tell what is burning in each sense.

9. Write a sentence using *carbohydrates* and *energy.*

Notes on Part B

Some additional *en-* words: enjoy, enroll, endorse, entitle.
Additional words with the assimilated prefix: embody, embankment, embitter, embroil.

Answer Key—Part B (19 points)

1. a. encourage
   b. endure
   c. encounter
   d. embroider
   e. energy
   f. emphasis
2. embroider, emphasis
3. a. eclipse
   b. excursion
   c. Exodus
   d. exile
   e. exclaim
   f. extraordinary
   g. example
4. a. eczema
   b. eccentric
   c. ecstatic
5. dissatisfied

Answer Key—Part C (25 points)

1. a. carbohydrates
   b. incense
   c. ascend, transcend
   d. emphasis
2. ordinary, extraordinary
3. a. installation
   b. dissatisfied
   c. encourage
4. a. courier
   b. surrender
   c. incense
   d. exile

   e. anticipate
   f. ascend
   g. ordinary
5. *Exodus* begins with a small *e* when it does not mean Israel leaving Egypt.
6. (kür' ē ər), (kėr' ē ər)
7. extraordinary
8. 1—a fragrant substance
   2—anger
9. (Sample sentence) *Carbohydrates* in your diet provide a source of *energy*.

D. LANGUAGE LINEAGE

MODERN DICTIONARIES

Language is a living, changing thing. Dictionaries and grammar books do not prevent speakers and writers from coining new words and using old ones in new ways. Some of the early dictionaries were published with the intention of preventing change and decay in the language. But the intent of modern dictionaries is not to fix usage. It is to provide a record of current accepted usage rather than the law for usage. When people change their speech, new dictionaries will publish the new standards.

One of the changeable aspects in language is the social acceptability of certain words. A dictionary will record a new word even if it is an offensive term, but warning is given of its classification with a usage label such as *slang, vulgar,* or *offensive.* With time, such words may grow common enough that the offensiveness wears off. An updated dictionary will change the labels according to the opinion of a panel of usage consultants.

Is a dictionary then the authority on what is correct and acceptable? Some linguists take the position that the final rule for correctness is popular usage. Accordingly, if enough educated people say "I seen" long enough, this will eventually be accepted as a correct usage.

Grammar change is not wrong in itself, but to accept something because "everybody does it" is a dangerous attitude that will filter into other areas of life. God's Word holds unchanging standards of right and wrong. No amount of man's opinion will ever change the wrongness or the consequences of sin. Though language may change, we should realize that part of the reason for change is man's natural laziness and his desire for self-exaltation. Language that is associated with ungodly attitudes should be shunned by the Christian, no matter how acceptable it becomes to society. "Whatsoever ye do in word . . . do all in the name of the Lord Jesus" (Colossians 3:17).

So, although dictionaries are valuable in helping us to understand words and use them effectively, we do not rely on a dictionary as the standard for what is morally right. The Bible is always the final authority on wholesome speech.

Exercises

1. What is the intent of dictionaries published today?

2. When do dictionaries change their classification of a word's acceptability?

3. What is wrong with the attitude that says, "It is all right if everyone says it"?

4. What guide other than the dictionary should regulate our speech?

Notes on Part D

Dictionaries should be used with discretion because they can be a source of undesirable terminology. Noah Webster felt a moral restraint about using such words, and he boasted that no other English dictionary was as free of vulgar and obscene words as his. Modern dictionary staffs are more likely to include such words for the claim of completeness.

The Oxford Dictionary, prepared on historical principle, listed the oldest definitions first. Modern dictionaries intended for common use will list first the definitions that are most prevalent.

Answer Key—Part D (4 points)

1. Modern dictionaries are published to *inform people according to current usage.*
2. Word classification changes when *popular opinion shifts* and usage consultants change the label.
3. This attitude could filter into other areas of life, but it must *never change Bible obedience.*
4. The *Bible* is the best guide to control our speech.

LESSON 20

A. UNEARTHING THE ROOTS

ROOT	MEANING	EXAMPLE
Greek *soma*	= body	somatic
Greek *psyche*	= soul, mind	psychology
Greek *pneuma*	= spirit, breath	pneumatic

NEW WORDS

abundance
algebra
amusing
borne
chord
environment
epidermis
epilepsy
epistles
insomnia
nineteenth
oblige
pneumonia
previous
psychology
quotations
recommend
refreshment
vague
warrior

REVIEW WORDS

epidemic
ridiculous
schedule
summon
threaten

Find words in the puzzle below for numbers 1–11. The number of the definition corresponds to a number in the puzzle, which marks the first letter of the word. If two words share the same first letter, two definitions are listed under the same number.

```
¹P  A  ²P  N  E  U  M  A  T  I  C
S  ³S  S  I  P  L  O  S  ⁴P  N  S
Y  O  Y  E  H  ⁵C  P  Y  S  ⁶S  ⁷P
C  M  C  C  O  H  N  C  Y  O  N
H  A  H  O  R  R  E  ⁸S  C  M  E
O  T  O  ⁹P  C  O  U  O  H  A  U
S  I  L  S  H  M  P  M  I  T  M
O  C  O  Y  R  O  O  A  A  I  O
M  C  G  C  O  S  N  N  T  C  N
A  E  Y  H  S  O  I  I  R  H  I
T  L  P  E  O  M  A  A  Y  N  A
I  L  H  ¹⁰P  N  E  U  M  A  S  L
C  ¹¹S  O  M  A  T  O  L  O  G  Y
```

1. a. Pertaining to interaction of mind and body.
   b. A mentally ill or unstable person.
2. a. Study of the mind*.
   b. Filled with air, as a tire.
3. Body cells of plants or animals (two words).
4. (mind) + (treatment)
5. Part within a cell that determines inherited traits.
6. Having to do with the body.
7. A lung disease.*
8. Root meaning "body."
9. Root meaning "soul."
10. Root meaning "spirit."
11. Study of the body.

12. "I pray God your whole *pneuma* and *psyche* and *soma* be preserved blameless unto the coming of our Lord Jesus Christ."
13. Do not confuse the Greek root *soma* with the Latin root *somn* (sleep). Write the NEW WORD with the *somn* root and the meaning "inability to sleep."
14. Use these two words for the definitions below.
    somnambulist   somniloquist
    a. One who talks in his sleep.
    b. One who walks in his sleep.

Lesson 20

(Total points: 87)

Notes on Part A

Selected Words With Lesson Roots

Gk. *soma:* chromosome, psychosomatic, somatic, somatology

Gk. *psyche:* **psychology,** psyche, psychiatry, psychopath, psychosomatic

Gk. *pneuma:* **pneumonia,** pneumatic

Puzzle words may run across, down, or diagonally.

Answer Key—Part A (19 points)

1. a. psychosomatic
   b. psychopath

2. a. psychology
   b. pneumatic

3. somatic cells

4. psychiatry

5. chromosome

6. somatic

7. pneumonia

8. soma

9. psyche

10. pneuma

11. somatology

12. spirit, soul, body

13. insomnia

14. a. somniloquist
    b. somnambulist

Lesson 20 Test Sentences

1. *warrior* Paul was a *warrior* for Christ. *warrior*
2. *epistles* His *epistles* give practical guidance. *epistles*
3. *borne* The eaglet was *borne* to safety by its mother. *borne*
4. *environment* They soared above a stormy *environment. environment*
5. *epidermis* Oil makes the *epidermis* waterproof. *epidermis*
6. *insomnia* Two nights of *insomnia* weakened Sue's health. *insomnia*
7. *pneumonia* Is that why she took *pneumonia? pneumonia*
8. *epilepsy* Medicines can control *epilepsy* to a degree. *epilepsy*
9. *nineteenth* The Civil War was in the *nineteenth* century. *nineteenth*
10. *epidemic* Save the field trip till the *epidemic* is past. *epidemic*
11. *threaten* We do not want to *threaten* the health of others. *threaten*
12. *refreshment* Singing brings *refreshment* to weary souls. *refreshment*
13. *chord* A beautiful *chord* is repeated throughout the song. *chord*
14. *abundance* There is an *abundance* of corn in the freezer. *abundance*
15. *recommend* Do you *recommend* that we plant more? *recommend*
16. *previous* Think of ways to use the *previous* supply. *previous*
17. *algebra* The thought patterns of *algebra* are very logical. *algebra*
18. *vague* Study the rules that are *vague* in your memory. *vague*
19. *summon* Try to *summon* your best skills for the test. *summon*
20. *quotations* Carefully punctuate all *quotations. quotations*
21. *psychology* The music in stores utilizes *psychology. psychology*
22. *schedule* Our *schedule* permits several reports. *schedule*
23. *oblige* You will *oblige* us by reading clearly. *oblige*
24. *amusing* It is *amusing* to compare impressions. *amusing*
25. *ridiculous* You need not answer a *ridiculous* question. *ridiculous*

B. AFFIXING AFFIXES

1. Write words with the prefix *epi-* to match the descriptions below. Choose from these words or the spelling list.

   epiglottis   episode
   epitaph   epicenter

   a. Spreading rapidly over the people, as an infectious disease.
   b. One incident in a series of events.
   c. Point on earth's surface over central point of earthquake.
   d. Messages sent over to someone.
   e. Inscription upon a *taphos* (tombstone).
   f. Outer layer of *derma* (skin) upon the deeper layer.
   g. Cartilage that closes the windpipe during swallowing.
   h. Convulsions that seize upon a person.

PREFIX	MEANING	EXAMPLE
epi-	upon, over	epilepsy

2. Write the spelling words derived from the words below. After each word write its part of speech.

   a. amuse   e. refresh
   b. ridicule   f. threat
   c. abound   g. nine
   d. quote   h. war

3. Most of the answers in number 2 have (inflectional, derivational) suffixes.

4. Write the spelling words with these etymologies.

   a. *en-* + *viron* (circle)
   b. *pre-* + *via* (way)

C. SOUND, STRUCTURE, AND MEANING

1. Write the spelling words that have these phonetic features.
   a. /j/ spelled *g* (3). Underline the letter after *g* in each word.
   b. /k/ spelled *ch* (3)
   c. final /g/ spelled *gue*
   d. silent *p* (2)
   e. /s/ spelled *ps*

2. Write the spelling words that begin with the prefix *re-*. Also write their root words.

3. Write the three principal parts of the verb *bear.*

4. Use six forms of *bear* for these answers.
   a. Jesus ____ our sins on the cross.
   b. Now He ____ the print of nails in His hands.
   c. We like to ____ good news.
   d. Several kinds of pollen were ____ in the air.
   e. The kittens were ____ under the porch.
   f. My cactus is ____ flowers this winter.

5. Use the same NEW WORD or a homonym for each blank.
   a. We practiced the difficult ____ in music class.
   b. A ____ of wood measures 4 feet by 4 feet by 8 feet.
   c. A diameter is a ____ that passes through the center of a circle.
   d. "A threefold ____ is not quickly broken" (Ecclesiastes 4:12).
   e. The missionary's account struck a ____ of generosity in the audience.

6. Write spelling words that are antonyms of these words.
   a. later   d. dismiss
   b. shortage   e. sobering
   c. distinct   f. slumber

Answer Key—Part B (27 points)

1. a. epidemic
   b. episode
   c. epicenter
   d. epistles
   e. epitaph
   f. epidermis
   g. epiglottis
   h. epilepsy

2. a. amusing—verb *or* adjective
   b. ridiculous—adjective
   c. abundance—noun
   d. quotations—noun
   e. refreshment—noun
   f. threaten—verb
   g. nineteenth—adjective *or* noun
   h. warrior—noun

3. derivational

4. a. environment
   b. previous

Notes on Part C

Exercise 5: The Speller Dictionary has two entries for *chord,* coming from two different sources. *Cord* is a homonym and a doublet of *chord²*.

Answer Key—Part C (34 points)

1. a. algebra, oblige, psychology
   b. chord, psychology, schedule
   c. vague
   d. pneumonia, psychology
   e. psychology

2. recommend, commend; refreshment, fresh

3. bear, bore, borne

4. a. bore
   b. bears
   c. bear
   d. borne
   e. born
   f. bearing

5. a. chord
   b. cord
   c. chord
   d. cord
   e. chord

6. a. previous
   b. abundance
   c. vague
   d. summon
   e. amusing (Accept *ridiculous.*)
   f. insomnia

D. LANGUAGE LINEAGE

THE BLUE-BACKED SPELLER

The first schoolbook that Noah Webster published was a speller. It did not have exercises with questions about words, but simply pages of word lists and short, character-building passages to read. Words were listed according to the number of syllables and the accent patterns. The words showed syllable divisions, for Webster believed: "Divide words according to pronunciation, and the smallest child can say them right." He promoted clear articulation of all the sounds, whether accented or unaccented. Each syllable was to be pronounced, so that one could easily hear the number of syllables in a word.

The little speller with the blue cover was usually studied by oral recitation. In unison, a class would read from the word list, spelling and pronouncing each syllable, building the word as they went. For the word printed *en-vi-ron-ment,* the class would chant as follows:

> e-n, en;
>
> v-i, vi, envi;
>
> r-o-n, ron, environ;
>
> m-e-n-t, ment, environment

Following this exercise, the pupils closed their books and the schoolmaster gave words for individuals to spell by memory. The deliberate and distinct pronunciation of every sound and syllable helped them to master the words.

Used nationwide, Webster's blue-backed speller helped generations of scholars to grow up with uniform and careful speech. Enthusiasm for spelling skill is also indicated by the popularity of spelling bees during the 1800s.

This spelling book sold widely, providing an income that supported Noah Webster the rest of his life. It continued in print well into the twentieth century, with total sales of more than eighty million copies.

Exercises

1. What features determined the grouping of words in Webster's spelling book?
2. Write the five REVIEW WORDS in this lesson, showing syllable divisions. Practice spelling them in the manner described above. If your teacher so directs, read them aloud with the class in unison.
3. The wide use of Webster's spelling book had what effect on American pronunciation?

Notes on Part D

Exercise 2: Follow this pattern for oral spelling exercise.
1. Spell the letters of a syllable.
2. Pronounce that syllable.
3. Repeat the accumulated syllables.

Answer Key—Part D (7 points)

1. Words were grouped according to the *number of syllables and the accent patterns.*

2. ep-i-dem-ic, ri-dic-u-lous, sched-ule, sum-mon, threat-en
   (optional oral work)
   e-p, ep;
   i, i, epi;
   d-e-m, dem, epidem;
   i-c, ic, epidemic

   r-i, ri;
   d-i-c, dic, ridic;
   u, u, ridicu;
   l-o-u-s, lous, ridiculous

   s-c-h-e-d, sched;
   u-l-e, ule, schedule

   s-u-m, sum;
   m-o-n, mon, summon

   t-h-r-e-a-t, threat;
   e-n, en, threaten

3. It helped to produce *uniform and careful speech.*

A. UNEARTHING THE ROOTS

ROOT	MEANING	EXAMPLE
Greek *philo*	= love	philosopher
Greek *sophos*	= wisdom	sophomore

LESSON 21

NEW WORDS

acceptable
accompanied
conspicuous
contemplate
dealt
frequently
hastily
inspection
parables
parachute
paradise
paralyze
parasite
perimeter
periodical
philosophy
precious
recognized
sophomore
urgent

REVIEW WORDS

angel
instruction
persuade
Philemon
sensible

1. a. Write the spelling word that contains both lesson roots.
   b. Write the etymology of this word.
2. Name the city in Pennsylvania whose name means "brotherly love," founded by William Penn for religious and political freedom.
3. Choose the correct word for each definition.
       bibliophile   xenophile
       philanthropist   philharmonic
   a. Lover of *anthrōpos* (mankind).
   b. Lover of *biblios* (books).
   c. Pertaining to love for music.
   d. Lover of *xenos* (strangers), translated "hospitality" in Romans 12:13.
4. _____* was a New Testament character whose name means "friendship."
5. Which spelling word names something that could lead a Christian astray? (See Colossians 2:8.)
6. Because of their love of wisdom, the _____ in Acts 17 desired to hear what Paul had to say.
7. a. Write the definition of *sophist*.
   b. Is a sophist wise?
   c. Which one of these Bible characters was a sophist?
       Onesiphorus (2 Timothy 1:16, 17)
       Hymenaeus (2 Timothy 2:16–18)
8. My cousin studied French during his _____* year in high school.
9. What does the etymology give as the meaning of the last part of *sophomore?*
10. Choose the correct word to complete this analogy.
        humble : haughty :: simple : _____
          (sophomoric, sophisticated)

Lesson 21

(Total points: 93)

Notes on Part A

Selected Words With Lesson Roots
Gk. *philo:* **Philemon, philosophy,** bibliophile, Philadelphia, philanthropist, philharmonic, Philip, philodendron, xenophile

Philip means "loving *hippos* (horses)." *Philodendron* means "loving trees."

Gk. *sophos:* **philosophy, sophomore,** sophist, sophisticated

Exercise 2: This item likely reviews a history detail from a former year. In the event that the students are uninformed, the name can be found in an atlas or reference book. Have them scan a map or index of cities, looking for a name that begins with the Greek root.

Exercise 7: A sophist is noted for subtle and misleading arguments. Onesiphorus brought Paul refreshing fellowship. Hymenaeus erred from the truth with profane and vain babblings.

Exercises 9 and 10: The "foolish wise" are overconfident. A sophomoric attitude is the opposite of wisdom.

Answer Key—Part A (16 points)

1. a. philosophy
   b. [<Gk. *philosophos* loving wisdom < *philos* loving + *sophia* wisdom]
2. Philadelphia
3. a. philanthropist
   b. bibliophile
   c. philharmonic
   d. xenophile
4. Philemon
5. philosophy
6. philosophers
7. a. One skilled in clever, misleading argument.
   b. no
   c. Hymenaeus
8. sophomore
9. foolish
10. sophisticated

Lesson 21 Test Sentences

1. *parables* Jesus often spoke in *parables.* *parables*
2. *instruction* His *instruction* was for all who would hear. *instruction*
3. *frequently* Everyday stories *frequently* hold spiritual truth. *frequently*
4. *precious* These truths are very *precious.* *precious*
5. *paradise* The pardoned thief gained *paradise* that day. *paradise*
6. *acceptable* His faith was *acceptable* to God. *acceptable*
7. *paralyze* A broken back could *paralyze* you. *paralyze*
8. *contemplate* Seriously *contemplate* safety measures. *contemplate*
9. *inspection* Give careful *inspection* to work areas. *inspection*
10. *sensible* A *sensible* approach will prevent many accidents. *sensible*
11. *periodical* Have a *periodical* review of safety rules. *periodical*
12. *philosophy* "Work before play" is a good *philosophy.* *philosophy*
13. *Philemon* Paul's letter to *Philemon* came from Rome. *Philemon*
14. *persuade* He wrote to *persuade* him to receive Onesimus. *persuade*
15. *dealt* As a Christian he surely *dealt* kindly with his slave. *dealt*
16. *angel* An *angel* appeared to Gideon. *angel*
17. *urgent* There was an *urgent* need for a leader. *urgent*
18. *recognized* Gideon *recognized* God's plan. *recognized*
19. *hastily* He *hastily* instructed his soldiers. *hastily*
20. *accompanied* Twelve disciples *accompanied* Jesus. *accompanied*
21. *perimeter* Conrad mowed the *perimeter* of the lawn first. *perimeter*
22. *sophomore* Are you ready for *sophomore* studies? *sophomore*
23. *parachute* The skydiver had a huge red *parachute.* *parachute*
24. *conspicuous* It made a *conspicuous* show in the sunshine. *conspicuous*
25. *parasite* The deer tick is an obnoxious *parasite.* *parasite*

B. AFFIXING AFFIXES

1. Use words with the prefix *para-* or *peri-* to replace the etymological definitions in these sentences.
   a. Jesus taught the people in (things thrown beside each other)* to help them understand spiritual truths.
   b. Each sentence in a (written beside) should support the main idea.
   c. Lines that are (beside one another) appear to come together in the distance.
   d. Do not let fear (completely remove power from)* you in a time of danger.
   e. A (beside feeder)* draws its nourishment from a host plant or animal.
   f. You need to know the (measure around)* of a field when you fence it in.
   g. When the submarine surfaced, two ships were seen through the (see around).

PREFIX	MEANING	EXAMPLE
para-	beside, near	parallel
peri-	around	periscope

   h. *The Christian Example* is a (thing going around)* that is printed every two weeks.
2. In two NEW WORDS, the beginning letters *para* are not prefixes. Write those words for the etymologies below.
   a. Iranian *pairi* (around) + *daēza-* (wall)
   b. French *parare* (to shield) + *chute* (a fall)
3. Write the two spelling words that end with *-ed.* Also write the root words with this suffix removed.
4. Write the two spelling words that end with *-ly.* Also write the root word of each.
5. Write the two words that end with *-ion.*
6. Write the NEW WORD that is past tense for an irregular verb.

C. SOUND, STRUCTURE, AND MEANING

1. Write the spelling words that have these sounds.
   a. /f/ spelled *ph* (3)
   b. /sh/ spelled *ch*
   c. /e/ spelled *ea*
   d. /j/ spelled *g* (2)
2. Write the two spelling words that end with *-ous.* In each one, circle the letter that comes before this ending.
3. Write the two spelling words that end with *-ble.* In each one, circle the letter that comes before this ending.
4. Write spelling words that are synonyms of these words.
   a. convince
   b. ponder
   c. reasonable
   d. obvious
   e. examination
   f. valuable
5. Write *angel* or *angle* for each sentence. (Remember that *g* usually spells /j/ when followed by *e.*)
   a. A right ____ has 90 degrees.
   b. An ____ shut the lions' mouths.
   c. The lake looks larger from this ____.
   d. We will ____ across the meadow to the hickory tree.
   e. Abraham's visitor was an ____.
6. Write a word that rhymes with *angle* and ends with *gle.*
7. Write a doublet of *recognize.*
8. What is the usage label for *precious* as used in the phrase "precious few words"?

Answer Key—Part B (21 points)

1. a. parables
   b. paragraph
   c. parallel
   d. paralyze
   e. parasite
   f. perimeter
   g. periscope
   h. periodical

2. a. paradise
   b. parachute

3. accompanied, accompany; recognized, recognize

4. frequently, frequent; hastily, haste (Accept *hasty.*)

5. inspection, instruction

6. dealt

Notes on Part C

   Exercise 8: A usage label does not refer to the part of speech but to social acceptability of a word as mentioned in *Language Lineage* of Lesson 19.

Answer Key—Part C (25 points)

1. a. philosophy, sophomore, Philemon
   b. parachute
   c. dealt
   d. urgent, angel

2. conspicuous, precious

3. acceptable, sensible

4. a. persuade
   b. contemplate
   c. sensible
   d. conspicuous
   e. inspection
   f. precious

5. a. angle
   b. angel
   c. angle
   d. angle
   e. angel

6. (Sample answers—any one) bangle, dangle, mangle, strangle, tangle, wrangle

7. reconnoiter

8. informal

D. LANGUAGE LINEAGE

SPELLING REVOLUTION

Because of changing pronunciations and adoption of foreign words, English is sprinkled with spelling inconsistencies that confuse school children as well as foreigners trying to learn the language. Why should a single sound be spelled in a variety of ways? Consider the long *a* sound, for instance.

They may take a bouquet to cheer the neighbor who has great pain in the veins.

And by what logic should *ough* have all the varying sounds in this sentence?

He had a rough cough all through the night, though he sought relief in several ways.

In the centuries since the printing press standardized spelling, various proposals have been made to improve the sound-to-spelling conformity. In 1568 Thomas Smith devised a 34-letter alphabet using new characters for sounds that do not have their own symbols. He advocated diacritical markings for long vowel sounds. His proposal, which was written in Latin, received little attention.

A year or two later, John Hart made another vain proposal. His plan included new characters to represent the sounds of *ch, sh,* and *th.*

In 1580 William Bullokar offered his plan for phonetic spelling. The earlier attempts were too radical for success, he thought. Instead of inventing new characters, Bullokar kept the same alphabet but indicated sound differences with accent marks, apostrophes, and various other jots and tittles attached to the letters. His bewhiskered alphabet found no more acceptance than did the others.

Richard Mulcaster, a teacher of the sixteenth century, advocated a more moderate approach to spelling reform. He believed there are so many subtle shades of sound variation that it is not logical to represent language in a totally phonetic manner. Besides, pronunciation will continue to change, but who wants spelling practices to shift with every speech variation? Some of Mulcaster's recommendations were the omission of unnecessary double letters and the use of final *e* to indicate long vowels. He respected the form established by common usage and did not urge strict phonetic consistency. Spelling revolution was evidently futile, but moderate spelling refinement was in progress.

Exercises

1. a. Write nine /ā/ words from the sentence that illustrates the long *a* sound. After each word, write the letters that represent long *a*.
   b. Write five *ough* words from the example sentence. After each one, print the phonetic sound(s) for the letters *ough*.
2. What did Thomas Smith and John Hart do to avoid having different sounds for the same symbol?
3. What did William Bullokar do to represent different sounds of the same letter?
4. Why would it not be practical to use a completely phonetic system of writing speech sounds?

Notes on Part D

To design a more consistent phonetic alphabet, what character changes would you make? Some students might enjoy analyzing the alphabet and proposing adjustments.

To begin with, consider the multiple sounds we now have for one character. If a vowel should always represent the same sound, there would need to be new characters for the other sounds that share that letter. Next consider the digraphs. Invent one character to represent each sound instead of using two letters (th, ch, sh, etc.).

The letter *c* has no sound unique to itself; therefore it could be assigned to represent one of the sounds that has no symbol of its own. The letters *q* and *x* also represent sounds that are made by other letters of the alphabet.

If anyone creates a proposed phonetic alphabet, have him write something in that system, or have him transcribe some familiar material, and let the class read it. They can probably identify with the response of those who considered the works of Smith, Hart, and Bullokar.

Answer Key—Part D (31 points)

1. a. (word)   (spelling)
   - They   *ey*
   - may   *ay*
   - take   *a-e*
   - a   *a*
   - bouquet   *et*
   - neighbor   *eigh*
   - great   *ea*
   - pain   *ai*
   - veins   *ei*

   b. (word)   (sound)
   - rough   /uf/
   - cough   /ôf/ *or* /of/
   - through   /ü/
   - though   /ō/
   - sought   /ô/ *or* /o/

2. Thomas Smith and John Hart *added new characters* to the alphabet.

3. William Bullokar *attached markings* such as accent marks and apostrophes to the letters.

4. There are too many small shades of *sound variation,* and *pronunciation changes.*

72

LESSON 22

ROOT	MEANING	EXAMPLE
Greek *physio*	= growth, nature	physical
Greek *geo*	= earth	geography
Greek *hydro*	= water	hydrant

NEW WORDS

Anabaptist

analysis

anatomy

assessment

beaten

commerce

crusade

dehydrate

flannel

geometry

hydrant

hydraulic

hydrogen

individual

magnificent

musician

occasional

passage

peasant

privilege

REVIEW WORDS

convenient

language

physical

satisfactory

visible

1. Complete each acrostic with words having the given lesson root. Choose from this list for answers that are not spelling words.

   geography   geology   hydroponics
   hydrotherapy   physician   physics
   physiography   physiology   physique

   a. Scientific study of how living things function.
   b. A doctor who treats diseases with medicine.
   c. Branch of science dealing with matter and energy.
   d. Of the body; not mental or spiritual*.
   e. Build and general appearance of the body.
   f. Physical geography.

   ```
   a. P - - - - - - - - -
   b. - H - - - - - - -
   c. - - Y - - - -
   d. - - - S - - - -
   e. - - - - I - - -
   f. - - - - - O - - - - - -
   ```

   g. The study of planes and solid figures*.
   h. Study of the earth's surface features.
   i. Study of the earth's crust.

   ```
   g. G - - - - - - -
   h. - E - - - - - - -
   i. - - O - - - -
   ```

   j. A colorless, odorless gas*.
   k. Having to do with water or other liquids*.
   l. A pipe with a valve for drawing water*.
   m. The raising of plants in water instead of soil.
   n. Use of water to treat certain diseases.

   ```
   j. H - - - - - -
   k. - Y - - - - - - -
   l. - - D - - - -
   m. - - - R - - - - - -
   n. - - - - O - - - - - -
   ```

2. H_2O is the chemical formula for water. It means that water is composed of two atoms of ____* and one atom of oxygen.

3. What is hydroelectricity?

4. Which NEW WORD means "remove moisture"?

Lesson 22

(Total points: 81)

Notes on Part A

Selected Words With Lesson Roots

Gk. *physio:* **physical,** physician, physics, physiography, physiology, physique

Gk. *geo:* **geometry,** geode, geography, geology (5), geothermal

Gk. *hydro:* **dehydrate, hydrant, hydraulic, hydrogen,** hydrangea, hydrophobia, hydroponics, hydrotherapy

Exercise 3: *Hydro* is *electricity* in Canadian vocabulary, shortened from *hydroelectricity.*

Answer Key—Part A (17 points)

1. a. Physiology
   b. pHysician
   c. phYsics
   d. phySical
   e. physIque
   f. physiOgraphy

   g. Geometry
   h. gEography
   i. geOlogy

   j. Hydrogen
   k. hYdraulic
   l. hyDrant
   m. hydRoponics
   n. hydrOtherapy
2. hydrogen
3. Electricity generated by the energy of falling water.
4. dehydrate

Lesson 22 Test Sentences

1. *geometry* Surveyors use *geometry* in their work. *geometry*
2. *language* Mary's second *language* is Swedish. *language*
3. *flannel* We can use this *flannel* for shirts. *flannel*
4. *visible* It has a barely *visible* flaw. *visible*
5. *satisfactory* The price is very *satisfactory*. *satisfactory*
6. *dehydrate* This drier will *dehydrate* any kind of fruit. *dehydrate*
7. *hydrogen* Use *hydrogen* peroxide to prevent infection. *hydrogen*
8. *peasant* An ordinary *peasant* could read the Bible. *peasant*
9. *individual* Baptism was by *individual* choice. *individual*
10. *Anabaptist* The *Anabaptist* way was severely persecuted. *Anabaptist*
11. *beaten* Many were *beaten,* burned, or drowned. *beaten*
12. *privilege* It was a *privilege* to suffer for Christ. *privilege*
13. *physical* They were willing to lose *physical* life. *physical*
14. *passage* Death was their *passage* to heaven. *passage*
15. *convenient* A protractor is a *convenient* tool. *convenient*
16. *anatomy* Alligator *anatomy* is similar to the crocodile's. *anatomy*
17. *assessment* Tax *assessment* was raised last year. *assessment*
18. *hydraulic* Keep *hydraulic* hoses in good repair. *hydraulic*
19. *hydrant* Water gushed out of the *hydrant.* *hydrant*
20. *occasional* We like an *occasional* change. *occasional*
21. *musician* King David was a skilled *musician.* *musician*
22. *commerce* Solomon had *commerce* with many lands. *commerce*
23. *magnificent* Tourists came for the *magnificent* scenery. *magnificent*
24. *analysis* Rangers made an *analysis* of their visits. *analysis*
25. *crusade* They launched a *crusade* for cleaner parks. *crusade*

B. AFFIXING AFFIXES

PREFIX	MEANING	EXAMPLE
ana-	again, up	Anabaptist

1. Write words beginning with *ana-* for these definitions.
   a. One who was baptized again as a believing adult, even though baptized as an infant*.
   b. A religious curse or ban mentioned by Paul in 1 Corinthians 16:22.
   c. A game played by arranging *gramma* (letters).
   d. The structure of a plant or an animal*.
   e. Systematic examination of the parts of a thing*.
   f. Comparison based on certain similarities, sometimes expressed in the form ___ : ___ :: ___ : ___.
2. Write words with the suffix *-ian* for these definitions.
   a. An expert in music*.
   b. A person in charge of a library.
   c. A person who eats only vegetables.
   d. An expert in technical work.
   e. One who follows Christ.
3. Write the NEW WORD that contains the suffix *-ment*. The suffix changes this word from a ____ to a ____.
4. Write the NEW WORD that contains the verb suffix *-en*.
5. Write the prefix of the NEW WORD that means "to remove moisture."
6. Use the prefix of number 5 with a word in each definition to write words for these meanings.
   a. To remove the horns.
   b. To get the message of something sent in code.
   c. To ruin fame; slander.
   d. To spoil the form of.
7. Write the spelling words that are derived from these root words.
   a. magnify   d. pass
   b. satisfy   e. divide
   c. occasion   f. baptize

C. SOUND, STRUCTURE, AND MEANING

1. Write the spelling words that have these phonetic features.
   a. /z/ spelled *s* and /sh/ spelled *ci*
   b. /g/ and /j/ spelled *g*
   c. /f/ spelled *ph*
   d. two sets of the same double letter
2. Write the five REVIEW WORDS, dividing them into syllables.
3. Write NEW WORDS for these definitions.
   a. A European farmer, especially in medieval times.
   b. Operated by a pressurized fluid.
   c. A soft, warm cloth made of wool or cotton.
   d. One person; not divisible.
   e. A vigorous movement for a certain cause.
4. a. When *crusade* is spelled with a capital letter, what does it mean?
   b. *Crusade* comes from the Latin word *crux* (cross). How are crosses related to crusades?
5. Use a NEW WORD and a word almost like it for each set of blanks.
   a. The hungry p__ roasted the p__ that he had caught in the field.
   b. The colonists had to produce marketable goods before c__ could c__ in the new colony.
6. Write NEW WORDS that are antonyms of these words.
   a. penalty   c. victorious
   b. frequent   d. crude

Answer Key—Part B (26 points)

1. a. Anabaptist
   b. Anathema
   c. anagrams
   d. anatomy
   e. analysis
   f. analogy
2. a. musician
   b. librarian
   c. vegetarian
   d. technician
   e. Christian
3. assessment, verb, noun

4. beaten
5. *de-*
6. a. dehorn
   b. decode
   c. defame
   d. deform
7. a. magnificent
   b. satisfactory
   c. occasional
   d. passage
   e. individual
   f. Anabaptist

Notes on Part C

Exercise 5: If students cannot identify an answer by the context, suggest that they scan an area in a dictionary where the partner word is found.

Answer Key—Part C (24 points)

1. a. musician
   b. language
   c. physical
   d. assessment
2. con-ven-ient
   lan-guage
   phys-i-cal
   sat-is-fac-to-ry
   vis-i-ble
3. a. peasant
   b. hydraulic
   c. flannel
   d. individual
   e. crusade
4. a. A military expedition to recover the Holy Land from the Muslims in the twelfth and thirteenth centuries.
   b. The Crusaders wore the cross symbol.
5. a. peasant, pheasant
   b. commerce, commence
6. a. privilege
   b. occasional
   c. beaten
   d. magnificent

D.   LANGUAGE LINEAGE

SPELLING REFINEMENT

Linguists continued seeking ways to overcome the phonetic inconsistencies of English. In America, Benjamin Franklin designed a new alphabet including six new characters so that each letter could always represent the same sound. He shared his plan with Noah Webster, seeking his promotional support. But Webster was not impressed. He opposed changing the "correct" spellings of the day.

The idea had its influence, however, and a few years later, Webster promoted a milder type of spelling reform. His dictionary encouraged new spelling practices such as these:

Omit the letter *u* in words like *honour* and *colour.*

Drop the final *k* in words like *musick* and *logick.*

Change final *re* to *er* in words like *fibre* and *centre.*

Change final *que* to *k* in a word like *masque* and to *ck* in a word like *cheque.*

Through lectures and writing, Webster campaigned for practical and economical spelling. He personally visited print shops to promote his spelling recommendations.

Some people adopted the new spelling forms, but the old ones remained in common use for a long time. In 1906 the Simplified Spelling Board was organized to promote simplicity and consistency in spelling. The first practical work of the board was to publish a list of 300 words of varied spelling, with recommendation to use the simpler forms. But changing so many spellings at once was too much, and further attempts at modifying American spellings were not well received. The Simplified Spelling Board passed out of existence in the 1930s.

Thus, although some adjustments have come to pass, our spelling is still basically the same as it was in the 1400s. This helps to keep writings from past ages meaningful to present-day readers. It also maintains the distinction between homonyms in writing, which would be lost if all words were spelled as they sounded.

A few etymological clues can be found in some apparent spelling quirks. The spelling of /ā/ in *bouquet* tells us the word has a French origin. In *mosquito,* the /ē/ spelled *i* and the final *o* are typical of Spanish words. And the *sch* combination in *schwa* signals a German word.

English remains a challenging language for children and foreigners to learn. But studying the structure and history of English helps to increase one's understanding and skill in correct usage.

Exercises

1. What may have influenced Noah Webster to take an interest in spelling reform?
2. Write the eight italicized words given after paragraph 2, using the modern American spellings.
3. a. What was the purpose of the Simplified Spelling Board?
   b. Why did it pass out of existence?
4. What are three advantages in continuing to use traditional spellings instead of changing to a purely phonetic system?

Answer Key—Part D (14 points)

1. Benjamin *Franklin's proposed new alphabet* may have influenced Webster to favor spelling reform.

2. honor, color, music, logic, fiber, center, mask, check

3. a. The Simplified Spelling Board was intended to *promote simplicity and consistency in spelling.*
   b. *People resisted changing* very much in spelling.

4. *Writings from long ago* are still meaningful.
   Homonyms can be distinguished.
   Etymological clues can be found in some spellings.

LESSON 23

A. UNEARTHING THE ROOTS

ROOT	MEANING	EXAMPLE
Latin *pract*	= do	practice
Greek *dyna*	= power	dynamite

NEW WORDS

anarchy
anxiety
certainty
curiosity
dreary
dynamic
humidity
inferiority
loyalty
maturity
moody
practical
reality
scratchy
strict
sufficient
theme
tyranny
unanimous
vengeance

REVIEW WORDS

Almighty
divinity
embroidery
necessity
security

1. Write the lesson roots and the spelling words derived from them.
2. Copy these verses, replacing the lesson roots with their meanings.
   a. "And as ye would that men should _pract_ to you, _pract_ ye also to them likewise."
   b. "There is no man that hath _dyna_ over the spirit to retain the spirit; neither hath he _dyna_ in the day of death: . . . neither shall wickedness deliver those that are given to it."
3. It takes much _pract_ to quote Bible verses from memory.
4. Knowledge has little value unless we put it to _pract_* use.
5. A medical (dynamist, practitioner) is someone who puts his knowledge of medicine to use.
6. The Greek word *cheir* (changed to *chiro*) means "hand." Combine the latter spelling with a lesson root and the suffix -*or* to name a doctor who "does (treatments) with his hands."
7. Choose the correct words for the sentences below.

   dynamic   dynamite
   dynamo   dynamometer
   dynasty   thermodynamics

   a. The miners used ____ to blast the coal loose.
   b. This huge ____ generates millions of watts of electricity.
   c. Paul was a ____ missionary after his conversion.
   d. Herod is the name of several rulers in the same ____.
   e. One law of ____ states that heat always flows from a warmer object to a cooler object.
   f. A ____ measures the power available at the shaft of an engine.

Lesson 23

(Total points: 76)

Notes on Part A

Selected Words With Lesson Roots

L *pract:* **practical,** chiropractor, practice, practitioner

Gk. *dyna:* **dynamic,** dynamist, dynamite, dynamo, dynamometer, dynasty, thermodynamics

Answer Key—Part A (18 points)	**Lesson 23 Test Sentences**

Answer Key—Part A (18 points)

1. *pract:* practical
   dyna: dynamic

2. a. "And as ye would that men should *do* to you, *do* ye also to them likewise."
   b. "There is no man that hath *power* over the spirit to retain the spirit; neither hath he *power* in the day of death: . . . neither shall wickedness deliver those that are given to it."

3. practice

4. practical

5. practitioner

6. chiropractor

7. a. dynamite
   b. dynamo
   c. dynamic
   d. dynasty
   e. thermodynamics
   f. dynamometer

Lesson 23 Test Sentences

1. *embroidery* Elsie does very fine *embroidery. embroidery*
2. *Almighty* The *Almighty* is a sure refuge. *Almighty*
3. *anxiety* That eases all our *anxiety. anxiety*
4. *security* This *security* is ours through Jesus. *security*
5. *vengeance* We leave all *vengeance* with God. *vengeance*
6. *curiosity* Leon's eyes sparkled with *curiosity. curiosity*
7. *scratchy* He heard *scratchy* noises in the trash can. *scratchy*
8. *theme* Does your program have a *theme? theme*
9. *dreary* A smile can change a *dreary* day. *dreary*
10. *sufficient* Everyone has *sufficient* time for politeness. *sufficient*
11. *maturity* Consistent kindness is a mark of *maturity. maturity*
12. *strict* Keep a *strict* control on words. *strict*
13. *divinity* Jesus' *divinity* accompanied His humanity. *divinity*
14. *practical* Take a *practical* approach to life. *practical*
15. *reality* Hard work is a *reality* for everyone. *reality*
16. *moody* Overcome *moody* feelings with a song. *moody*
17. *dynamic* Brother Seth displays *dynamic* Christianity. *dynamic*
18. *loyalty* All can see his *loyalty* to Christ. *loyalty*
19. *certainty* He has faith in the *certainty* of God's guidance. *certainty*
20. *inferiority* Do you see the *inferiority* of reasoning to faith? *inferiority*
21. *necessity* Water is a *necessity* of life. *necessity*
22. *unanimous* The plan was accepted by *unanimous* vote. *unanimous*
23. *tyranny* A revolt threw off the *tyranny* of the despot. *tyranny*
24. *anarchy* The people soon found that *anarchy* was worse. *anarchy*
25. *humidity* Heat is less stressful when the *humidity* is low. *humidity*

B. AFFIXING AFFIXES

1. Use spelling words with the suffix *-ity* for these answers.
   a. Three words that had no spelling change in the root when *-ity* was added.
   b. Three words in which final *e* was dropped from the root word.
   c. A word with *ious* changed to *ios* before *-ity* was added.
2. If *-ity* is removed from one of the spelling words, a suffix such as *-ary* must replace it because the root cannot stand alone. Write this spelling word and its *-ary* form.
3. Write the two spelling words in which the roots had no spelling change when *-ty* was added.
4. Write the spelling word with the suffix *-ety*. Also write its *-ous* form.
5. Use spelling words with the suffix *-y* for these exercises.
   a. Three NEW WORDS that are adjectives.
   b. A proper noun or adjective with a prefix and a suffix.
   c. A word in which *-ant* in the root was

Noun- and Adjective-forming Suffixes

SUFFIX	MEANING	EXAMPLE
-y		thorny
-ty	condition	royalty
-ity	or quality	solidity
-ety		variety

changed to *ann* before *-y* was added.
   d. Words with assimilated forms of *a-* and *en-*.
6. Write the NEW WORDS that are derived from these root words.
   a. suffice
   b. practice
7. Add a prefix meaning "not" to form an antonym for each of these words.
   a. certainty
   b. loyalty
   c. maturity
   d. practical
   e. sufficient
8. Change *practical* to an adverb by adding *-ly,* and to a noun by adding a lesson suffix.

C. SOUND, STRUCTURE, AND MEANING

1. Write the NEW WORDS that have these phonetic features.
   a. /k/ spelled *ch*
   b. /sh/ spelled *ci*
   c. soft *g* and soft *c*
2. Write NEW WORDS for these definitions.
   a. Of one mind.
   b. Enough to satisfy.
   c. Punishment for wrongdoing.
   d. Topic; main idea.
   e. Exact; precise.
3. Write spelling words that are antonyms of these words.
   a. cheery
   b. sluggish
   c. betrayal
   d. confidence
   e. fantasy
4. One word in Matthew 7:13 is a doublet to one of your NEW WORDS. Write both words.
5. One word in Genesis 43:9 is a doublet to one of your REVIEW WORDS. Write both words.
6. The Speller Dictionary has run-on entries for these words. Write a sentence using the run-on entry for each one.
   a. vengeance
   b. almighty

Notes on Part B

Exercise 7: Review some prefixes that mean "not," such as *dis-, un-, in-, im-, anti-*.

Answer Key—Part B (29 points)

1. a. humidity, inferiority, reality
   b. maturity, divinity, security
   c. curiosity
2. necessity, necessary
3. certainty, loyalty
4. anxiety, anxious
5. a. dreary, moody, scratchy
   b. Almighty
   c. tyranny
   d. anarchy, embroidery
6. a. sufficient
   b. practical
7. a. uncertainty
   b. disloyalty
   c. immaturity
   d. impractical
   e. insufficient
8. practically, practicality

Notes on Part C

Exercise 6: A run-on entry gives the word in a commonly used phrase that specializes its meaning.

Answer Key—Part C (19 points)

1. a. anarchy
   b. sufficient
   c. vengeance
2. a. unanimous
   b. sufficient
   c. vengeance
   d. theme
   e. strict
3. a. dreary (Accept *moody.*)
   b. dynamic
   c. loyalty
   d. anxiety
   e. reality
4. strait, strict
5. surety, security
6. (Sample sentences)
   a. For half an hour we pulled weeds *with a vengeance.*
   b. Scientific laws are decrees of *the Almighty.*

D. LANGUAGE LINEAGE

SEMANTIC STUDY: EUPHEMISM

The word *euphemism* comes from the Greek *euphēmos,* which means "good speech." Euphemism is the use of good words in referring to things that are distasteful or improper to mention directly. It is kind to speak gently of things that hurt deeply. It is polite to speak modestly when we need to mention things associated with indecency.

Death is a sensitive subject. Because of sinners' reluctance to talk about death, and because of sympathy for the grief that death brings, euphemisms are common in discussing this subject.

"When did Mr. Smith depart this life?"

"He expired soon after one o'clock on Thursday."

"He said his books should be donated to the school if something happens to him."

Undertaker literally means "one who takes upon himself a task." You can undertake to do a great variety of things, but the term has become so strongly associated with death that many people have come to avoid even that euphemism in favor of terms like *mortician* and *funeral director. Burial grounds, cemetery,* and *memorial gardens* are often preferred over *graveyard.*

Modesty has produced such terms as *restroom* and *washroom.* We understand their meanings by association rather than by literal interpretation. Through frequent use, terms like these soon mean nothing else; and polite society invents new expressions to mention the little room in a nice way.

Euphemisms are used for respectfulness in many areas. Clothing is not labeled in sizes for "fat" customers but in "king" or "queen" sizes. An unwanted dog is "put to sleep" instead of being "killed." Deer are "harvested" by hunters, and laboratory animals are "sacrificed."

Because the Bible forbids profanity, many people try to avoid direct use of the Lord's Name in exclamations of surprise or disgust. But they may use altered forms as euphemisms (such as *gee* for *Jesus*), and that is still wrong. These people may not realize the meaning of the expressions they use, or perhaps they think euphemism makes the violation less serious.

It is sometimes necessary to speak of death and other delicate matters. But it is never in order to take God's Name in vain. We should be careful to keep our speech free from any light or profane reference to God.

Exercises

1. What is euphemism?
2. a. When is euphemism good?
   b. When is it bad?
3. a. Write three expressions used in the lesson as euphemisms for death.
   b. Give some other euphemisms for death that you can think of.
4. Copy the *least* euphemistic expression in each group.
   a. relieved of his duties, fired from his job, given his walking papers
   b. old woman, senior citizen, golden ager
   c. was retained, repeated a grade, failed a grade

Notes on Part D

Do the students recognize *the little room* as a euphemism in the paragraph about *restroom* and *washroom?* Quite a string of polite society terms have been applied to the toilet, all of them respectable in the literal meaning: *outhouse, water closet, W. C., ladies' lounge, men's room, powder room, and privy. Lavatory* comes from the Latin root *lavāre* (to wash).

You may want to point out some euphemisms for profanity, especially if you hear them in the speech of your students. The best victory over such speech habits is to overcome emotions that need to be vented in such expression. Many people use terms such as the following, probably without realizing what they represent.

blamed, darned, darnation, tarnation—damned, damnation

doggone—damn

drat—God rot

gee, jeez, gee whiz, jeepers, jeepers creepers—Jesus, Jesus Christ

golly, gosh—God

Answer Key—Part D (10 points)

1. Euphemism is using *nice words* for something distasteful or undesirable to talk about.
2. a. Euphemism is good when it helps one speak *kindly or modestly.*
   b. Euphemism is bad when it excuses using *God's name in vain.*
3. a. depart this life, expired, something happens to him
   b. (Sample answers) breathe one's last, pass away, pass on, fall asleep, cross the river, entered eternity
4. a. fired from his job
   b. old woman
   c. failed a grade

LESSON 24

19	20	21	22	23
anticipate	abundance	acceptable	Anabaptist	anarchy
ascend	algebra	accompanied	analysis	anxiety
carbohydrates	amusing	conspicuous	anatomy	certainty
courier	borne	contemplate	assessment	curiosity
discourse	chord	dealt	beaten	dreary
dissatisfied	environment	frequently	commerce	dynamic
eclipse	epidermis	hastily	crusade	humidity
embroider	epilepsy	inspection	dehydrate	inferiority
emphasis	epistles	parables	flannel	loyalty
endure	insomnia	parachute	geometry	maturity
energy	nineteenth	paradise	hydrant	moody
exclaim	oblige	paralyze	hydraulic	practical
excursion	pneumonia	parasite	hydrogen	reality
exile	previous	perimeter	individual	scratchy
Exodus	psychology	periodical	magnificent	strict
extraordinary	quotations	philosophy	musician	sufficient
incense	recommend	precious	occasional	theme
installation	refreshment	recognized	passage	tyranny
occurred	vague	sophomore	peasant	unanimous
transcend	warrior	urgent	privilege	vengeance

A. UNEARTHING THE ROOTS

L *scend*	= climb	Gk. *soma*	= body
L *curr, curs*	= run	Gk. *psyche*	= soul, mind
		Gk. *pneuma*	= spirit, breath
Gk. *philo*	= love		
Gk. *sophos*	= wisdom	Gk. *physio*	= growth, nature
		Gk. *geo*	= earth
L *pract*	= do	Gk. *hydro*	= water
Gk. *dyna*	= power		

Lesson 24

(Total points: 71)

Lesson 24 Test Sentences

1. *dissatisfied* Mother was *dissatisfied* with the garden. *dissatisfied*
2. *energy* We all put some *energy* into weeding. *energy*
3. *anticipate* Now we *anticipate* better production. *anticipate*
4. *incense* Prayer is a sweet *incense* to God. *incense*
5. *emphasis* There should be more *emphasis* on sacrifice. *emphasis*
6. *excursion* Absalom's *excursion* ended in an oak. *excursion*
7. *courier* An eager *courier* carried the news. *courier*
8. *eclipse* Ray saw notice of an *eclipse* in the news. *eclipse*
9. *installation* The door comes with free *installation*. *installation*
10. *endure* We can *endure* extra noise and dust for a while. *endure*
11. *epistles* Peter wrote two *epistles*. *epistles*
12. *nineteenth* Be sure to read the *nineteenth* verse. *nineteenth*
13. *warrior* An Indian in *warrior* costume rode the pony. *warrior*
14. *amusing* They led an *amusing* train. *amusing*
15. *previous* It gave a glimpse of *previous* days. *previous*
16. *vague* There was a *vague* bank of fog on the hill. *vague*
17. *pneumonia* Grandfather is prone to *pneumonia*. *pneumonia*
18. *abundance* He had an *abundance* of visitors. *abundance*
19. *oblige* He will always *oblige* you with a smile. *oblige*
20. *chord* A minor *chord* has a mournful tone. *chord*
21. *periodical* Take a *periodical* survey of the pantry. *periodical*
22. *hastily* The *hastily* made cookies were delicious. *hastily*
23. *acceptable* Buttermilk is an *acceptable* substitute. *acceptable*
24. *urgent* Carl's summons was *urgent* but gentle. *urgent*
25. *contemplate* Did you *contemplate* the schedule? *contemplate*
26. *dealt* Winter *dealt* some harsh blows. *dealt*
27. *paralyze* Ice will *paralyze* the fan. *paralyze*
28. *precious* Silence is a *precious* commodity. *precious*
29. *conspicuous* A cricket gave two *conspicuous* chirps. *conspicuous*
30. *parachute* George reached the cliff by *parachute*. *parachute*
31. *flannel* He carried *flannel* for the victim. *flannel*
32. *dehydrate* How quickly would he *dehydrate*? *dehydrate*
33. *geometry* First grade has *geometry* by learning shapes. *geometry*
34. *privilege* It is a *privilege* to live in the country. *privilege*
35. *occasional* Take an *occasional* fresh-air walk. *occasional*
36. *individual* The children had *individual* garden plots. *individual*
37. *magnificent* Samuel grew a *magnificent* pumpkin. *magnificent*
38. *analysis* Carver did intense *analysis* of the peanut. *analysis*
39. *commerce* Cotton helped to build *commerce* in the South. *commerce*
40. *hydraulic* A hose nozzle demonstrates *hydraulic* force. *hydraulic*
41. *dreary* The hall was a *dreary* gray. *dreary*
42. *unanimous* There was *unanimous* consent to paint it. *unanimous*
43. *practical* Choose a *practical* color. *practical*
44. *strict* Mark keeps *strict* watch over the flock. *strict*
45. *curiosity* One lamb's *curiosity* led it astray. *curiosity*
46. *anxiety* Mark's *anxiety* increased as it grew later. *anxiety*
47. *sufficient* God's grace is *sufficient* to endure wrong. *sufficient*
48. *vengeance* We leave *vengeance* in His hands. *vengeance*
49. *theme* Peace is the *theme* of our relationships. *theme*
50. *inferiority* Submission does not indicate *inferiority*. *inferiority*

— PUPIL —

1. Write words from Lesson 19 to fill these blanks.
   a. A balloon may *scend* several miles, but a rocket can *scend* the atmosphere.
   b. The *curr* gave a long *curs* about how the accident *curr* .
   c. Our *curs* ended with a picnic beside the lake.

2. Write words from Lesson 20 for these meanings or etymologies.
   a. sleeplessness
   b. lung disease
   c. unclear
   d. (mind) + *-logia* (study)
   e. (in) + *viron* (circle) + *-ment*
   f. *ob-* (to) + *ligāre* (to bind)
   g. *prae-* (before) + *via* (way)

3. Write words from Lesson 21 for these meanings or etymologies.
   a. study carefully
   b. easily noticeable
   c. (loving) + (wisdom)
   d. (wise) + *mōros* (fool)

4. Write words from Lesson 22.
   a. *de-* (away) + (water) + *-ate*
   b. Ann washed the vegetables at an outdoor *hydro* .
   c. Without *hydro* there would be no water.
   d. (water) + *aulos* (pipe) + *-ic*
   e. (earth) + *metron* (measure)

5. Write words from Lesson 23.
   a. a synonym for *powerful*
   b. (do) + *-al*

B. AFFIXING AFFIXES

1. Write words from Lesson 19 for these definitions. Write *A* after each one that has an assimilated prefix.
   a. Decorate with stitches.
   b. Bear hardship.
   c. Banishment from one's native country.
   d. The obscuring of a heavenly body.
   e. Special forcefulness or attention.
   f. Short pleasure outing.

2. Write words from Lesson 20 for these etymologies.
   a. (over) + *dēmos* (people) (REVIEW WORD)
   b. (over) + *stellein* (to send)
   c. (upon) + *lambanein* (to seize)
   d. (upon) + *derma* (skin)

3. Write words from Lesson 21 for these etymologies.
   a. (around) + (measure)

en-, em-	on, in
ex-, ec-	out
epi-	upon, over
para-	beside, near
peri-	around
ana-	again, up
-y, -ty, -ity, -ety	condition or quality

   b. *pairi* (around) + *daēza* (wall)
   c. (going around) + *-al*
   d. *parare* (to shield) + *chute* (a fall)
   e. (beside) + *sitos* (feeder)
   f. (beside) + *ballein* (to throw)

4. Write words from Lesson 22 for these etymologies.
   a. (again) + (to baptize)
   b. (up) + *luein* (to loosen)
   c. (up) + *tomē* (a cutting)

Answer Key—Part A (24 points)

1. a. ascend, transcend
    b. courier, discourse, occurred
    c. excursion

2. a. insomnia
    b. pneumonia
    c. vague
    d. psychology
    e. environment
    f. oblige
    g. previous

3. a. contemplate
    b. conspicuous
    c. philosophy
    d. sophomore

4. a. dehydrate
    b. hydrant
    c. hydrogen
    d. hydraulic
    e. geometry

5. a. dynamic
    b. practical

Answer Key—Part B (38 points)

1. a. embroider, A
    b. endure
    c. exile
    d. eclipse, A
    e. emphasis, A
    f. excursion

2. a. epidemic
    b. epistles
    c. epilepsy
    d. epidermis

3. a. perimeter
    b. paradise
    c. periodical
    d. parachute
    e. parasite
    f. parables

4. a. Anabaptist
    b. analysis
    c. anatomy

5. Write words from Lesson 22 that have these suffixes.
   a. *-ment*
   b. *-en*
   c. *-ian*
   d. *-al*
   e. *-age*
   f. *-cent*

6. Write the words from Lesson 23 that are forms of these words.
   a. anxious   f. certain
   b. curious   g. humid
   c. mature   h. real
   d. tyrant   i. loyal
   e. suffice   j. inferior

D.   LANGUAGE LINEAGE

REVIEW

1. a. What is the purpose of modern dictionaries?

   b. What view of dictionary publication should not be applied to life in general?

2. How did Webster's blue-backed speller influence American speech?

3. Describe two plans, proposed in the 1500s, by which words would be spelled exactly as they sound.

4. Why would a completely phonetic spelling system be impractical?

5. a. What man campaigned actively for spelling refinement?

   b. What organization also helped improve spelling consistency?

6. When is euphemism appropriate?

5. a. assessment
   b. beaten
   c. musician
   d. occasional
   e. passage
   f. magnificent

6. a. anxiety
   b. curiosity
   c. maturity
   d. tyranny
   e. sufficient
   f. certainty
   g. humidity
   h. reality
   i. loyalty
   j. inferiority

Answer Key—Part D (9 points)

1. a. The purpose of modern dictionaries is to provide a record of *current usage*.
   b. The idea that something is *right because everybody does it* should not be applied to life in general.

2. The speller was so widely used, many people learned the same *careful pronunciation*.

3. One plan had *extra characters* so that each sound could have its own symbol. Another plan had *added marks* such as accents and apostrophes attached to the letters.

4. There are too many *fine sound variations, and pronunciations change*.

5. a. *Noah Webster* campaigned actively for spelling refinement.
   b. The *Simplified Spelling Board* helped improve spelling consistency.

6. Euphemism is appropriate when it helps one speak *kindly and modestly*.

LESSON 25

NEW WORDS

applicant
architect
consultant
defendant
generate
inhabitant
nitrogen
ornament
responsibility
scientist
solvent
superintendent
susceptible
testimony
therapist
tourist
triumph
typist
unregenerate
violent

REVIEW WORDS

attendant
enthusiastic
hydrogen
immigrant
oxygen

A.   UNEARTHING THE ROOTS

ROOT	MEANING	EXAMPLE
Greek *gen*	= produce, begin	generate
Greek *arch*	= begin, lead	archangel

1. Write the lesson roots and the six spelling words derived from them.
2. Falling water is used to (produce)* electricity.
3. When a person is born again, he experiences _gen_ (Titus 3:5).
4. If a person is not born again, he is _gen_ *.
5. Which book of the Bible is the "book of beginnings"?
6. Write a REVIEW WORD that might be defined as "the beginning of water."
7. A major element in the atmosphere and a part of all living tissues is _____*.
8. Write the REVIEW WORD whose etymology reveals a mistaken idea about acids.
9. Choose the correct word for each definition.

   allergen   hallucinogen
   carcinogen   pathogen

   a. A substance that causes cancer.
   b. A substance that causes disease.
   c. A substance that causes hallucinations.
   d. A substance that causes an allergic reaction.
10. Hereditary qualities are reproduced by (arches, genes).
11. God is the (designer)* of the universe. Write the etymology of this word.
12. *Shew* and *thine* are examples of _arch_ words.
13. Write a word with the *arch* root for the italicized phrase in each sentence.

   a. The *leading angel* is Michael (Jude 9).
   b. Abraham was a *leading father* of the Israelite nation (Hebrews 7:4).
   c. Herod was a *leader over one-fourth of a province* (Matthew 14:1).

Lesson 25

(Total points: 79)

Notes on Part A

Selected Words With Lesson Roots

Gk. *gen:* **generate, hydrogen, nitrogen, oxygen, unregenerate,** allergen, carcinogen, Genesis, hallucinogen, pathogen

Gk. *arch:* **architect,** archaic, archetype, partiarch, tetrarch

Arch- is a prefix for combining forms such as *archangel, archbishop, archenemy.*

Exercise 6: Recall the root *hydro* from Lesson 22.

Exercise 9: Choose answers by matching similarities in word parts or by familiar root meanings (*patho*—Lesson 3). Check remaining possibilities with a dictionary.

Answer Key—Part A (26 points)

1. *gen:* generate, nitrogen, unregenerate, hydrogen, oxygen
   arch: architect
2. generate
3. regeneration
4. unregenerate
5. Genesis
6. hydrogen
7. nitrogen
8. oxygen
9. a. carcinogen
   b. pathogen
   c. hallucinogen
   d. allergen
10. genes
11. architect [< L *architectus* < Gk. *arkhitektōn* < *archi-* chief + *tektōn* builder]
12. archaic
13. a. archangel
    b. patriarch
    c. tetrarch

Lesson 25 Test Sentences

1. *immigrant* Each *immigrant* had a health examination. *immigrant*
2. *susceptible* Children are *susceptible* to mischief. *susceptible*
3. *unregenerate* Christ came to save *unregenerate* man. *unregenerate*
4. *nitrogen* Read the *nitrogen* content of the fertilizer. *nitrogen*
5. *defendant* Jesus had no *defendant* before Pilate. *defendant*
6. *inhabitant* One thief is now an *inhabitant* of heaven. *inhabitant*
7. *testimony* His *testimony* of guilt was sincere. *testimony*
8. *triumph* He shares in the *triumph* of the resurrection. *triumph*
9. *architect* Who was the *architect* of this staircase? *architect*
10. *superintendent* Contact the building *superintendent*. *superintendent*
11. *tourist* It is a popular *tourist* attraction. *tourist*
12. *scientist* Faith is mystery to a *scientist*. *scientist*
13. *generate* Faith can *generate* miracles. *generate*
14. *enthusiastic* There was *enthusiastic* scrubbing in the hall. *enthusiastic*
15. *solvent* A bit of *solvent* erased black marks. *solvent*
16. *responsibility* We'll take *responsibility* to keep it clean. *responsibility*
17. *typist* Hudson Bank needs a new *typist*. *typist*
18. *applicant* Has there been any *applicant* for the job? *applicant*
19. *attendant* The governor's *attendant* called a taxi. *attendant*
20. *consultant* A special *consultant* shared the ride. *consultant*
21. *therapist* His *therapist* called for more exercise. *therapist*
22. *oxygen* Get more *oxygen* in your lungs. *oxygen*
23. *ornament* Wear the *ornament* of meekness. *ornament*
24. *hydrogen* The largest element of water is *hydrogen*. *hydrogen*
25. *violent* The shed collapsed in *violent* winds. *violent*

B.   AFFIXING AFFIXES

1. Write words with the *-ant* or *-ent* suffix for these meanings.
   a. One who defends*.
   b. One who opposes.
   c. One who inhabits*.
   d. One who attends*.
   e. One who studies.
   f. One who applies*.
   g. One who consults or is consulted*.
   h. One who supervises*.
   i. One who immigrates*.
   j. That which adorns*.
   k. That which dissolves another substance*.
2. Write the spelling word with *-ent* that means "fierce."
3. Write words with the *-ist* suffix for these meanings.
   a. One who has knowledge in science*.
   b. One who gives therapy*.
   c. One who tours*.
   d. One who types*.
   e. One who baptizes.
   f. One who produces art.
   g. One who evangelizes.

Noun- and Adjective-forming Suffixes

SUFFIX	MEANING	EXAMPLE
-ant,	one who	informant
-ent		student
-ist	one who has	artist
-ast	or does	enthusiast

   h. One who colonizes.
   i. One who studies languages. (See *Language Lineage*, Lesson 22.)
4. a. Use the suffix *-ast* to write a word that means "one who has enthusiasm."
   b. Write the spelling word that is the adjective form of this word.
   c. Write the adjective form with an ending that changes it to an adverb.
5. Write the NEW WORD derived from *responsible*.
6. Write *susceptible* with the suffix you added in number 5.
7. a. Write the REVIEW WORD that has an assimilated form of the prefix *in-*. Circle the last letter of the prefix and the first letter of the root word.
   b. Write a word with the same root word and the prefix *e-* which means "out."

C.   SOUND, STRUCTURE, AND MEANING

1. Write the spelling words that have these phonetic features.
   a. /f/ spelled *ph*
   b. /s/ spelled *sc* (2)
   c. /ī/ spelled *y* (2)
2. Write the six-syllable spelling word.
3. Write three five-syllable spelling words.
4. Write three NEW WORDS that have a syllable division between two vowels.
5. Write NEW WORDS that are antonyms of these words.
   a. gentle
   b. plaintiff
   c. immune
   d. defeat
   e. visitor
6. What name was given to the box that held the tables of stone on which God wrote the Ten Commandments? (Exodus 31:7).
7. Write a sentence using *testimony* with definition 3 in the Speller Dictionary.
8. Write a sentence using *ornament* as a verb.

Answer Key—Part B (28 points)

1. a. defendant
   b. opponent
   c. inhabitant
   d. attendant
   e. student
   f. applicant
   g. consultant
   h. superintendent
   i. immigrant
   j. ornament
   k. solvent

2. violent

3. a. scientist
   b. therapist
   c. tourist
   d. typist
   e. baptist
   f. artist
   g. evangelist
   h. colonist
   i. linguist

4. a. enthusiast
   b. enthusiastic
   c. enthusiastically

5. responsibility

6. susceptibility

7. a. immigrant
   b. emigrant

Answer Key—Part C (20 points)

1. a. triumph
   b. scientist, susceptible
   c. typist, hydrogen

   c. susceptible
   d. triumph
   e. inhabitant

2. responsibility

3. superintendent, unregenerate, enthusiastic

4. scientist, triumph, violent

5. a. violent
   b. defendant

6. ark of the testimony

7. (Sample sentence) For many Anabaptists, their *testimony* cost their life.

8. (Sample sentence) Good works *ornament* your life better than gold.

D.   LANGUAGE LINEAGE

AMERICAN ENGLISH AND BRITISH ENGLISH

The English language came to America with the Pilgrims and other English settlers. There, a frontier culture, strange plants and animals, and new associations added new terms to their speech. Back home in England, the language also changed, as any living language will. Both factors caused the language to diverge until American English became distinctly different from British English.

Although the differences do not cause serious communication difficulties, they easily reveal the nationality of the speaker or writer. Grammar is basically the same in both countries, but some spelling patterns and pronunciation habits differ. Lesson 26 discusses some interesting vocabulary differences.

The spelling changes described in Lesson 22 were American changes. The British still use older forms such as *favour, centre,* and *cheque.*

Noah Webster's speller trained Americans to give full pronunciation to all the syllables of a word, but British speech tends to clip words. For example, *dictionary* and *stationary* become three-syllable words, pronounced /dik′ shən ri/ and /stā′ shən ri/.

Another British characteristic is omission of the /r/ sound at the end of a syllable or word. An agricultural worker without riches is called a /pü ə fä′ mə/. Final *r* is usually replaced with the schwa sound.

Final *r* is pronounced, however, if the next word begins with a vowel sound. "Far to go" is /fä tü gō/, but "far ahead" is /fä rə hed/. Furthermore, an extra *r* sound is tucked in, though none is written, to separate a vowel sound at the end of one word from a vowel sound at the beginning of the next word. "Saw ahead" is /sô rə hed/.

A significant difference in vowel pronunciation is the broad *a.* Short *a* is pronounced at the back of the mouth with lowered tongue, making it sound very much like the American short *o.* For a demonstration, read the following sentence with the same vowel sound in *half* and *past* as you say in *watch.* "My watch shows half past four." (Did you say *four* with or without a final *r?*)

Exercises

1. a. What influenced language changes in America?
   b. Why did the language change in England?
2. What are some differences between British spelling and American spelling?

3. a. What letter sounds have significantly different pronunciations?
   b. What pronunciation change happens in many multisyllable words?

Notes on Part D

Americans are also losing the distinction of careful speech. In the pronunciations for *superintendent,* the Speller Dictionary shows the tendency to clip syllables. The first pronunciation has five syllables, and the second one, only four.

Answer Key—Part D (5 points)

1. a. Americans faced *new culture,* plants, animals, and associations.
    b. Any living *language will change*.
2. British spelling uses some *older forms* that Americans have changed.
3. a. The British do not pronounce the final *r.* Their short *a* sounds more like the American short *o*.
    b. The British tend to *clip longer words* to fewer syllables.

LESSON 26

A. UNEARTHING THE ROOTS

> ROOTS
> Words of French origin

NEW WORDS

beige
bouquet
brochure
camouflage
career
chaperon
chauffeur
compliment
corsage
croquet
employee
fatigue
gourmet
lieutenant
parliament
referee
restaurant
revenue
silhouette
sunset

REVIEW WORDS

amateur
available
engineer
juvenile
souvenir

1. Write words in which /ā/ has the French spelling *et*.
    a. A game of hitting balls through wickets*.
    b. One skilled in evaluating fine foods*.
    c. An arrangement of flowers*.
    d. To make with yarn and a hooked needle: <u>croc</u> .
    e. To bounce off a flat surface: <u>rico</u> .
    f. A perfumed powder: <u>sac</u> .
    g. A man who compiled a thesaurus: <u>Rog</u> .
2. What NEW WORD with /ā/ spelled *ei* means "a light tan color"?
3. Write words with French spelling of /ēg/ for these definitions.
    a. Weariness*.
    b. Secret scheming: <u>intr</u> .
4. Write the NEW WORD with a French spelling of /ü/ that names a military officer.
5. Write other words with the same spelling of /ü/ for these definitions.
    a. French word for *good-by:* <u>ad</u> .
    b. Instead of: in <u>l</u> of.
    c. Environment: <u>mil</u> .
6. Write spelling words for these etymologies.
    a. *brocher* (to stitch) < *broche* (knitting needle)
    b. *camoufler* (to disguise) < Ital. *camuffare*
    c. *chaperon* (hood) < *chape* (covering)
    d. *cors* (body) < L *corpus*
    e. *parler* (to talk)
    f. *restaurer* (to restore)
    g. *revenir* (to return) < L *re-* back + *venīre* (to come)
    h. *subvenīre* (come to mind) < *sub-* (under) + *venīre* (to come)
7. A French finance minister of the 1700s was noted for cutting back state finances. His name was eventually applied to the ____*, a substitute for expensive paintings.

Lesson 26

(Total points: 78)

Notes on Part A

The Norman Conquest brought the French language into supremacy in England. Several hundred years later when English overcame the "foreign language," it had absorbed thousands of French words. These are some that began to be used in English during the Middle Ages.

authority	government	mayor	proof	state
charity	judge	minister	public	traitor
clergy	justice	pastor	rebel	treaty
crime	liberty	piety	religion	verdict

Answer Key—Part A (23 points)

1. a. croquet
   b. gourmet
   c. bouquet
   d. crochet
   e. ricochet
   f. sachet
   g. Roget

2. beige

3. a. fatigue
   b. intrigue

4. lieutenant

5. a. adieu
   b. lieu
   c. milieu

6. a. brochure
   b. camouflage
   c. chaperon
   d. corsage
   e. parliament
   f. restaurant
   g. revenue
   h. souvenir

7. silhouette

Lesson 26 Test Sentences

1. *career* Describe your *career* in the kitchen. *career*
2. *brochure* Read this *brochure* on canning. *brochure*
3. *restaurant* Some tips were used in the *restaurant.* *restaurant*
4. *available* They are *available* to all the workers. *available*
5. *juvenile* Debbie is a *juvenile* cook. *juvenile*
6. *corsage* Kim gave Mother a *corsage* of violets. *corsage*
7. *croquet* She found them during the *croquet* game. *croquet*
8. *amateur* Frank is an *amateur* carpenter. *amateur*
9. *fatigue* Heavy work causes *fatigue. fatigue*
10. *employee* Each *employee* can help encourage the others. *employee*
11. *referee* Do the ants have a *referee? referee*
12. *beige* Please clean the *beige* carpet again. *beige*
13. *bouquet* The daffodil *bouquet* drank all its water. *bouquet*
14. *sunset* We sang until *sunset. sunset*
15. *engineer* The *engineer* let us blow the whistle. *engineer*
16. *chaperon* Uncle Ben was our *chaperon* at the zoo. *chaperon*
17. *lieutenant* He met a *lieutenant* from his service days. *lieutenant*
18. *parliament* The last session of *parliament* was short. *parliament*
19. *revenue* They will need more *revenue* next year. *revenue*
20. *chauffeur* The new *chauffeur* missed his road. *chauffeur*
21. *compliment* Jean gave him a *compliment* for safe driving. *compliment*
22. *silhouette* The tree was a *silhouette* in the moonlight. *silhouette*
23. *camouflage* Shadows helped to *camouflage* the antelope. *camouflage*
24. *gourmet* Bees in the desert make *gourmet* honey. *gourmet*
25. *souvenir* We took a tiny cactus as a *souvenir. souvenir*

B. AFFIXING AFFIXES

1. Write words ending with -*eer* or -*eur* for these definitions.
   a. One who operates engines*.
   b. One who drives a chariot.
   c. One who conducts auctions.
   d. One hired to drive a private vehicle*.
   e. One who engages in an activity as a pastime rather than a profession*.
   f. One who lives in the mountains.
2. Write the spelling word in which -*eer* is not a suffix meaning "one who."
3. Use the -*ee* form of another word in the sentence to fill each blank.
   a. The employer gave each ____* a raise in pay.
   b. The dispute was referred to the ____* for settlement.
   c. The ____ quickly mastered the skills

French Suffixes

SUFFIX	MEANING	EXAMPLE
-*eer*	one who	auctioneer
-*eur*		
-*ee*	one who is	payee

that his trainer taught.
4. Answer with lesson suffixes: A word ending with ____ or ____ names a doer, and one ending with ____ names a receiver.
5. Write each of these words with a prefix that changes it to the opposite meaning.
   a. available
   b. complimentary
6. a. Write the REVIEW WORD that means "young."
   b. Remove the last three letters, and rewrite the word with the prefix *re-* and the suffix -*ate*, meaning "to make young again."

C. SOUND, STRUCTURE, AND MEANING

1. Write the NEW WORDS that have these phonetic features.
   a. /ā/ spelled *ei*
   b. /ā/ spelled *et* (3)
   c. /ō/ spelled *au*
   d. /ü/ spelled *ieu*
   e. final /äzh/ (2)
2. Write the compound spelling word.
3. Write spelling words that are synonyms of these words.
   a. hireling
   b. obtainable
   c. occupation
   d. nonprofessional
   e. immature
4. Write *compliment* or *complement* for the blank in each sentence. (Remember to associate *complement* with "complete" and *compliment* with "praise.")
   a. A ____ is an expression of admiration or praise.
   b. A ____ is a sentence part that completes the meaning of a verb.
   c. The first *e* in ____ can be associated with the first *e* in *complete*.
   d. The letter *i* appears in ____ and in *praise*.
   e. A sincere ____ can be greatly encouraging.
   f. The expression "Mother bought" needs a ____.
   g. We should ____ Mark for his thorough work.
5. a. Look up the NEW WORD *croquet*, and write the French variant of this word.
   b. If you add *te* to this NEW WORD, you will spell the name of a small cake of fried food. Write that word.
6. Look up the etymology of *bouquet*. Does it have the thought of a loosely arranged group or a close bunch?
7. Write an alternate spelling for *chaperon*.

Notes on Part B

Other *-eur* words: colporteur, entrepreneur, provocateur.

Other *-ee* words: absentee, addressee, appointee, devotee, entree, licensee, nominee, refugees (31), transferee.

Answer Key—Part B (17 points)

1. a. engineer
   b. charioteer
   c. auctioneer
   d. chauffeur
   e. amateur
   f. mountaineer

2. career

3. a. employee
   b. referee
   c. trainee

4. -eer, -eur, -ee

5. a. unavailable
   b. uncomplimentary

6. a. juvenile
   b. rejuvenate

Notes on Part C

Exercise 4: *I* like a compl*i*ment. *E* makes compl*e*te.

Answer Key—Part C (25 points)

1. a. beige
   b. bouquet, croquet, gourmet
   c. chauffeur
   d. lieutenant
   e. camouflage, corsage

2. sunset

3. a. employee
   b. available
   c. career
   d. amateur
   e. juvenile

4. a. compliment
   b. complement
   c. complement
   d. compliment
   e. compliment
   f. complement
   g. compliment

5. a. crochet
   b. croquette

6. close bunch

7. chaperone

D.   LANGUAGE LINEAGE

BRITISH VOCABULARY

British and American people exchange words. Terms originating in one country are often adopted in the other. But many words are typically American or British and do not come into common use in the other country. The following paragraphs contain some British terms.

George lives in a tower block in London. Last summer he spent a fortnight visiting Bruce in his caravan on the moor. Bruce is a market gardener, and vegetable marrow was in season at the time. On market day, they went to the field with a torch and started picking the marrow before daylight.

On the way to market in the lorry, they came upon a car stalled by the motorway with the bonnet raised. Bruce stopped to offer help. When nothing seemed to be amiss with the engine, Bruce suggested that perhaps the petrol tank was empty. The man had a petrol can in his boot, but there was nothing in it.

Bruce and George took him to the nearest petrol station to fill the can, and then they returned to the stranded car. That proved to be the solution, for the car started normally, and the motorist thanked his helpers. They climbed back into the lorry and waved to him through the windscreen as he drove away.

Exercises

Judging from the context of the paragraphs above, choose the correct definition for each of the British terms in the left column.

1. tower block	a. high-rise building	b. prison	c. street of stores
2. fortnight	a. winter holiday	b. two weeks	c. overnight baggage
3. caravan	a. mobile home	b. train of camels	c. near relatives
4. moor	a. swamp	b. boat dock	c. broad tract of open land
5. market gardener	a. construction worker	b. merchant	c. truck farmer
6. vegetable marrow	a. type of large squash	b. corn cobs	c. vegetable and mutton stew
7. torch	a. garden cart	b. flashlight	c. hot drink
8. lorry	a. truck	b. foggy weather	c. sleigh
9. motorway	a. field lane	b. repair garage	c. superhighway
10. bonnet	a. car hood	b. umbrella	c. lady's hat
11. petrol	a. pet food	b. gasoline	c. policeman
12. boot	a. tool box	b. foot gear	c. car trunk
13. windscreen	a. tall grass	b. windshield	c. smoke

Notes on Part D

Here are some additional vocabulary differences between British and American English.

British	American
railway	railroad
goods	freight
wireless	radio
boiler	furnace
milliard	billion
post	mail
fun fair	carnival
biscuit	cracker
dustbin	trash can
porridge	oatmeal
geyser	water heater
lift	elevator
mackintosh	raincoat
pram	baby carriage
reel	spool

Lesson 30 in *A Time of Peace* (Rod and Staff's Eighth Reader) has some British terminology. Exercise 7 in that lesson focuses on that vocabulary.

Answer Key—Part D (13 points)

1. a. high-rise building
2. b. two weeks
3. a. mobile home
4. c. broad tract of open land
5. c. truck farmer
6. a. type of large squash
7. b. flashlight
8. a. truck
9. c. superhighway
10. a. car hood
11. b. gasoline
12. c. car trunk
13. b. windshield

LESSON 27

A.   UNEARTHING THE ROOTS

> **ROOTS**
> Words of French origin

NEW WORDS

accompany
adjourned
alarm
anoint
asterisk
campaign
deem
exhibition
flourish
fraud
galloped
galvanized
guaranteed
madam
maneuver
mutton
picturesque
reservoir
sabotage
warrant

REVIEW WORDS

boulevard
bureau
camouflage
garage
prairie

1. Write the REVIEW WORD containing the French spelling *oul.*
2. Write words beginning with *poul* for these definitions.
   a. Chickens, ducks, and turkeys.
   b. A soft, moist mass of herbs applied to the body.
3. Write the French spelling for *mold.*
4. Which REVIEW WORD ends with a French spelling of /ō/?
5. Write other words with the same spelling of /ō/.
   a. A high plain: pla__ .
   b. A large country house in Europe: chat__ .
   c. An attractive scene: tabl__ .
   d. A bride's outfit of clothes: trous__ .
6. Write three spelling words containing the French spelling of /äzh/.
7. Write other words containing that spelling for these definitions.
   a. A bombardment of shots or words in rapid succession: bar__ .
   b. An optical illusion caused by the bending of light rays: mir__ .
8. Write words containing the French spelling of /esk/ for these definitions.
   a. Like a picture*.
   b. Like a statue.
   c. Having distorted, unnatural features: gro__ .
9. Write NEW WORDS of French origin to match these definitions.
   a. To go as a companion.   c. My lady.
   b. To apply oil.   d. A series of battles.
10. Write the NEW WORD that refers to a process named for Luigi Galvani, an Italian physician.
11. Write the two NEW WORDS of French origin that are synonyms. (One is past tense.)
12. Write the NEW WORD that was originally a battle cry meaning "to arms."

Lesson 27

(Total points: 76)

Notes on Part A

English absorbed many French words during the Middle Ages. These are some additional words that have come from French more recently.

alloy	casserole	croutons	explore	patrol	routine
bouillon	chowder	dentist	gourmet	progress	surpass
brunette	cohesion	detail	menu	publicity	ticket
cartoon	comrade	equip	omelet	ridicule	trophy

Answer Key—Part A (25 points)

1. boulevard
2. a. poultry
   b. poultice
3. mould
4. bureau
5. a. plateau
   b. chateau
   c. tableau
   d. trousseau
6. sabotage, camouflage, garage
7. a. barrage
   b. mirage
8. a. picturesque
   b. statuesque
   c. grotesque
9. a. accompany
   b. anoint
   c. madam
   d. campaign
10. galvanized
11. guaranteed, warrant
12. alarm

Lesson 27 Test Sentences

1. *flourish* Joel swings his bat with a *flourish.* *flourish*
2. *boulevard* The *boulevard* was littered with leaves. *boulevard*
3. *accompany* Did the kitten *accompany* the rabbit? *accompany*
4. *alarm* The fire *alarm* rang. *alarm*
5. *galloped* Frantic children *galloped* down the hall. *galloped*
6. *maneuver* We need to practice that *maneuver* again. *maneuver*
7. *camouflage* Flowers can *camouflage* a weathered fence. *camouflage*
8. *warrant* Bad paint does not *warrant* a new fence. *warrant*
9. *guaranteed* Use paint that is *guaranteed* to cover rust. *guaranteed*
10. *sabotage* The property showed signs of *sabotage.* *sabotage*
11. *picturesque* Roses make a *picturesque* arbor. *picturesque*
12. *prairie* Summer was dry on the *prairie.* *prairie*
13. *reservoir* The pond made a *reservoir* for irrigating. *reservoir*
14. *anoint* God asked Samuel to *anoint* a new king. *anoint*
15. *deem* He did not *deem* Saul worthy to continue. *deem*
16. *exhibition* Patrick held an *exhibition* of metals. *exhibition*
17. *galvanized* Chemical reaction *galvanized* the nails. *galvanized*
18. *garage* He sold them at the *garage* sale. *garage*
19. *bureau* I found a used *bureau* in the corner. *bureau*
20. *campaign* Moses did not *campaign* for his charge. *campaign*
21. *fraud* Pharaoh's magicians were a *fraud.* *fraud*
22. *adjourned* The king's court *adjourned* in embarrassment. *adjourned*
23. *madam* Let the *madam* go first. *madam*
24. *mutton* She ordered *mutton* from the butcher. *mutton*
25. *asterisk* An *asterisk* marks this week's special. *asterisk*

B. AFFIXING AFFIXES

1. Most words ending with -*eau* can be made plural by adding *x*. Use *x* to write the plural form of the following words.
    a. bureau
    b. chateau
    c. plateau
    d. tableau
    e. trousseau

2. It is also correct to spell the plurals in number 1 with *s* instead of *x*. Write the plural of the same five words with *s*.

3. Use words that end with -*oir* for these meanings.
    a. A place where water is kept in reserve*.
    b. A French farewell: <u>au re</u>.

4. Write words with the French ending -*ois* for these clues.
    a. The name of an Indian confederation and a central state of the United States.

French Endings

	EXAMPLE
-*eau*	chateau
-*oir*	au revoir
-*ois*	chamois

b. Indian confederation of the New York region: <u>Iroqu</u>.
c. European antelope, or a soft leather made from its hide: <u>cham</u>.
d. V-shaped frame used by Plains Indians to carry goods: <u>trav</u>.

5. Write the present-tense form of the four NEW WORDS that end with -*ed*.

6. Add the suffix -*ing* to these words.
    a. accompany
    b. alarm
    c. flourish
    d. maneuver

C. SOUND, STRUCTURE, AND MEANING

1. Write the spelling words that have these phonetic features.
    a. two words that end with /sk/
    b. /ü/ spelled *eu*
    c. final /ān/ spelled *aign*
    d. /g/ spelled *gu*
    e. /e/ spelled *ai*
    f. correctly spelled forward or backward

2. Use spelling words that come from French for these answers.
    a. Ferns ____ in shady spots.
    b. Arthur likes ____ better than pork.
    c. The board meeting ____ just before midnight.
    d. The pony express carried mail across the ____.
    e. Express ponies ____ ten to fifteen miles in each relay.

3. Use NEW WORDS to complete these analogies.
    a. work : labor :: display : ____
    b. know : realize :: consider : ____
    c. health : sickness :: honesty : ____
    d. drought : wither :: rain : ____

4. a. What is a bulwark?
    b. How does that relate to the meaning of *boulevard?*

5. a. What is a sabot?
    b. How does that relate to the meaning of *sabotage?*

6. Write a word that is a doublet of *gallop*.

7. a. Write *exhibition,* dividing it into syllables and showing the accents.
    b. Write the root word of *exhibition,* dividing it into syllables and marking the accent.

Notes on Part B

Exercises 1 and 2: The two plural forms are pronounced alike—the way you would naturally say the word with *s* on the end.

Other words with French endings

-ois   Illinois

In *Illinois* the French spelling and pronunciation are applied to the Indian word *Iliniwek,* which meant "superior men."

-oir   abattoir, boudoir

An abattoir is a slaughterhouse.

Answer Key—Part B (24 points)

1. a. bureaux
   b. chateaux
   c. plateaux
   d. tableaux
   e. trousseaux

2. a. bureaus
   b. chateaus
   c. plateaus
   d. tableaus
   e. trousseaus

3. a. reservoir
   b. au revoir

4. a. Illinois
   b. Iroquois
   c. chamois
   d. travois

5. adjourn, gallop, galvanize, guarantee

6. a. accompanying
   b. alarming
   c. flourishing
   d. maneuvering

Notes on Part C

Exercise 5: Note that the word *sabot* is pronounced /sa bō'/, as is characteristic of French endings.

Answer Key—Part C (23 points)

1. a. asterisk, picturesque
   b. maneuver
   c. campaign
   d. guaranteed
   e. prairie
   f. madam

2. a. flourish
   b. mutton
   c. adjourned
   d. prairie
   e. galloped

3. a. exhibition
   b. deem

   c. fraud
   d. flourish

4. a. a wall raised for defense
   b. *Boulevard* was originally a passage along a bulwark.

5. a. a wooden shoe
   b. A wooden shoe could be used to damage machinery.

6. wallop

7. a. (ex' hi bi' tion)
   b. (ex hib' it)

D. LANGUAGE LINEAGE

AMERICAN DIALECTS

Peter tried to hide his identity at the time of Jesus' trial, but his speech betrayed him as a Galilean. He was not using a different language, but characteristics of his speech identified the region he was from. Similarly, your pronunciation and terminology are indicators of where you live.

A number of factors caused language variations in America. Different sections of the country were settled by people from different places, who brought their language characteristics with them. Interchange with natives or other immigrants also influenced the development of dialects in America.

The settlers of New England came from the southern counties of England. Their religious strictness caused a relative isolation that preserved their dialect. To this day the speech of New England resembles that of southern Britain. The New England Dialect has the broad *a* and omits the final *r* sound except when the next word begins with a vowel sound. Word endings are also clipped short. Can you read this clause from Proverbs 4:14 with the New England accent? (Drop the /r/ from *enter,* and say /ô/ in *not* and /ä/ in *path.*)

Enter not into the path of the wicked.

The southern seacoast was settled by an assortment of English-speaking people. The dialects from different areas of England blended as religious, political, and economic advantages drew colonists to this area from various parts of England. African slaves were also a significant part of the population. Southern speech has a slow, unhurried drawl. Final *r* is dropped regardless whether the following word begins with a consonant or vowel sound. Long *i* resembles the short *a* sound in *laugh.* Use Southern pronunciation as you read this verse from Proverbs 15:31.

The ear that heareth the reproof of life abideth among the wise.

Between the North and South may be found the Midland Dialect, which also has some distinctive characteristics. This area was settled by a mixture of immigrants from different European backgrounds. Quakers brought the dialect of northern England. Dutch and German settlers and the English-speaking Scotch and Irish colonists blended in the mid-Atlantic region. The Midland Dialect retains a strong *r* pronunciation in all positions, and it uses the flat, short *a.* Read both quotations from Proverbs above with the pronunciation of the Midland Dialect.

Westward expansion extended the various dialect regions. The Midland Dialect, especially, has spread over most of the West, and it is sometimes called the General American Dialect.

Besides pronunciation, there are some typical vocabulary differences in the American regions. The following sentences illustrate a few varying terms from different parts of the country.

New England	A peach has a stone in the middle. A fritter can be fried in a spider.
Midland	A peach has a seed in the middle. Pancakes are fried in a skillet. A sack or poke is used to carry something.
Southern	The peach seed may be called a kernel. Pancakes are battercakes. A sack or poke is used to tote something.

Exercises

1. What are three general dialects of American English?

2. Which American dialect is most nearly like British speech?

Notes on Part D

Linguists have studied in detail the regional differences in American speech, both of pronunciation characteristics and vocabulary. The findings have been published in the *Dictionary of American Regional English* (unique vocabulary) and *The Linguistic Atlas of the United States.* Each region has also been divided into many subregions. Someone skilled in the study of the areas could identify a Hudson Valley resident or New York City resident by his speech. These dividing lines are very vague because there is always a blending area between sections.

The large western areas also have their regional speech characteristics resulting from who settled the areas, who the natives were, and what the economical pictures were. But because settlement of these areas is comparatively recent, local distinction has not had time to develop to the degree that it has in the parts of the country settled earlier.

Some interesting vocabulary differences appear in names for the dragonfly.

Northern—darning needle, sewing needle, ear sewer, stinger

Midland—snake feeder, snake doctor

Southern—mosquito hawk, skeeter hawk.

Cottage cheese was a common household product in the days before refrigeration. It has the following colorful regional terms.

Northern—curds, curd cheese, sour milk cheese, pot cheese, Dutch cheese

Midland—smearcase, shmearcase, farmer's cheese, clabber cheese

Southern—curd, curd cheese, cream cheese.

Answer Key—Part D (4 points)

1. New England, Midland, Southern
2. New England Dialect

90

A. UNEARTHING THE ROOTS

NEW WORDS

alligator
ambitious
associated
barbarous
barbecue
continuously
coyote
hammock
maiden
miscellaneous
occasionally
pamphlets
pirate
plaza
preparation
recommended
resources
strenuous
tendency
voluntary

REVIEW WORDS

cafeteria
conscientious
continuous
desirous
valuable

1. The answers for these blanks are spelling words that come from the Spanish language.
   a. Spaniards were not familiar with the ____ until they explored the swamplands of the New World.
   b. Especially in Spanish America, people like to ____ meat by roasting it over live coals.
   c. Venders spread their wares in the ____ on market day.
   d. Visitors could eat meals at the ____.
   e. Prairie chickens were easy prey to the ____.
   f. While Mother planted corn, the baby slept in a ____.

2. Here are some additional words of Spanish origin. Write these words for the following definitions.

adobe	alfalfa	fiesta
lariat	llama	mesa
mustang	siesta	sombrero

   a. Spanish holiday.
   b. Wild horse of American West.
   c. High, flat tableland.
   d. Broad-brimmed hat.
   e. Sun-dried clay brick.
   f. Rope; lasso.
   g. Plant raised to make hay.
   h. Midday rest.
   i. Humpless camellike animal.

3. Write spelling words for these etymologies.
   a. *barbacoa* (framework of sticks)
   b. *platea* (wide street)
   c. *el lagarto* (the lizard)
   d. *café* (coffee)
   e. *hamaca* (swinging bed)
   f. *pīrāta* (to attempt)
   g. *voluntās* (choice)
   h. *Pamphilus* (title of a popular poem)
   i. *re-* + *surgere* (to rise)

Lesson 28

(Total points: 101)

Notes on Part A

Spanish colonies in the South and Southwest planted the Spanish language in America. English picked up these words during the colonial period.

armadillo	cockroach	tapioca
banana	Negro	tobacco
cannibal	potato	tomato

Answer Key—Part A (24 points)

1. a. alligator
   b. barbecue
   c. plaza
   d. cafeteria
   e. coyote
   f. hammock
2. a. fiesta
   b. mustang
   c. mesa
   d. sombrero
   e. adobe
   f. lariat
   g. alfalfa
   h. siesta
   i. llama
3. a. barbecue
   b. plaza
   c. alligator
   d. cafeteria
   e. hammock
   f. pirate
   g. voluntary
   h. pamphlets
   i. resources

Lesson 28 Test Sentences

1. *ambitious* One *ambitious* gopher ventured too far. *ambitious*
2. *coyote* He provided dinner for a *coyote*. *coyote*
3. *cafeteria* The meadow *cafeteria* was wide and sunny. *cafeteria*
4. *pirate* A swarthy *pirate* boarded the victim ship. *pirate*
5. *recommended* The captain *recommended* that he repent. *recommended*
6. *resources* Seek more honorable *resources* than theft. *resources*
7. *desirous* Aren't we all *desirous* of a good conscience? *desirous*
8. *maiden* We saw a frail *maiden* in a grove. *maiden*
9. *hammock* She was swinging her sister in a *hammock*. *hammock*
10. *continuously* They were *continuously* smiling. *continuously*
11. *alligator* Fashion has endangered the *alligator*. *alligator*
12. *valuable* Its hide made *valuable* leather. *valuable*
13. *miscellaneous* It was used in *miscellaneous* articles. *miscellaneous*
14. *tendency* Resist the *tendency* to criticize. *tendency*
15. *conscientious* A *conscientious* effort deserves reward. *conscientious*
16. *plaza* The shop across the *plaza* opened early. *plaza*
17. *continuous* There was a *continuous* flow of customers. *continuous*
18. *strenuous* The merchant had a *strenuous* day. *strenuous*
19. *pamphlets* His free *pamphlets* were gone by noon. *pamphlets*
20. *barbecue* Jason fixed *barbecue* for dinner. *barbecue*
21. *preparation* The *preparation* took longer than usual. *preparation*
22. *voluntary* Susan gave some *voluntary* help. *voluntary*
23. *associated* This menu is often *associated* with picnics. *associated*
24. *barbarous* A picnic is no excuse for *barbarous* manners. *barbarous*
25. *occasionally* Check your records *occasionally*. *occasionally*

B.   AFFIXING AFFIXES

1. Write spelling words with the *-ous* suffix for these definitions.
   a. Full of ambition.
   b. Full of desire.
   c. Varied; assorted.
   d. Heeding the conscience.
   e. Showing great effort.
   f. Showing coarseness or cruelty.
   g. Unceasing (adj.).
   h. In an unceasing manner (adv.).
2. Copy these root words. After each one write its part of speech, the form of this word from the spelling list, and the part of speech of the spelling word.

Adjective-forming Suffix

SUFFIX	MEANING	EXAMPLE
-ous	full of, quality of	marvelous

Example: continue
Answer: continue—v.
         continuously—adv.

a. occasion   e. resource
b. pamphlet   f. tend
c. prepare   g. volunteer
d. recommend   h. value

3. Write the spelling words from number 2 that have derivational suffixes.

C.   SOUND, STRUCTURE, AND MEANING

1. Write spelling words that have these phonetic features.
   a. the letters *uou* (3)
   b. the letters *iou* (2)
   c. the letters *eou*
   d. /ī/ spelled *oy*
   e. a letter *c* that may be pronounced /sh/ or /s/
   f. a final *e* that may be pronounced or silent
2. a. Write the NEW WORD in which the first two syllables have the same letters.
   b. Write a word that is pronounced the same as these two syllables and means "one who cuts hair." What vowel change did you make?
3. a. The word *miscellaneous* is commonly abbreviated to save space. Write its abbreviation.
   b. Drop *eous* from *miscellaneous* and add *y* to write a noun that means "a collection of various items, especially writings."
4. Change the suffix of *barbarous* to form nouns with these definitions.

   a. A person of an uncivilized tribe.
   b. A word or form not approved in standard language.
5. For each blank, write a spelling word that is a form of another word in the sentence.
   a. We prepared salad as part of our ____ for dinner.
   b. Can we continue to feed the ____ growing flock?
   c. A resourceful person can manage with limited ____.
   d. Twelve kitchen maids served on the ____ voyage of the ship.
   e. My grandparents are ____ present for special occasions.
6. Look up the etymology for *barbarous*.
   a. What people were the Greeks referring to when they used their form of this word?
   b. *Barbarous* simply meant "foreign" at first (as in Acts 28:2), but later it meant "crude and uncivilized." What attitude does this suggest that the Greeks had about themselves?

Answer Key—Part B (45 points)

1. a. ambitious
   b. desirous
   c. miscellaneous
   d. conscientious
   e. strenuous
   f. barbarous
   g. continuous
   h. continuously

2. a. occasion—n.
      occasionally—adv.
   b. pamphlet—n.
      pamphlets—n.
   c. prepare—v.
      preparation—n.

   d. recommend—v.
      recommended—v. *or* adj.
   e. resource—n.
      resources—n.
   f. tend—v.
      tendency—n.
   g. volunteer—v. *or* n.
      voluntary—adj.
   h. value—n. *or* v.
      valuable—adj.

3. occasionally, preparation, tendency, voluntary, valuable (*Recommended* may be derivational or inflectional.)

Answer Key—Part C (23 points)

1. a. continuously, strenuous, continuous
   b. ambitious, conscientious
   c. miscellaneous
   d. coyote
   e. associated
   f. coyote

2. a. barbarous
   b. barber
      The *a* in the second syllable changes to *e*.

3. a. misc.
   b. miscellany

4. a. barbarian
   b. barbarism

5. a. preparation
   b. continuously
   c. resources
   d. maiden
   e. occasionally

6. a. foreign people
   b. The Greeks considered themselves refined and cultured.

D.   LANGUAGE LINEAGE

PIDGIN ENGLISH

Special situations lead to specially altered forms of language. Commercial trade may compel the natives of one land to communicate with foreigners who buy their products. Conquest by a foreign nation can also create the need for communication between strange tongues. A pidgin language develops to bridge the gap between the two languages. This marginal language uses the grammatical structure and basic vocabulary of one language but is strongly influenced by words and pronunciation patterns from the other. Communication is kept as simple as possible, and word inflections are ignored. English traders shared such "Business English" with the Chinese in the 1800s. The Chinese pronunciation of *business* gave rise to the term *pidgin*.

Many varieties of pidgin English have developed in scattered parts of the world. There are several varieties within Australia. The Africans of Cameroon and eastern Nigeria use Cameroon Pidgin. Hawaiians also use a pidgin English.

A pidgin language is native to no one. It is a third language, spoken in common by those whose native languages are foreign to each other. However, if this common language is used long enough, a new generation may grow up speaking pidgin as their native tongue. When it is established that well, the language becomes a creole instead of pidgin. The creole language will expand and develop its own inflections and refinements to meet the needs of full expression and finer shades of meaning. Thus languages begin and develop in the flow of human exchange and interaction.

Pidgin and creole languages have developed from base languages other than English. The language of Jamaica is an English-based creole. In the Bahama Islands, another English-based creole is used. But French is the base of the Haitian Creole used in Haiti, and the Chabakano creole spoken in the Philippines is based on Spanish.

Exercises

1. Describe two situations that can give rise to a pidgin language.
2. What features does a pidgin language take from the two strange languages that it bridges?
3. When does a pidgin language become a creole language?
4. Name the base language for each of these creole languages.
   a. The creole spoken in Jamaica.
   b. The creole spoken in Bahama Islands.
   c. Haitian Creole.
   d. Chabakano.

Notes on Part D

A pidgin language is very simple, with mutual abandonment of grammatical complexities from both sides. But when the language becomes a creole, complexities necessarily arise to make the language effective.

Gullah is an English creole spoken on the sea islands at the coast of South Carolina, Georgia, and Florida. It accommodates some West African languages brought to America with the slaves in the 1700s and early 1800s.

Haitian Creole was formed from French settlers and the former African slaves.

Chabakano is pronounced /chä' bə kä' nō/.

Answer Key—Part D (9 points)

1. *Commercial trade* between foreign nations, or foreign occupation in *military conquest* can give rise to a pidgin language.

2. Basic *vocabulary and grammatical structure* come from one language, with influence of *words and pronunciation* from the other.

3. When a generation grows up using a pidgin language as their *native tongue,* it is called a creole.

4. a. English
   b. English
   c. French
   d. Spanish

LESSON 29

NEW WORDS

avocado
canyon
capitalism
communism
criticism
hurricane
iguana
meter
mosquito
omitted
outstanding
partial
patio
preference
propaganda
rheumatism
stampede
submarine
suicide
tornado

REVIEW WORDS

Anabaptist
attached
maintenance
unnecessary
visitors

A. UNEARTHING THE ROOTS

ROOTS
Words of Spanish origin

1. The spelling words that end with *o* come from the Spanish language. Write them.
2. Some Spanish words came originally from American Indian languages. Write the NEW WORDS that had these Indian origins.
   a. *ahuacatl* (a fruit)
   b. *huracán* (a storm)
   c. *iwana* (an animal)
3. The NEW WORDS with these meanings come from the Spanish language. Write them.
   a. Sudden wild flight.
   b. A storm cloud with a whirlwind funnel.
   c. A tropical Atlantic storm.
   d. A deep ravine.
4. The etymology in the Speller Dictionary gives the Spanish form and its meaning for each of these words. Write the meaning of the Spanish word.
   a. canyon
   b. mosquito
   c. stampede
5. Write the spelling words for these etymologies.
   a. *prae-* (before) + *ferre* (to carry)
   b. *prō-* (forth) + *pangare* (to fasten a graft)
   c. *sub-* (under) + *mare* (sea)
   d. *manus* (hand) + *tenēre* (to hold)
6. For each answer in exercise 5, write the language from which the word came into English.
7. Write the spelling words with these meanings.
   a. not needed
   b. self-killing
   c. fastened
   d. incomplete

Lesson 29

(Total points: 88)

Notes on Part A

More Spanish words came into general English usage as the United States expanded westward in the 1800s.

bronco	cinch	lasso
burro	garbanzo	mosey
chaps	hacienda	pronto
chili	jerky	ranch

Answer Key—Part A (26 points)

1. avocado, mosquito, patio, tornado

2. a. avocado
   b. hurricane
   c. iguana

3. a. stampede
   b. tornado
   c. hurricane
   d. canyon

4. a. tube (*Reed* is the meaning of the Latin root.)
   b. small fly
   c. to stamp

5. a. preference
   b. propaganda
   c. submarine
   d. maintenance

6. a. Latin
   b. Italian
   c. Latin
   d. French (Old French)

7. a. unnecessary
   b. suicide
   c. attached
   d. partial

Lesson 29 Test Sentences

1. *iguana* You will not find the *iguana* in the Arctic. *iguana*
2. *hurricane* Neither is a *hurricane* from the north. *hurricane*
3. *Anabaptist* Jan is well read in *Anabaptist* history. *Anabaptist*
4. *omitted* The state church *omitted* some basic truths. *omitted*
5. *propaganda* *Propaganda* was used against believers. *propaganda*
6. *visitors* The factory will give *visitors* a tour any time. *visitors*
7. *unnecessary* Previous notice is *unnecessary*. *unnecessary*
8. *partial* Some days they have only *partial* operation. *partial*
9. *capitalism* Factories thrive under *capitalism*. *capitalism*
10. *patio* We relaxed on the *patio* after dark. *patio*
11. *mosquito* Itchy *mosquito* bites spoiled the pleasure. *mosquito*
12. *avocado* Have you tried *avocado* salad? *avocado*
13. *preference* Bill's *preference* is tomato salad. *preference*
14. *outstanding* Combine them for an *outstanding* treat. *outstanding*
15. *submarine* Mark painted a *submarine* view. *submarine*
16. *attached* Many barnacles were *attached* to the rocks. *attached*
17. *stampede* Indians used the *stampede* as a hunting aid. *stampede*
18. *canyon* They ran buffalo over a *canyon* rim. *canyon*
19. *communism* The tribal system was a form of *communism*. *communism*
20. *suicide* Could the wreck have been a *suicide?* *suicide*
21. *criticism* Surrounding evidence puts *criticism* on that idea. *criticism*
22. *tornado* God gave the *tornado* unique power. *tornado*
23. *rheumatism* A dry climate eases *rheumatism*. *rheumatism*
24. *meter* The wise person will *meter* his spending. *meter*
25. *maintenance* A working budget takes *maintenance*. *maintenance*

B.   AFFIXING AFFIXES

1. Write a spelling word with the suffix *-ism* for each answer.
    a. ____ is a political system that allows individual control of capital and property.
    b. ____ is a political system that emphasizes common ownership of goods.
    c. ____ produces stiffness and pain in muscles and joints.
    d. ____ can be helpful or damaging.
2. Write the REVIEW WORD with the suffix *-ist,* and write its etymological meaning.
3. An *-ist* is one who does or has an *-ism.* Change the suffix of a word in each sentence to form a word for the blank.
    a. An evangelist practices ____.
    b. An optimist is given to ____.
    c. A pacifist promotes ____.
    d. A terrorist practices ____.

Noun-forming Suffix

SUFFIX	MEANING	EXAMPLE
-ism	act, doctrine, system	communism

e. A Calvinist supports ____.
f. An atheist follows ____.
g. A euphemist practices ____.
h. A catechist studies a ____.

4. Write the spelling words formed from these words. After each word, write whether the suffix is inflectional (*I*) or derivational (*D*).
    a. omit   e. maintain
    b. stand   f. visitor
    c. part   g. prefer
    d. attach
5. In two words that you wrote for number 4, the accent shifts from the second syllable to the first syllable when the suffix is added. Write those two spelling words again.

C.   SOUND, STRUCTURE, AND MEANING

1. Write three NEW WORDS in which /ē/ is spelled *i.*
2. Write the NEW WORD in which final /shəl/ is spelled *tial.*
3. Write the spelling word that begins with /r/ spelled *rh.*
4. Write other words that begin with *rh* for these definitions.
    a. An animal with a horn on its nose.
    b. A state in New England.
    c. A plant with tart, edible stalks.
    d. Matching sounds in word endings.
    e. Accent pattern in syllables of poetry.
5. Which NEW WORD is compound?
6. Write NEW WORDS to finish these analogies.
    a. temple : courtyard :: house : ____
    b. bird : airplane :: fish : ____
    c. quart : liter :: yard : ____
7. Find *unnecessary* in the Speller Dictionary.
    a. From the etymology, write the English prefix that means "not."
    b. Write the Latin prefix that means "not."
    c. Write the Latin word that means "to withdraw."
8. Find *canyon* in the Speller Dictionary. Write the Spanish spelling that is sometimes used.
9. *Meter* has multiple entries in the Speller Dictionary. Show which entry is correct for each blank below by writing meter[1], meter[2], or meter[3].
    a. A ____ is a little longer than 39 inches.
    b. The nurse will carefully ____ the intravenous feeding.
    c. The iambic ____ is suited to a joyful theme.
    d. An error in reading the ____ resulted in a high electric bill.
    e. The Middle English word *meten* (to measure) is the source of ____ .

Answer Key—Part B (30 points)

1. a. Capitalism
   b. Communism
   c. Rheumatism
   d. Criticism

2. Anabaptist, to baptize again

3. a. evangelism
   b. optimism
   c. pacifism
   d. terrorism
   e. Calvinism
   f. atheism
   g. euphemism
   h. catechism

4. a. omitted, I *or* D
   b. outstanding, D
   c. partial, D
   d. attached, I *or* D
   e. maintenance, D
   f. visitors, I
   g. preference, D

5. maintenance, preference

Notes on Part C

   Exercise 7: The word *unnecessary* is a hybrid that forms a double negative. Something that is not to be withdrawn is not dispensable—it is necessary. That which is *not* not dispensable can be dispensed with—it is unnecessary.

Answer Key—Part C (23 points)

1. mosquito, patio, submarine

2. partial

3. rheumatism

4. a. rhinoceros
   b. Rhode Island
   c. rhubarb
   d. rhymes
   e. rhythm

5. outstanding

6. a. patio
   b. submarine

   c. meter

7. a. *un-*
   b. *ne*
   c. *cedere*

8. cañon

9. a. meter^2
   b. meter^3
   c. meter^1
   d. meter^3
   e. meter^3

D.   LANGUAGE LINEAGE

SEMANTIC STUDY: FOLK ETYMOLOGY AND BACK-FORMATION

One kind of semantic change, called *folk etymology,* affects the form of words more than it affects meaning. It results in changes through the common folk's use of language rather than through scholarly decrees from linguists. When people hear new words, their natural response is to associate them with familiar words. For example, when pioneers wanted to spell *otcheck,* the name that the Cree Indians gave to a certain type of marmot (which has nothing to do with wood), they wrote *woodchuck* because that is what it sounded like to them.

Ten-gallon hat is another example of folk etymology. This expression appears to be based on a huge liquid measure, but the etymology has nothing to do with measurement. Rather, *gallon* represents the Spanish word *galon,* which means "braid." In a literal sense, a ten-gallon hat is simply a hat with ten rows of braid above the brim. But since *galon* resembled the English word *gallon,* Americans used that familiar word in their name for the hat.

Asparagus comes from the Greek *asparagos.* To English ears it resembled "sparrow grass," and around 1800, it was commonly said and written that way. But linguists put enough emphasis on the incorrectness of *sparrow grass* that the expression gradually faded from general use.

Because certain words look and sound alike, folk etymology makes connections between words that are totally unrelated in meaning. The pen name *A. Nonnie Mouse,* used to represent an anonymous author, is another example of folk etymology.

A process called *back-formation* produces new words by reversing the normal process of word formation. Instead of beginning with a short word and adding affixes, it begins with a longer word and removes what appears to be an affix.

The word *edit* is a back-formation of *editor,* which comes from Latin *edere*—"to publish." Back-formation has made what seems to be a root word by removing *-or* and leaving *edit.*

Statistics is a singular noun, as are *measles* and *mathematics.* But back-formation has coined the word *statistic* to mean one numerical fact. In that sense, *statistics* may be used as a plural form.

By the logic of back-formation, *gusted* and *gruntled* should be the opposite of *disgusted* and *disgruntled,* and *beave* should be what a *beaver* does.

Exercises

1. Name the language that was the source of each expression below, which has the form shown because of folk etymology.
   a. woodchuck
   b. ten-gallon hat
   c. sparrow grass
2. How is folk etymology misleading?
3. How does back-formation produce new words?

4. The following words originated through back-formation. Write the longer word that is the source of each one.
   a. greed
   b. peeve
   c. resurrect
   d. diagnose

Notes on Part D

Exercise 4: A classroom dictionary should have etymologies that give the source words for these back-formations. If it does not, change the exercise to making a guess at what the source word is.

A pun or play on words is often an illustration of the kind of change that makes folk etymology. The students may enjoy collecting examples.

trousseau—true sew	sacrifice—sack of rice
parachute—pair of shoes	mountaineers—my own tin ears

Following are some other words that have come by way of folk etymology:

frontispiece—often thought of as the piece in front, but its origin actually means "a face to look at." [< OF *frontispice* a building's principal façade < L *frontispicium* < *frons* façade + *specere* to look at]

hangnail—The original *nail* of *hangnail* was a hard spot like an iron nail head. [< OE *angnægl* corn on the foot < *ang-* painful + *nægl* nail (of iron)]

helpmate—Folk etymology from Genesis 2:18: "an help meet for him."

Jerusalem artichoke—The familiar-sounding name *Jerusalem* was used in place of the Italian word for sunflower. [< Ital. *girasole* sunflower < *girare* to turn + *sole* sun] The plant is not a true artichoke, but the edible root resembles artichoke in flavor.

shamefaced—alteration of *shamefast* (same structural ending as *steadfast*). Shame does usually show on the face.

Most back-formations begin as jokes or through ignorance, and they are likely to be disapproved as proper words. The following examples are back-formations that have become established as standard usage.

Back-formation	*Source word*
automate	automatic
donate	donation
greed	greedy
jell	jelly
peddle	peddler
peeve	peevish

Answer Key—Part D (9 points)

1. a. Cree Indian
   b. Spanish
   c. Greek

2. Folk etymology gives the *appearance that words are related in meaning* when they are not.

3. Back-formation makes new words by *removing letters* that resemble prefixes or suffixes.

4. a. greedy
   b. peevish
   c. resurrection
   d. diagnostic

— PUPIL —

LESSON 30

25	26	27	28	29
applicant	beige	accompany	accompanying	avocado
architect	bouquet	adjourned	alligator	canyon
consultant	brochure	alarm	ambitious	capitalism
defendant	camouflage	anoint	associated	communism
generate	career	asterisk	barbarous	criticism
inhabitant	chaperon	campaign	barbecue	hurricane
nitrogen	chauffeur	deem	continuously	iguana
ornament	compliment	exhibition	coyote	meter
responsibility	corsage	flourish	maiden	mosquito
scientist	croquet	fraud	miscellaneous	omitted
solvent	employee	galloped	occasionally	outstanding
superintendent	fatigue	galvanized	pamphlets	partial
susceptible	gourmet	guaranteed	pirate	patio
testimony	lieutenant	madam	plaza	preference
therapist	parliament	maneuver	preparation	propaganda
tourist	referee	mutton	recommended	rheumatism
triumph	restaurant	picturesque	resources	stampede
typist	revenue	reservoir	strenuous	submarine
unregenerate	silhouette	sabotage	tendency	suicide
violent	sunset	warrant	voluntary	tornado

A. UNEARTHING THE ROOTS

Gk. *gen*	= produce, begin
Gk. *arch*	= begin, lead
Words of French origin	
Words of Spanish origin	

1. Write words from Lesson 25.
    a. Write the word that means "cause or make" and the related word that means "not made anew."
    b. *archi-* (chief) + *tektōn* (builder) = _____
    c. *nitron* + *gen* = _____

Lesson 30

(Total points: 103)

Answer Key—Part A (36 points)

1. a. generate, unregenerate
   b. architect
   c. nitrogen

Lesson 30 Test Sentences

1. *testimony* Stephen's *testimony* angered the crowd. *testimony*
2. *violent* He met a *violent* death. *violent*
3. *susceptible* The righteous are *susceptible* to persecution. *susceptible*
4. *ornament* Parental instruction is an *ornament* of grace. *ornament*
5. *inhabitant* Each *inhabitant* must pay tax. *inhabitant*
6. *applicant* He was an *applicant* for baptism. *applicant*
7. *responsibility* Privilege brings *responsibility*. *responsibility*
8. *solvent* Love is a *solvent* for life's gritty irritants. *solvent*
9. *tourist* The new *tourist* center was perfect. *tourist*
10. *architect* A clever *architect* designed it to fit the scene. *architect*
11. *chauffeur* Our grandparents should have a *chauffeur*. *chauffeur*
12. *restaurant* Judy bakes pies for a *restaurant* in town. *restaurant*
13. *employee* She is the only *employee* who works at home. *employee*
14. *beige* I lost my *beige* sweater. *beige*
15. *bouquet* Put your *bouquet* on the bookshelf. *bouquet*
16. *camouflage* It will *camouflage* the stained wallpaper. *camouflage*
17. *silhouette* Could you identify everyone by his *silhouette*? *silhouette*
18. *revenue* Income is reported to the *revenue* service. *revenue*
19. *parliament* The meeting resembled a *parliament* session. *parliament*
20. *fatigue* Orderly meetings cause less *fatigue*. *fatigue*
21. *adjourned* The meeting *adjourned* in good time. *adjourned*
22. *flourish* Some special flowers *flourish* in the desert. *flourish*
23. *picturesque* Spring is a very *picturesque* time. *picturesque*
24. *reservoir* Memorized verses are a *reservoir* of inspiration. *reservoir*
25. *asterisk* The *asterisk* guides you to some notes below. *asterisk*
26. *maneuver* It was hard to *maneuver* between the trees. *maneuver*
27. *galloped* The herd *galloped* across the pasture. *galloped*
28. *guaranteed* This salve is *guaranteed* to relieve itching. *guaranteed*
29. *anoint* You should *anoint* the rash twice daily. *anoint*
30. *fraud* The peddler's *fraud* was exposed. *fraud*
31. *pirate* He tried to *pirate* his neighbor's poems. *pirate*
32. *barbecue* After the *barbecue*, the boys slept outside. *barbecue*
33. *ambitious* They were *ambitious* about rigging up a tent. *ambitious*
34. *preparation* It was dark before the *preparation* was done. *preparation*
35. *coyote* A yapping *coyote* startled them. *coyote*
36. *resources* Did they have *resources* for building a fence? *resources*
37. *voluntary* There was plenty of *voluntary* labor. *voluntary*
38. *occasionally* Jack *occasionally* gets a few spare bricks. *occasionally*
39. *continuously* Water flows *continuously* over these falls. *continuously*
40. *associated* Waterfalls are *associated* with hydroelectricity. *associated*
41. *rheumatism* Fido had *rheumatism* in his last years. *rheumatism*
42. *canyon* There is a clear echo in the *canyon*. *canyon*
43. *meter* The wind carried our velocity *meter* away. *meter*
44. *hurricane* It was blowing with *hurricane* force. *hurricane*
45. *tornado* A *tornado* is smaller but stronger. *tornado*
46. *suicide* It could be *suicide* to walk in its path. *suicide*
47. *preference* Which storm would be your *preference*? *preference*
48. *criticism* Jesus had some *criticism* for the Pharisees. *criticism*
49. *omitted* They *omitted* the most important part of the Law. *omitted*
50. *partial* God does not accept *partial* obedience. *partial*

2. Write words from Lesson 26 for these meanings that have etymological hints.
   a. Color of natural wool.
   b. Cluster of flowers resembling a thicket.
   c. Small stitched book.
   d. To disguise.
   e. Person who protects like a hood.
   f. Flowers worn upon the body.
   g. To tire.
   h. Taster of wines (and fine foods).
   i. An officer who can hold the place of another.
   j. Assembly that speaks about national concerns.
   k. Money coming back.
3. Write a word from Lesson 27 for each blank.
   a. Please ____ us on our hike.
   b. We have found a ____ spot for a picnic.
   c. Espionage (spying) and ____ are techniques of warfare.
   d. We saw the art projects at an ____ of schoolbooks.
   e. The wood stove had a ____ for heating water.

4. Write the words that have these meanings with etymological hints.
   a. My lady.
   b. Operation done by hand.
   c. To smear with an oily substance.
   d. To bloom; grow well.
   e. Small star.
5. Match NEW WORDS from Lesson 28 with these meanings with etymological hints.
   a. The lizard (of southern swamps).
   b. Framework of sticks for smoking meat.
   c. Mixed; assorted.
   d. Joined in companionship.
6. Write the words that come from these Spanish origins.
   a. *cóyotl*
   b. *platea*
7. Match NEW WORDS from Lesson 29 with these meanings with etymological hints.
   a. Tube (between cliffs).
   b. Small fly.
   c. To stamp and run.
   d. Thundering windstorm.
   e. Pasture; small open space.

B. AFFIXING AFFIXES

1. Write the part of speech for each word. Then write a word from Lesson 25 that is derived from it, and name that part of speech.

   > Example: tour
   > Answer: v., tourist—n.

   a. type
   b. apply
   c. therapy
   d. responsible
   e. science
   f. inhabit
   g. consult
2. Use words from Lesson 26.
   a. Write two words that have the French

-ant, -ent	one who
-ist, -ast	one who has or does
-eer, -eur	one who
-ee	one who is
-eau, -oir, -ois	French endings
-ous	full of, quality of
-ism	act, doctrine, system

ending *ee*. After each word write its definition.
   b. Write four words that have the /ā/ sound but do not contain that letter.
   c. Write three words in which /sh/ is spelled c*h*.
   d. Write the word that contains a silent *h*.

2. a. beige
   b. bouquet
   c. brochure
   d. camouflage
   e. chaperon
   f. corsage
   g. fatigue
   h. gourmet
   i. lieutenant
   j. parliament
   k. revenue

3. a. accompany
   b. picturesque
   c. sabotage
   d. exhibition
   e. reservoir

4. a. madam
   b. maneuver
   c. anoint
   d. flourish
   e. asterisk

5. a. alligator
   b. barbecue
   c. miscellaneous
   d. associated

6. a. coyote
   b. plaza

7. a. canyon
   b. mosquito
   c. stampede
   d. tornado
   e. patio

Answer Key—Part B (60 points)

1. a. v. *or* n., typist—n.
   b. v., applicant—n.
   c. n., therapist—n.
   d. adj., responsibility—n.
   e. n., scientist—n.
   f. v., inhabitant—n.
   g. v., consultant—n.

2. a. employee—one who is employed
      referee—one to whom something is referred
   b. beige, bouquet, croquet, gourmet
   c. brochure, chaperon, chauffeur
   d. silhouette

98 *Lesson 30*

3. Use words from Lesson 27.
   a. Write the one-syllable words.
   b. Write the words containing past-tense suffixes.
   c. Write the word with /ān/ spelled *aign*.
4. Use words from Lesson 28.
   a. Write four words that have the suffix *-ous*.
   b. Write two words that contain adverb-forming suffixes.

c. Write the six words that have double letters.
5. Write the words from Lesson 29 that have these suffixes.
   a. *-ism* (4)
   b. *-ed*
   c. *-ing*
   d. *-ial*
   e. *-ence*

D. LANGUAGE LINEAGE

REVIEW

1. In which of these four aspects is there the least difference between American and British English? (spelling, pronunciation, grammar, vocabulary)
2. What is a basic cause for language variation in different parts of the United States?
3. What is a pidgin language?
4. Where did the term *pidgin English* originate?
5. What is a pidgin language called when it is established so well that it becomes the native tongue of some people?
6. How does folk etymology cause language changes?
7. What is back-formation?

3. a. deem, fraud
   b. adjourned, galloped, galvanized, guaranteed
   c. campaign

4. a. ambitious, continuously, miscellaneous, strenuous
   b. continuously, occasionally
   c. accompanying, alligator, associated, miscellaneous, occasionally, recommended

5. a. capitalism, communism, criticism, rheumatism
   b. omitted
   c. outstanding
   d. partial
   e. preference

Answer Key—Part D (7 points)

1. grammar
2. Language varies within the United States because different parts were settled by *people from different places.*
3. A pidgin language is a mixture developed for *communication between two different languages.*
4. The term *pidgin* comes from the *Chinese pronunciation* of *business.*
5. When a pidgin language becomes the native tongue of a generation, it is called a *creole.*
6. In folk etymology, *association is made between words with totally different meanings,* because of their sound.
7. Back-formation is the *forming of a new word by removing some letters that appear to be an affix.*

LESSON 31

NEW WORDS

dachshund
diesel
plunder
poodle
refugees
resolution
responsible
roommate
satisfactorily
sauerkraut
separately
sheer
smallpox
successor
supplement
tender
trifle
undoubtedly
university
unusually

REVIEW WORDS

aquarium
communicate
kindergarten
salesman
voyage

A.   UNEARTHING THE ROOTS

ROOTS
Words of German origin

1. Write the NEW WORD that refers to an engine named for the German who invented it.
2. Write the spelling words that have these etymologies.
    a. *sauer* (sour) + *Kraut* (cabbage)
    b. *Kinder* (children) + *Garten* (garden)
    c. *plündern* (household goods)
    d. *Dachs* (badger) + *Hund* (dog)
    e. *Pudelhund* (puddle dog)
3. Match these words of German origin to the clues below.

    autobahn   blitzkrieg
    delicatessen   gesundheit
    hinterland   quartz
    spritz   verboten

    a. To squirt or spray.
    b. Expressway, from (car) + *Bahn* (road).
    c. Swift, sudden invasion, from *Blitz* (lightning) + *Krieg* (war).
    d. Delicacies to eat.
    e. Prohibited; forbidden.
    f. A hard, crystalline mineral.
    g. Back country, from (back) + (land).
    h. Good health, wished on someone who has sneezed.
4. *Trifle* and *trivial* have similar meanings, but the word origins are completely different. Write the correct word for each etymology.
    a. From Latin roots referring to a meeting of roads.
    b. From an Old French root meaning "mockery" or "deception."
5. a. Write the REVIEW WORD that names a container for water creatures.
    b. Use the first four letters to write a word for *water*.

Lesson 31

(Total points: 66)

Notes on Part A

Exercise 3e: English pronunciation of /v/ and /f/ are similar, one being voiced and the other voiceless. In German *v* is pronounced /f/. *Volks*wagon is a wagon for folks.

Additional words that have come from German:

dollar	noodle	swindle
ecology	pretzel	yodel
hoodlum	quartz	zinc
nickel	semester	

Answer Key—Part A (18 points)

1. diesel
2. a. sauerkraut
   b. kindergarten
   c. plunder
   d. dachshund
   e. poodle
3. a. spritz
   b. autobahn
   c. blitzkrieg
   d. delicatessen
   e. verboten
   f. quartz
   g. hinterland
   h. gesundheit
4. a. trivial
   b. trifle
5. a. aquarium
   b. aqua

Lesson 31 Test Sentences

1. *communicate* How did God *communicate* to Solomon? *communicate*
2. *tender* Two women claimed a *tender* child. *tender*
3. *responsible* He was *responsible* to settle the dispute. *responsible*
4. *satisfactorily* His judgment answered it *satisfactorily*. *satisfactorily*
5. *unusually* God gave him *unusually* great wisdom. *unusually*
6. *plunder* Piles of *plunder* filled the robbers' den. *plunder*
7. *resolution* The board passed a *resolution* about tardiness. *resolution*
8. *kindergarten* Children brought pets to *kindergarten*. *kindergarten*
9. *poodle* Jamie's *poodle* licked everyone's hands. *poodle*
10. *aquarium* Susan brought a little *aquarium* with goldfish. *aquarium*
11. *voyage* The fish made a circling *voyage* all day. *voyage*
12. *dachshund* A sleepy *dachshund* lay on Maggie's sweater. *dachshund*
13. *salesman* A kettle *salesman* came to our door. *salesman*
14. *separately* He would not sell his items *separately*. *separately*
15. *roommate* Dale was my *roommate* for three years. *roommate*
16. *university* Now he is a *university* teacher. *university*
17. *successor* He is the *successor* of Mr. Turnbay. *successor*
18. *undoubtedly* He has *undoubtedly* forgotten us. *undoubtedly*
19. *sauerkraut* Will the *sauerkraut* cure in two weeks? *sauerkraut*
20. *refugees* Where will the *refugees* stay? *refugees*
21. *smallpox* Some were afraid of the *smallpox* virus. *smallpox*
22. *supplement* A vitamin *supplement* was given. *supplement*
23. *trifle* We should not *trifle* with health risks. *trifle*
24. *sheer* They sang for *sheer* delight. *sheer*
25. *diesel* Cold weather makes it harder to start a *diesel*. *diesel*

B.   AFFIXING AFFIXES

1. The digraph *ei* in German words is pronounced /ī/. Write these words with the *ei* digraph for the definitions below.

    Fahrenh__t   Schl__th__m
           Albert __nst__n

    a. Famous physicist of the early 1900s.
    b. City associated with an Anabaptist confession of faith.
    c. German inventor of the mercury thermometer.

2. The digraph *ie* in German words is pronounced /ē/. Write words with *ie* for the clues below.

    sitzkr__g   sp__gel   w__ner

    a. Frankfurter.
    b. War with little fighting; "sitting war."
    c. Mirror made of shiny metal.
    d. Engine fired by the heat of compression*.

3. The German word *fest* has been used to add the idea of festivity to several words. Write words ending with *fest* to match the descriptions below.

    a. Informal gathering for singing: song__ .

German Endings

SUFFIX	EXAMPLE
-heit	gesundheit
-fest	songfest

    b. A long, enjoyable conversation: talk__ .
    c. A festival in autumn: Oktober__ .

4. Write the root word of *undoubtedly*. Then write its three affixes.

5. Write another NEW WORD that has a prefix and a suffix.

6. Use forms of the word *satisfy* in these blanks.

    a. Wanda takes great ____ in designing a flower bed.
    b. Is the van in ____ condition for the trip?
    c. Do you know the language well enough to communicate ____?

7. Write spelling words for these definitions.

    a. One who succeeds another in office.
    b. That which is resolved to be done.
    c. That which supplies additional material or information.
    d. An institution of higher learning.
    e. Obligated to give account; answerable.

C.   SOUND, STRUCTURE, AND MEANING

1. Write two NEW WORDS that have two sets of double letters.

2. Write three compound words from the spelling list.

3. Write *separately*. Draw a line to connect the two *a*'s, which are near the middle of the word. Draw another line connecting the two *e*'s, which are near the ends of the word.

4. Write spelling words for these definitions.
    a. People seeking refuge.
    b. To exchange ideas or knowledge.
    c. Journey on water.
    d. Something of small importance.
    e. Not unitedly; individually.

5. *Tender* has multiple entries in the Speller Dictionary. Write *tender¹, tender², or tender³* for each definition.

    a. Kind and gentle.
    b. A railroad car supplying coal and water for a steam engine.
    c. To present payment.
    d. Sore and painful to the touch.

6. Etymologies indicate that *sheer* entered our language in two different ways.

    a. Write a sentence using the word *sheer* from the Middle English source.
    b. Write a sentence using the word *sheer* from the Dutch source.

Notes on Part B

Exercise 7c: The double *p* in *supplement* comes from assimilation of the prefix *sub-* in the Latin word *supplēre*.

Answer Key—Part B (23 points)

1. a. Albert Einstein
   b. Schleitheim
   c. Fahrenheit
2. a. wiener
   b. sitzkrieg
   c. spiegel
   d. diesel
3. a. songfest
   b. talkfest
   c. Oktoberfest
4. doubt, *un-, -ed, -ly*
5. unusually
6. a. satisfaction
   b. satisfactory
   c. satisfactorily
7. a. successor
   b. resolution
   c. supplement
   d. university
   e. responsible

Notes on Part C

Exercise 3: Students may conquer this frequently misspelled word if they remember that two *a*'s separate two *e*'s.

Exercise 5: Have the students noticed the statement on U.S. currency, "This note is legal tender for all debts, public and private"?

Answer Key—Part C (17 points)

1. roommate, successor
2. roommate, smallpox, salesman
3. separately
4. a. refugees
   b. communicate
   c. voyage
   d. trifle
   e. separately
5. a. tender¹
   b. tender³
   c. tender²
   d. tender¹
6. a. (Sentence with *sheer* meaning "thin," "pure," or "very steep.")
   b. (Sentence with *sheer* meaning "to swerve" or "a ship's curve or position.")

D.   LANGUAGE LINEAGE

MODERN COMMUNICATION

Some early Americans predicted that their speech would eventually become so different from the language of England that people would need interpreters to communicate. That was a logical conclusion in a day when the ocean was a major barrier, for the same thing had happened many times before in history. For example, in the centuries after the Roman Empire fell, Latin developed into the Romance languages of today: French, Italian, Portuguese, Romanian, and Spanish.

But the barrier between England and America lost its dividing power. As shipbuilding technology advanced, it became easier to cross the ocean. The transatlantic cable permitted rapid telegraph communication between Europe and America. Soon the telephone transmitted actual voice sounds. Tape recordings reproduce speech with all its dialectal inflections and accents. And the radio and television have carried spoken language worldwide.

New words are constantly being formed with advancing technology in medical fields, computer programs, space exploration, and many other areas. But the new words are soon known far and wide because of mass-produced books, newspapers, and magazines. In addition, sound-carrying media allow people to hear the spoken sounds of many different localities. With this exchange, differences are likely to diminish rather than increase.

Long-distance travel is growing more and more common. Young people cross dialectal regions to blend at Bible schools. Families travel to visit relatives, and ministers preach in distant places. Many people move to communities in different parts of the country. All these things keep large numbers of people in communication with each other, thus slowing the divergence of speech variations.

Exercises

1. Why did early Americans expect that their speech would become a foreign language to England?
2. Name five technological advances that helped to bridge the barrier between England and America.
3. What is one occasion that could bring a different variety of English into your hearing?
4. Why are new words needed in our day?

Answer Key—Part D (8 points)

1. They thought there would *little communication* between England and America.

2. (Any five)
   ship building
   telegraph and transatlantic cable
   telephone
   tape recorders
   radio
   television
   air travel (Not mentioned in the lesson)

3. (Individual answers may refer to Bible school, travel, telephone, tape recordings, etc.)

4. New words are still needed because of *advancing technology*.

LESSON 32

A. UNEARTHING THE ROOTS

ROOTS
Words of Italian origin relating to music

NEW WORDS

alto
arrangements
crescendo
indefinitely
limestone
motto
opportunities
peaceable
penicillin
repentance
sergeant
serial
shouted
skiing
so-called
soprano
sufficiently
temporary
tenor
volcano

REVIEW WORDS

artificial
bass
buffalo
unbeliever
zero

1. Write music-related NEW WORDS of Italian origin for these etymologies.
   a. *altus* (high)
   b. *crescere* (to increase)
   c. *sopra* (above)
2. Three other spelling words, ending with *o,* come from Italian. Write those words for these etymologies.
   a. *mōttum* (word)
   b. *Vulcānus* (god of fire)
   c. *sifr* (empty)
3. Write spelling words relating to music that have the following origins.
   a. A Middle English word meaning "low."
   b. A Latin word meaning "to hold on."
4. *Tempo* comes from an Italian word meaning "time." Write the related NEW WORD.
5. Write the word that has Italian origin from this group. (Hint: Consider your answers to numbers 1 and 2.)
       choir   guitar   piano   clarion
6. Which NEW WORD refers to the results of organizing things?
7. *Pencil* is derived from the Latin word *penicillus* (brush). Write the related NEW WORD that names a drug obtained from a brush-shaped mold.
8. a. Which NEW WORD comes from the Old Norse word *skiō?*
   b. Which NEW WORD comes from a French word derived from Latin *serviēns* (serving)?
9. A____* consists of a series of items.
10. Match these definitions to spelling words whose roots are the italicized words.
   a. Made by *art.*
   b. Blowing toward *port;* favorable.

Lesson 32

(Total points: 79)

Notes on Part A

Stylistic notes in music are Italian words.

accelerando—gradually faster

adagio—very slowly

allegro—fast

andante—slowly

a tempo—return to normal speed

crescendo—gradually louder

decrescendo—gradually softer

diminuendo—gradually softer

forte—loudly

fortissimo—very loud

legato—gently

marcato—strongly accented

mezzo—half voice

moderato—moderate speed

piano—softly

pianissimo—very softly

presto—very fast

ritardando—gradually slower

staccato—short, choppy

Answer Key—Part A (17 points)

1. a. alto
   b. crescendo
   c. soprano
2. a. motto
   b. volcano
   c. zero
3. a. bass
   b. tenor
4. temporary
5. piano
6. arrangements
7. penicillin
8. a. skiing
   b. sergeant
9. serial
10. a. artificial
    b. opportunities

Lesson 32 Test Sentences

1. *opportunities* Make good use of *opportunities*. *opportunities*
2. *arrangements* We practiced new music *arrangements*. *arrangements*
3. *soprano* Connie often sings *soprano*. *soprano*
4. *alto* She will practice *alto* today. *alto*
5. *bass* We need a strong *bass* singer. *bass*
6. *zero* Begin with *zero* at the bottom of your graph. *zero*
7. *sergeant* An army *sergeant* visited the orchard. *sergeant*
8. *sufficiently* Some apples were *sufficiently* ripe to sample. *sufficiently*
9. *shouted* The farmer *shouted* at the strangers. *shouted*
10. *tenor* Suddenly the *tenor* of their visit changed. *tenor*
11. *peaceable* They parted on *peaceable* terms. *peaceable*
12. *penicillin* A British scientist discovered *penicillin* in 1928. *penicillin*
13. *buffalo* Indians made many things from *buffalo* materials. *buffalo*
14. *artificial* Today we use *artificial* products. *artificial*
15. *crescendo* The singers' voices rose to a *crescendo*. *crescendo*
16. *skiing* Watch the water bugs *skiing* on a puddle. *skiing*
17. *limestone* Sit on the *limestone* wall and dream a bit. *limestone*
18. *volcano* A roaring *volcano* spewed fire and lava. *volcano*
19. *temporary* There was *temporary* panic in the city. *temporary*
20. *unbeliever* Such an event makes an *unbeliever* tremble. *unbeliever*
21. *so-called* Many *so-called* Christians also turned to God. *so-called*
22. *repentance* God longs for the *repentance* of every sinner. *repentance*
23. *indefinitely* The bridge was closed *indefinitely*. *indefinitely*
24. *serial* A new *serial* begins in this issue. *serial*
25. *motto* Each story is based on the *motto* of a famous person. *motto*

B. AFFIXING AFFIXES

Words of Italian origin that end with *o* usually form the plural by adding -*s,* especially if they are musical terms. Sometimes either -*s* or -*es* is correct.

1. Write the plural form of all the NEW and REVIEW WORDS that end with *o*.
2. Write the plural form of these words. They are not all of Italian origin.
   a. solo
   b. trio
   c. patio
   d. potato
   e. tomato
   f. Eskimo
3. Find two NEW WORDS that are plural. Write their singular forms.

> Plural of Italian Words Ending With O

4. Write the REVIEW WORD that has a prefix and a suffix.
5. a. Write the two NEW WORDS that end with adverb-forming suffixes.
   b. By adding or removing prefixes, write the opposite of each word.
6. Write a part-of-speech label for each of these words. Then write the spelling word derived from it, and label its part of speech.
   a. peace
   b. repent
   c. shout
   d. believe

C. SOUND, STRUCTURE, AND MEANING

1. a. Write the NEW WORD that contains *ii*.
   b. Remove the suffix and write the root word.
2. Write the NEW WORD in which *sc* spells /sh/.
3. Write the NEW WORD in which *er* spells /är/.
4. Write two five-syllable words from your spelling list.
5. Write the NEW WORD that has *ea* twice. Underline the *ea* that is a vowel digraph. Draw a vertical line between the other *e* and *a* to divide the root word from the suffix.
6. Write the two NEW WORDS that are compound words. Circle the hyphen in the hyphenated compound.
7. Write these words correctly as compounds. Hyphenate three of them.
   a. earth quake
   b. high minded
   c. law abiding
   d. out doors
   e. over turn
   f. self pity
   g. water fall
8. Write a NEW WORD or its homonym for each blank.
   a. Mother served hot ____ for breakfast.
   b. We enjoyed reading the ____ about Menno Simons's life.
9. Use the same spelling word to fill the blank in each sentence.
   a. The minister spoke of judgment, but the ____ of his message was mercy.
   b. A few more people in our class should sing ____.
10. Heteronyms are words with identical spellings but different pronunciations and meanings. Write the REVIEW WORD that is a heteronym in which the letter *a* could be long or short.
11. Write the word that is a doublet of *zero*.

Answer Key—Part B (32 points)

1. altos, crescendos, mottos *or* mottoes, sopranos, volcanos *or* volcanoes, buffalo *or* buffalos *or* buffaloes, zeros *or* zeroes

2. a. solos
   b. trios
   c. patios
   d. potatoes
   e. tomatoes
   f. Eskimos *or* Eskimo

3. arrangement, opportunity

4. unbeliever

5. a. indefinitely, sufficiently
   b. definitely, insufficiently

6. a. n., peaceable—adj.
   b. v., repentance—n.
   c. v. *or* n., shouted—v. *or* adj.
   d. v., unbeliever—n.

Notes on Part C

Exercise 5: Retain final *e* on the root word to protect soft *c*.

Answer Key—Part C (22 points)

1. a. skiing
   b. ski

2. crescendo

3. sergeant

4. indefinitely, opportunities

5. peace/able

6. limestone, so-called

7. a. earthquake
   b. high-minded
   c. law-abiding
   d. outdoors
   e. overturn
   f. self-pity
   g. waterfall

8. a. cereal   b. serial

9. a. tenor   b. tenor

10. bass

11. cipher

D.   LANGUAGE LINEAGE

BABEL IN REVERSE?

With the increasing travel and communication of today, people around the world are seeing and hearing more of each other. Everyone seems to be closer together, and it matters more when people cannot understand each other. Is it feasible to think that there might some-day be a world language? Which language would it be?

Learning to write English is not easy for foreigners, because spelling is so irregular. But English is an efficient language with respect to grammar and inflections. Also, the numerous words borrowed from other languages provide a touch of the familiar for many foreigners. The status of many English-speaking people has made English popular, and people of many nationalities now know it as a second language.

Hundreds of attempts have been made through the centuries to devise a language for universal speech. A version of English with simplified spelling, called Anglic, was promoted in the early 1900s. Another proposal, Basic English, has a restricted vocabulary. Its selection of 850 words is supposed to be sufficient for expressing any idea.

Perhaps the most successful artificial language of all time is Esperanto, which was devised in 1887 by L. L. Zamenhof. (*Esperanto* is based on the Latin word for "hope.") For basic vocabulary, Zamenhof used root words common to the widely familiar Indo-European lan-guage family. Singular nouns end with -*o* and plural nouns end with -*oj* (pronounced /oi/). In the objective case, nouns have -*n* tacked on after the -*o* or -*oj*. Adjectives end with -*a*. They also take the -*j* or -*n* ending to match the number and case of the noun they are describing. Verbs end with -*s* and have no inflection. Adverbs end with -*e*. Today about one million people know Esperanto as a second language, and some magazines and newspapers are printed in Esperanto.

No artificial language is likely to replace any mother tongue, but as a second language it could be a means of communication for a broad range of people. As technology advances in many other fields, will scientists also break the language barrier and unite all peoples in a common exchange? Only God knows. It was He who looked down upon the builders at Babel and said, "Let us go down, and there confound their language, that they may not understand one another's speech" (Genesis 11:7).

Exercises

1. a. What are some points in favor of English as a world language?
   b. What is against English for becoming a world language?
2. a. Name two versions of English that were designed for use as a world language.
   b. Tell what changes were made in devis-ing each of these versions.
3. Why would Esperanto words seem famil-iar to people of many different languages?
4. In Esperanto, what helps to make it easy to understand the function of a word in a sentence?

Notes on Part D

A world language need not be anyone's native tongue. It could be a simplified language that everyone agrees upon for a second language, thus making possible communication anywhere in the world.

Anglic

This version of the opening sentences of the Gettysburg Address is a sample of Anglic. When the accent falls on a syllable other than the first, that vowel is in boldface.

Forskor and sevn yeerz ag**oe** our faadherz braut forth on this kontinent a nue naeshon, kon-**see**vd in liberti, and dedikaeted to the propo**zi**shon that aul men ar kreeated eequel.

Now we ar eng**ae**jd in a graet sivil wor, testing whedher that naeshon, or eni naeshon soe kon-**see**vd and soe dedikaeted, kan long end**u**er. We ar met on a graet batl-feeld of that wor.

Esperanto

1. Adjectives take inflective endings to match the nouns.

singular adjective:	bona = good
singular noun:	amiko = friend
	bona amiko
plural:	bonaj amikoj
singular objective:	bonan amikon
plural objective:	bonajn amikojn

2. Basic roots adapt to different parts of speech.

verb:	ridi (to laugh)
noun:	rido (a laugh)
adjective:	ridinda (funny)

3. About fifty affixes provide a system for building derivatives that enables rapid vocabulary expansion for beginners.

arbo—tree

arbaro—woods (collection of trees)

arbarego—forest (big collection of trees)

arbaregano—forest dweller (inhabitant of a big collection of trees)

A sample of Esperanto: (The bold syllables are roots that are taught in seventh or eighth grade.)

Je *un*ua rigardo, Esperanto ŝajnas sufiĉe simpla. La lingvo havas nur 16 facile memoreblajn gramatikajn regulojn—sen iuj ajn esceptoj—kaj bazan vortaron kon*stru*itan el plejparte hindeŭropaj radikoj. Fakuloj pretendas, ke preskaŭ iu ajn persono povas lerni Esperanton en *cent* horoj aŭ *malpli.**

Esperantistoj estas troveblaj tra la tuta mondo. Cinio subtenas *ak*tivan eldonprogramon. En Japanio la lingvo estis foje uzata por diskutoj inter *sci*entistoj, kiuj parolas *mals*amajn naciajn lingvojn.

* *mal* (bad) + *ple* (fill) = anti-fill, or less

English translation of Esperanto sample:

At a glance, Esperanto seems simple enough. It has only 16 easily memorized rules of grammar—no exceptions—and a basic vocabulary built from mostly Indo-European roots. Experts claim that virtually anyone can learn Esperanto in 100 hours or less.

Esperantists can be found all around the world. China supports an active publishing program. In Japan the language has sometimes been used for discussions by scientists who speak different languages.

Answer Key—Part D (8 points)

1. a. English is efficient in grammar and inflections. English has many borrowed words that are familiar to different languages. Some English-speaking nations have high status in the world.
   b. English is difficult to learn because the *spelling is so irregular.*
2. a. Anglic and Basic English were two versions of English designed for a world language.
   b. Anglic had *simplified spelling.* Basic English has a *restricted vocabulary.*
3. Esperanto basic vocabulary uses *roots common to the Indo-European language family.*
4. *Word endings* indicate the *part of speech.*

LESSON 33

A. UNEARTHING THE ROOTS

> **ROOTS**
> Words borrowed from American Indians

NEW WORDS

canoe
caribou
classify
itemize
jaguar
llama
moccasin
opossum
pressurize
raccoon
realize
reign
sanctify
simplify
spiritualize
tapioca
tobacco
tomahawk
tying
utilize

REVIEW WORDS

chocolate
emphasize
identify
justify
prophesy

1. Write the NEW WORDS that come from these Indian words.
   a. *mohkussin*
   b. *tipiog*
   c. *aposoum*
   d. *tamahaac*
   e. *arathkone*
2. Which REVIEW WORD comes from an Indian word for "bitter water"?
3. Maya Indians worshiped the _____*, a catlike animal that symbolized strength and courage to them.
4. Indians of South America used the ____* as a beast of burden.
5. Indian tribes of the far North used the ____* for meat, tools, and clothing.
6. In the eastern woodlands, an Indian ____* was often made of birch bark.
7. Columbus found the Indians of the Caribbean region smoking ____*.
8. Write the word that developed by folk etymology from the Cree Indian word *otcheck*. (See *Language Lineage,* Lesson 29.)
9. Some other words from Indian languages are listed here. Match them to the descriptions below.

chipmunk	hickory
skunk	squash
succotash	toboggan

   a. *segākw* (striped cat-sized animal)
   b. *ajidamoon* (striped rodent)
   c. *msíckquatash* (dish of corn and lima beans)
   d. *askútasquash* (hard-shelled fruit of a low-growing vine)
   e. *pocohiquara* (nut-bearing tree)
   f. *topaghan* (device for sliding)

Lesson 33

(Total points: 90)

Notes on Part A

Exercise 1: The most likely way to recognize the spelling word is to try pronouncing the Indian word as it is written. The Indian word and English counterpart do not always have similar beginnings. If pronunciation does not give the clue, the words can be found by trial-and-error checking in the Speller Dictionary.

Exercise 9: Let students try giving phonetic pronunciations for the Indian words. In some of them you can hear similarity to the English word. Can the students guess the match without reading the definition?

Answer Key—Part A (18 points)

1. a. moccasin
   b. tapioca
   c. opossum
   d. tomahawk
   e. raccoon
2. chocolate
3. jaguar
4. llama
5. caribou
6. canoe
7. tobacco
8. woodchuck
9. a. skunk
   b. chipmunk
   c. succotash
   d. squash
   e. hickory
   f. toboggan

Lesson 33 Test Sentences

1. *identify* How did Adam *identify* all the animals? *identify*
2. *jaguar* The *jaguar* was tame in the beginning. *jaguar*
3. *caribou* The *caribou* is a large deer. *caribou*
4. *llama* A *llama* is useful for mountain travel. *llama*
5. *opossum* Nighttime is when the *opossum* roams. *opossum*
6. *raccoon* The *raccoon* also hunts at night. *raccoon*
7. *classify* We *classify* animals by structure. *classify*
8. *tomahawk* Was the *tomahawk* used in hunting? *tomahawk*
9. *tapioca* Cassava roots yield *tapioca*. *tapioca*
10. *chocolate* Cacao beans produce *chocolate*. *chocolate*
11. *utilize* Can they *utilize* the dry hulls? *utilize*
12. *tobacco* Some value is found in *tobacco*. *tobacco*
13. *justify* Does that *justify* raising the crop? *justify*
14. *sanctify* We cannot *sanctify* harmful habits. *sanctify*
15. *realize* Most people *realize* the harm of nicotine. *realize*
16. *canoe* See the brown *canoe* on the beach. *canoe*
17. *moccasin* A water *moccasin* was hiding beneath it. *moccasin*
18. *prophesy* Which city did Jonah *prophesy* against? *prophesy*
19. *emphasize* Their actions *emphasize* their repentance. *emphasize*
20. *spiritualize* The Indians *spiritualize* their harvest. *spiritualize*
21. *simplify* Plain obedience will *simplify* life. *simplify*
22. *reign* God's *reign* is eternal. *reign*
23. *pressurize* Don't *pressurize* the balloon too much. *pressurize*
24. *tying* We are *tying* up the loose ends. *tying*
25. *itemize* Then we can *itemize* our summer plans. *itemize*

B.   AFFIXING AFFIXES

1. Write words containing the lesson suffixes for these definitions.
    a. To arrange according to class*.
    b. To make glorious.
    c. To cause terror.
    d. To list as individual items*.
    e. To put under pressure*.
    f. To give clarity.
    g. To give sanctity to*.
    h. To make simple*.
    i. To give spiritual meaning*.
    j. To put to use*.
    k. To make beautiful.
    l. To make sterile.
    m. To recognize as being real*.
    n. To reduce to a minimum.

Verb-forming Suffixes

SUFFIX	MEANING	EXAMPLE
-ify	make,	justify
-efy	become	liquefy
-ize		emphasize

2. Write the *-ed* and *-ing* forms of the REVIEW WORDS that have lesson suffixes.
3. Write the root word of *tying*.
4. Write the *-ed* and *-ing* forms of these words.
    a. die
    b. lie
    c. vie
5. Write the two plural forms of each word.
    a. caribou
    b. llama

C.   SOUND, STRUCTURE, AND MEANING

1. Write the spelling words that have these phonetic features.
    a. /f/ spelled *ph* (2)
    b. /ān/ spelled *eign*
    c. /ü/ spelled *oo*
    d. /ü/ spelled *oe*
    e. /ü/ spelled *ou*
    f. initial double letter
    g. double letter *c* (3)
2. Two of the NEW WORDS that name animals may be pronounced with two syllables or with three. Write the words. After each one, write the pronunciation that best matches the spelling.
3. Write a spelling word or its homonym for each blank.
    a. King David did not ____ as long as King Uzziah.
    b. We will plant potatoes today if it does not ____.
    c. The hikers can catch up if you ____ in the pony for a rest.
4. Write spelling words for these definitions.
    a. Fastening with rope.
    b. Declare guiltless.
    c. Understand.
    d. A dark brown color.
5. Write NEW WORDS to complete these analogies.
    a. alcohol : wine :: nicotine : ____
    b. expand : contract :: complicate : ____
    c. glitter : sparkle :: hallow : ____
    d. baby : papoose :: ax : ____
    e. candy : chocolate :: pudding : ____
6. Write sentences using *prophesy* and *prophecy* correctly.

Notes on Part B

Exercises 3 and 4: Instead of changing *y* to *i,* in these derivations we change *ie* to *y* to add *-ing.*

Answer Key—Part B (31 points)

1. a. classify
   b. glorify
   c. terrify *or* terrorize
   d. itemize
   e. pressurize
   f. clarify
   g. sanctify
   h. simplify
   i. spiritualize
   j. utilize
   k. beautify
   l. sterilize
   m. realize
   n. minimize

2. emphasized, emphasizing
   identified, identifying
   justified, justifying

3. tie

4. a. died, dying
   b. lied, lying
   c. vied, vying

5. a. caribou, caribous
   b. llamas, llama

Answer Key—Part C (28 points)

1. a. emphasize, prophesy
   b. reign
   c. raccoon
   d. canoe
   e. caribou
   f. llama
   g. moccasin, raccoon, tobacco

2. jaguar (jag' yü är')
   opossum (ə pos' əm)

3. a. reign
   b. rain
   c. rein

4. a. tying
   b. justify
   c. realize
   d. chocolate

5. a. tobacco
   b. simplify
   c. sanctify
   d. tomahawk
   e. tapioca

6. (Sample sentences)
   It is easy to *prophesy* failure when you see chores being neglected.
   Those who heeded the *prophecy* were spared.

D.   LANGUAGE LINEAGE

SEMANTIC STUDY: COMMON PROPER NOUNS

In the late 1700s, a malfunctioning steam engine was brought to the Scottish engineer James Watt. He repaired it, but the inefficiency of the machine troubled him. So he tried to build a better model, and within a few years he developed a steam engine that was practical for ships, railroads, and a broad range of other applications. His name was eventually used to designate a standard unit of power. Have you seen it printed on light bulbs to show how much electricity they use?

Timothy Hanson, a farmer of the 1700s, introduced a certain kind of grass in the Carolinas. Today many farmers raise timothy hay.

On the northwest coast of Africa lies the narrow nation of Morocco. Sheep, goats, and dairy cattle are its chief livestock, and leather is one of its major manufactured products. Here was developed a soft, fine leather made from goatskin tanned with sumac. When you buy a Bible bound with morocco, the name of the leather comes from Africa, if the product itself does not.

The luxurious vehicle called a limousine is named for Limousin, a region in France. The city of Hamburg, Germany, has given its name to the ground meat we call hamburger.

These are just a few examples of the many words that originally were proper names for people and places. As the examples show, the proper nouns often grow so common that they are no longer capitalized.

The same thing happens with trademarks. A trade name is capitalized, officially registered, and restricted to the company authorized to use that name. Other manufacturers selling similar items are not allowed to use the same name for their products. But sometimes a trademark becomes a generic name for the product and is written as a common noun. This is what happened to *yo-yo* and *pogo stick,* which were formerly trademarks.

Some trademarks in photography today are *Agfa, Fuji,* and *Kodak.* When buying facial tissues, you may choose *Scotties, Kleenex,* or *Puffs.* Do you use any of these names as common nouns? Trademark owners try to protect their names from becoming general vocabulary, but they do not always succeed. *Escalator, linoleum,* and *zipper* are other words that originally were trade names.

Exercises

1. a. Name two people whose names have become common nouns.
    b. Name three places that are the source of common nouns.
    c. Write five common nouns that originally were trademarks.

2. Check a dictionary and write what is the source of each of these words.
    a. diesel
    b. aspirin
    c. sandwich

Notes on Part D

Do we use trade names improperly? These names are not common nouns:

Band-Aid   Thermos   Scotch (tape)

Additional examples of words that originated as trade names:

nylon   kerosene   cellophane

Additional examples of words that originated from names of people:

derrick—Derick, a London executioner around 1600. His gallows was a framework with a hoisting apparatus.

pasteurize—Louis Pasteur, a French scientist of 1822–1895

raglan—Baron Raglan, an officer in the Crimean War who wore a coat with sleeves that extended to the neckline

silhouette—Étienne de Silhouette, a French finance minister (See Lesson 26)

wisteria—Caspar Wistar, an American anatomist 1761–1818

Additional examples of words that originated from names of places:

bologna—Bologna, a city in Italy

calico—Calicut, a city in India

frankfurter—Frankfort, a city in Germany

tabasco—Tabasco River in Mexico

tarantula—Taranto, an ancient seaport inside the heel of Italy

Another source of names that have become common nouns is the stories of Greek and Roman mythology.

atlas—In Greek mythology, Atlas was a giant who held up the heavens.

mercury—In Roman mythology, Mercury was the messenger among the gods.

money—The Romans minted coins in the temple of their goddess Moneta.

panic—Pan was the Greek god of woods, fields, and flocks.

volcano—Vulcan was the Roman god of fire.

Answer Key—Part D (13 points)

1. a. James *Watt, Timothy* Hanson
    b. Morocco, Limousin, Hamburg
    c. yo-yo, pogo stick, escalator, linoleum, zipper
2. a. *Diesel* was the last *name of the man* who invented the diesel engine.
    b. *Aspirin* was formerly a *trade name.*
    c. *Sandwich* was a *region in England.*

LESSON 34

31	32	33
dachshund	alto	canoe
diesel	arrangements	caribou
plunder	crescendo	classify
poodle	indefinitely	itemize
refugees	limestone	jaguar
resolution	motto	llama
responsible	opportunities	moccasin
roommate	peaceable	opossum
satisfactorily	penicillin	pressurize
sauerkraut	repentance	raccoon
separately	sergeant	realize
sheer	serial	reign
smallpox	shouted	sanctify
successor	skiing	simplify
supplement	so-called	spiritualize
tender	soprano	tapioca
trifle	sufficiently	tobacco
undoubtedly	temporary	tomahawk
university	tenor	tying
unusually	volcano	utilize

A. UNEARTHING THE ROOTS

Words of German origin
Words of Italian origin
Words borrowed from American Indians

1. Write words with German roots for these exercises.

   a. A German inventor built the first _____ engine.

   b. Which dog is longer, a _____ or a _____?

   c. Cabbage is used to make _____.

   d. David recovered all the _____ as well as people that were captured at Ziklag.

   e. The _____ class learned two short psalms. (REVIEW WORD)

ﾠ

ﾠ

ﾠﾠ

Page 217

Lesson 34

(Total points: 74)

Answer Key—Part A (30 points)

1. a. diesel
   b. dachshund, poodle
   c. sauerkraut
   d. plunder
   e. kindergarten

Lesson 34 Test Sentences

1. *responsible* You are *responsible* for great influence. *responsible*
2. *separately* Wash dark clothes *separately* from white. *separately*
3. *diesel* The old *diesel* gave good service. *diesel*
4. *satisfactorily* The loose shingle was *satisfactorily* nailed. *satisfactorily*
5. *refugees* Flood *refugees* crowded the school. *refugees*
6. *plunder* All their *plunder* was swept downstream. *plunder*
7. *trifle* Open the window a *trifle*. *trifle*
8. *unusually* The wind is *unusually* cold. *unusually*
9. *tender* What spoiled the *tender* grapes? *tender*
10. *undoubtedly* It was *undoubtedly* some little foxes. *undoubtedly*
11. *resolution* We need fresh *resolution* to keep them out. *resolution*
12. *successor* The captain's *successor* painted his ship. *successor*
13. *sauerkraut* He always has *sauerkraut* with his sausage. *sauerkraut*
14. *poodle* The clipped *poodle* looked much different. *poodle*
15. *university* We visited the *university* library. *university*
16. *supplement* I got two books to *supplement* my study. *supplement*
17. *sheer* The hillside is too *sheer* for mowing. *sheer*
18. *arrangements* Flight *arrangements* should be made early. *arrangements*
19. *opportunities* Make the most of your *opportunities*. *opportunities*
20. *sufficiently* Is the paint *sufficiently* dry? *sufficiently*
21. *alto* Karen memorized her *alto* music. *alto*
22. *tenor* She sang a duet with the *tenor* part. *tenor*
23. *temporary* There will be a *temporary* detour. *temporary*
24. *indefinitely* We may use the garden *indefinitely*. *indefinitely*
25. *limestone* Add *limestone* dust to improve the soil. *limestone*
26. *serial* Janet is writing a *serial* about pioneers. *serial*
27. *peaceable* Indians were *peaceable* with some. *peaceable*
28. *volcano* They thought the *volcano* was God's wrath. *volcano*
29. *soprano* There was a prominent *soprano* voice. *soprano*
30. *crescendo* It rang out in the *crescendo*. *crescendo*
31. *shouted* Terry *shouted* above the noise. *shouted*
32. *motto* A *motto* is a good reminder. *motto*
33. *repentance* John preached *repentance*. *repentance*
34. *penicillin* Alexander Fleming discovered *penicillin*. *penicillin*
35. *raccoon* We caught a *raccoon* in the corn patch. *raccoon*
36. *classify* Would you *classify* him as a robber? *classify*
37. *realize* Now we *realize* what damaged the corn. *realize*
38. *spiritualize* We can *spiritualize* our work. *spiritualize*
39. *sanctify* Singing helps to *sanctify* our hearts. *sanctify*
40. *reign* Jesus will not *reign* in a defiled heart. *reign*
41. *pressurize* They must *pressurize* highflying jets. *pressurize*
42. *moccasin* There is a hole in Alma's *moccasin*. *moccasin*
43. *caribou* Here is a piece of *caribou* leather. *caribou*
44. *utilize* See if you can *utilize* it for a patch. *utilize*
45. *simplify* Let's *simplify* the supper plans. *simplify*
46. *itemize* Will you *itemize* the menu? *itemize*
47. *tapioca* Jane will bring *tapioca* pudding. *tapioca*
48. *llama* Pedro led his *llama* to market. *llama*
49. *tying* He was *tying* it when the load fell off. *tying*
50. *tobacco* Keep the air clear of *tobacco* smoke. *tobacco*

2. Write other words from Lesson 31 for these etymologies.
   a. *re-* (back) + *fugere* (to flee)
   b. *satis* (enough) + *facere* (to do)
   c. *sub-* (up from under) + *plēre* (to fill)
   d. *trufle* (mockery, deception)

3. Write words that end with *o* and have Italian roots.
   a. Daniel's ____ might have been "In every thing give thanks."
   b. There were few ____ voices because most of the girls sang ____.
   c. The ____ enhances the meaning of the triumphant phrase at the end of the song.

d. The cloud of ash and gases from the ____ spread for miles.

4. Write other words from Lesson 32 for these definitions.
   a. A story printed in monthly installments.
   b. A police or military officer.
   c. An antibiotic made from a mold.
   d. For a limited time; not permanent.

5. Answer with spelling words derived from Indian sources.
   a. Name five animals.
   b. Name three food or drug substances. (One is a REVIEW WORD.)
   c. Name three items made by Indians to be used or worn.

B. AFFIXING AFFIXES

1. Write words with *-heit* or *-fest* for these definitions.
   a. A scale for measuring heat.
   b. A festival of song.
   c. An exclamation meaning "good health."

2. Write words from Lesson 31 that are derived from these words.
   a. resolve
   b. satisfy
   c. separate
   d. succeed
   e. supply
   f. doubt
   g. universe
   h. usual

3. Write the plural form of the words from Lesson 32 that end with *o*.

4. Write words from Lesson 32 that are derived from these words.
   a. arrange
   b. definite

-heit	
-fest	
-ify, -efy, -ize	make, become

   c. peace
   d. repent
   e. suffice

5. Write four words from Lesson 32 with inflectional suffixes.

6. Write words from Lesson 33 for these definitions.
   a. To make use of.
   b. To organize in classes.
   c. To put under pressure.
   d. To make simple.
   e. To list as individual items.
   f. To give sanctity to.
   g. To recognize as being real.
   h. To give spiritual meaning.
   i. To rule.
   j. Fastening.

2. a. refugees
    b. satisfactorily
    c. supplement
    d. trifle

3. a. motto
    b. alto, soprano
    c. crescendo
    d. volcano

4. a. serial
    b. sergeant
    c. penicillin
    d. temporary

5. a. caribou, jaguar, llama, opossum, raccoon
    b. tapioca, tobacco, chocolate
    c. canoe, moccasin, tomahawk

Answer Key—Part B (35 points)

1. a. Fahrenheit
    b. songfest
    c. Gesundheit

2. a. resolution
    b. satisfactorily
    c. separately
    d. successor
    e. supplement
    f. undoubtedly
    g. university
    h. unusually

3. altos, crescendos, mottos *or* mottoes, sopranos, volcanos *or* volcanoes

4. a. arrangements
    b. indefinitely
    c. peaceable
    d. repentance
    e. sufficiently

5. arrangements, opportunities, shouted, skiing

6. a. utilize
    b. classify
    c. pressurize
    d. simplify
    e. itemize
    f. sanctify
    g. realize
    h. spiritualize
    i. reign
    j. tying

D. LANGUAGE LINEAGE

REVIEW

1. What kept British and American English from developing into separate languages?

2. Why do some people want a world language?

3. What international language is being used in some newspapers and magazines?

4. Describe something that has been named for each of these people or places.

    a. James Watt

    b. Timothy Hanson

    c. Morocco, Africa

    d. Limousin, France

    e. Hamburg, Germany

5. One kind of language change is disliked by manufacturers because it affects their trademarks. What language change is that?

Answer Key—Part D (9 points)

1. Increasing *communication* by technological advances kept British and American English from drifting into separate languages.

2. Today's technology permits contact *all over the world,* and a world language would enable one to communicate everywhere.

3. Some newspapers and magazines are published in *Esperanto.*

4. a. a unit of power
   b. a type of grass
   c. fine leather from goat skin
   d. a luxury vehicle
   e. ground meat

5. Manufacturers do not like to have their *trade names change to common nouns.*

222

Final Test

1. *infallible* God's prophecies are *infallible*. *infallible*
2. *enthusiastic* Balaam was *enthusiastic* about rewards. *enthusiastic*
3. *perished* He *perished* with the Midianites. *perished*
4. *suspicion* Habitual honesty keeps one clear of *suspicion*. *suspicion*
5. *anticipation* Live with *anticipation* of eternity. *anticipation*
6. *evangelist* Paul was a traveling *evangelist*. *evangelist*
7. *malicious* He faced *malicious* persecution. *malicious*
8. *acquaintance* Develop *acquaintance* with the elderly. *acquaintance*
9. *preceding* *Preceding* experiences gave them wisdom. *preceding*
10. *instinct* Birds migrate by *instinct*. *instinct*
11. *conveniently* Can you *conveniently* mail my note? *conveniently*
12. *protein* A dog needs *protein* in its diet. *protein*
13. *procedure* Use a consistent training *procedure*. *procedure*
14. *miniature* Grandfather carves *miniature* furniture. *miniature*
15. *advisable* It is *advisable* to keep his knife sharp. *advisable*
16. *ceremony* Visitors appeared without *ceremony*. *ceremony*
17. *eligible* Who is *eligible* for the prize? *eligible*
18. *scheme* Our gardening *scheme* was successful. *scheme*
19. *assurance* Goliath had a false *assurance* of power. *assurance*
20. *efficient* David was *efficient* with his sling. *efficient*
21. *financial* Credit cards bring *financial* snares. *financial*
22. *dedicate* We will *dedicate* this poem to Grandmother. *dedicate*
23. *literature* She enjoys our *literature*. *literature*
24. *indefinite* We saw *indefinite* forms in the fog. *indefinite*
25. *civilized* Cultivate *civilized* manners. *civilized*
26. *inconvenience* Frozen pipes cause major *inconvenience*. *inconvenience*
27. *energy* Direct your *energy* into useful channels. *energy*
28. *occurred* An eclipse *occurred* during the battle. *occurred*
29. *vague* Don't be *vague* with your suggestions. *vague*
30. *recommend* Can you *recommend* an improvement? *recommend*
31. *precious* An honest friend is a *precious* treasure. *precious*
32. *occasional* You will face *occasional* misunderstandings. *occasional*
33. *frequently* Do not *frequently* analyze your friend's trust. *frequently*
34. *crusade* The neighbors staged a *crusade* against litter. *crusade*
35. *certainty* No one has the *certainty* of tomorrow. *certainty*
36. *superintendent* A *superintendent* must be on time. *superintendent*
37. *testimony* Your hobbies are a *testimony* of your interests. *testimony*
38. *career* A farming *career* takes many skills. *career*
39. *bouquet* My lilac *bouquet* drooped quickly. *bouquet*
40. *exhibition* Orderly children are an *exhibition* to the world. *exhibition*
41. *tendency* Resist the *tendency* to slouch. *tendency*
42. *preparation* Good meals take *preparation*. *preparation*
43. *criticism* We cannot cure faults by *criticism*. *criticism*
44. *stampede* Thunder triggered the *stampede*. *stampede*
45. *refugees* Storm *refugees* stayed in the school. *refugees*
46. *temporary* It was a *temporary* shelter. *temporary*
47. *peaceable* Did everyone have *peaceable* neighbors? *peaceable*
48. *separately* Part of the order will be shipped *separately*. *separately*
49. *sanctify* Prayer will *sanctify* your thoughts. *sanctify*
50. *canoe* Keep your *canoe* out of the rapids. *canoe*

The Speller Dictionary

The Speller Dictionary

Full Pronunciation Key

Each entry word in the Speller Dictionary is followed by a phonetic spelling that shows its pronunciation. This pronunciation key lists all the symbols used in the phonetic spellings, and it shows how they should be pronounced.

A heavy accent mark is placed after the syllable that receives the primary accent. A light accent mark follows a syllable with a secondary accent. Observe the primary and secondary accents in the word *pronunciation:* (prə nun′ sē ā′ shən).

a	man, had	oi	oil, point	
ā	ate, made	ou	loud, round	
ä	car, father	p	pay, dip	
b	boy, tab	r	rod, near	
ch	choose, such	s	saw, gas	
d	deer, lid	sh	she, dish	
e	red, then	t	top, wet	
ē	me, east	th	thank, with	
ër	herd, search	ᴛʜ	the, weather	
f	for, if	u	bud, sun	
g	girl, peg	u̇	pull, took	
h	have, his	ü	blue, pool	
i	it, dim	v	very, over	
ī	hide, wire	w	we, away	
j	jar, rejoice	y	you, canyon	
k	kin, week	z	zone, daze	
l	lot, deal	zh	treasure, vision	
m	my, some	ə	represents	
n	need, win		*a* in ago	
ng	sing, rang		*e* in open	
o	not, fox		*i* in pencil	
ō	home, so		*o* in wagon	
ô	fall, or		*u* in cactus	

Abbreviations

adj.	adjective
adv.	adverb
conj.	conjunction
interj.	interjection
n.	noun
prep.	preposition
pron.	pronoun
v.	verb
abbr.	abbreviation
cap.	capitalized
def.	definition
esp.	especially
etc.	et cetera
pl.	plural
sing.	singular
<	from
Afr.	African
Am. Sp.	American Spanish
E	English
F	French
G	German
Gk.	Greek
Ital.	Italian
L	Latin
Mex. Sp.	Mexican Spanish
M	Middle
O	Old
Port.	Portuguese
Scand.	Scandinavian
Sp.	Spanish

A

a ban don (ə ban′ dən), *v.* 1. To cease from supporting or helping; to forsake responsibility; desert. 2. To give up one's rights: *abandon oneself to God's will.* —*n.* 3. A yielding to one's feelings: *preaching with abandon.* [< OF *abandoner* < *à bandon* < *à* at + *bandon* control]

ab hor (ab hôr′), *v.* **-horred, -hor ring** Look upon with horror or disgust; hate thoroughly. [< L *abhorrēre* to shrink from < *ab-* from + *horrēre* to shudder]

ab nor mal (ab nôr′ məl), *adj.* Not normal; not average; irregular. [< L *abnormis* < *ab-* away from + *norma* rule] —**ab nor′ mal ly** *adv.*

a bol ish (ə bol′ ish), *v.* To do away with; stamp out; destroy. [< ME *abolisshen* < F *aboliss-* < L *abolēre* destroy < *ab-* from + *ōlescere* to grow]

ab so lute (ab′ sə lüt′, ab′ sə lüt′), *adj.* 1. To fullest degree; ultimate: *absolute darkness.* 2. Complete; unconditional: *absolute trust.* 3. Not limited by any restriction: *absolute freedom.* —*n.* Unchangeable truth: *eternal absolute.* [< L *absolūtus* ended < *absoluere* to finish < *ab-* from + *solvere* to loose] —**ab so lute′ ly** *adv.*

ab stain (ab stān′, əb stān′), *v.* To keep oneself back from something; avoid. [< L *abstinēre* to hold back < *ab-* away + *tenēre* to hold]

ab sti nence (ab′ stə nəns), *n.* 1. The practice of abstaining, or refraining, from certain appetites. 2. Denial of alcoholic beverages, also called total abstinence. [< L *abstinēre*]

ab stract (ab strakt′, ab′ strakt′), *adj.* Having reality that cannot be seen or touched: *an abstract noun.* [< L *abstractus* < *abstrahere* to draw away < *ab-* away + *trahere* to draw]

a bun dance (ə bun′ dəns), *n.* A plentiful or overflowing amount. [< L *abundāns* < *abundāre* to overflow < *ab-* from + *undāre* to flow (< *unda* wave)]

ac cept a ble (ak sep′ tə bəl), *adj.* 1. Good enough to be accepted; pleasing. 2. Meeting the requirements, but not outstanding: *an acceptable job.* [< L *acceptāre* < *accipere* to receive < *ad-* to + *capere* to take]

ac cess (ak′ ses′), *n.* 1. The right to enter or use: *access to the library.* 2. Means of approach to people or places: *The only access to the farm was flooded.* [< L *accessus* < *accēdere* to arrive < *ad-* to + *cēdere* to come]

ac com mo date (ə kom′ ə dāt′), *v.* **-dat ed, -dat ing** 1. To have room for: *accommodate the crowd.* 2. To help out; do a favor: *accommodate him with a ride to the airport.* 3. Adapt; adjust: *accommodate to tropical climate.* [< L *accomodāre* to fit < *ad-* to + *commodus* suitable]

ac com mo da tion (ə kom′ ə dā′ shən), *n.* That which meets a need, shows a favor, or gives help. [< L *accomodāre*]

ac com pa ny (ə kum′ pə nē), *v.* **-nied, -ny ing, -nies** 1. To go along; join in. 2. To occur at the same time: *Thunder accompanies lightning.* [< ME *accompanien* < OF *acompagnier* < *à* to + *compaignon* companion. See COMPANION.]

ac cord ing ly (ə kôr′ ding lē), *adv.* Correspondingly; in manner fitting to a situation: *pray accordingly.* [< L *accordāre* < *ad-* to + *cor* heart]

ac knowl edg ment (ak nol′ ij mənt), *n.* 1. The act of admitting. 2. A response for something given or done: *acknowledgment for the grocery shower.* [< OE *oncnāwan* to know] Also **ac knowl′ edge ment.**

ac quain tance (ə kwān′ təns), *n.* 1. A person whom one knows, but not a close friend. 2. Knowledge of an individual or a thing: *acquaintance in Bible languages.* [< ME *aqueinten* < OF *acointier* < ML *adcognitāre* < *accognoscere* to know perfectly < *ad-* to + *cognoscere* to know]

ac tor (ak′ tər), *n.* A person who acts, as in a play; performer. [< L *āctor* doer < *agere* to do]

ad di tion al (ə dish′ ən əl), *adj.* More; added; extra. [< L *additiō* < *additus* < *addere* to add < *ad-* to + *dare* to give]

ad dress (*n.* ə dres′, ad′ res; *v.* ə dres′), *n.* 1. The writing on a letter or package that directs it to the receiver. 2. A formal speech. —*v.* 1. To write an address on (an envelope or a package). 2. To

---

had, māde, cär; then, mē, hėrd; dim, hīde; not, hōme, ôr; oil, loud; sun, pull, blüe; ch, such; ng, sing; sh, she; th, with; ᴛH, the; zh, vision;

ə represents *a* in ago, *e* in open, *i* in pencil, *o* in wagon, *u* in cactus.

adjourn   114   amphibian

adj.	adjective	*n.*	noun
adv.	adverb	*prep.*	preposition
conj.	conjunction	*pron.*	pronoun
interj.	interjection	*v.*	verb
sing.	singular	*pl.*	plural

speak to, esp. in a formal manner: *The president addressed the lawmakers.* 3. To devote energy to; apply (oneself to): *address oneself to solving a problem.* [< OF *adresser* < *a-* to + *dresser* to arrange]

ad journ (ə jėrn′), *v.* To suspend until another time or place. [< MF *ajourner* < *a* to + *jour* day (< L *diurnum*)]

ad mis sion (ad mish′ ən), *n.* 1. The act of admitting or granting entrance; acceptance. 2. A fee charged for entering: *Pay admission at the gate.* 3. Acknowledgment that something is true: *admission of the theft.* [< L *admissiō* < *admittere* to admit < *ad-* to + *mittere* to send]

ad o les cence (ad′ əl es′ əns), *n.* The period of growth between childhood and adulthood. [< L *adolēscēns* < *adolēscere* to grow up < *ad-* toward + *alēscere* to grow]

ad o ra tion (ad′ ə rā′ shən), *n.* 1. Strong love and respect. 2. Worship. [< L *adōrāre* to pray to < *ad* to + *ōrāre* to pray]

ad vis a ble (ad vī′ zə bəl), *adj.* Worthy of being offered as good advice; according to good counsel; prudent: *an advisable thing to do.* [< OF *aviser* < *avis* < L *advisus* < *ad-* to + *vīsum* something seen (< *vidēre* to see)]

ad vi so ry (ad vī′ zə rē), *adj.* Authorized to advise: *the advisory panel.* —*n. pl.* **-ries** A report giving facts, esp. in warning: *a weather advisory.* [< OF *aviser*]

aer o nau tics (er′ ə nô′ tiks), *n.* The knowledge or act of planning, building, or flying of aircraft. [< Gk. *aēr* air + *nautēs* sailor]

a larm (ə lärm′), *n.* 1. Sudden fear because of danger. 2. A warning signal because of danger. 3. An instrument that gives a signal. —*v.* To cause alarm. [< OF *alarme* < Ital. *all' arme* to arms < L *ad illam* to that + *arma* arms]

al ge bra (al′ jə brə), *n.* A branch of mathematics in which symbols (usually letters) are used instead of numbers to solve problems. [< Arabic *al-jebr* the (science of) reuniting < *al* the + *jabr* reunification]

al le giance (ə lē′ jəns), *n.* Loyalty to a nation, sovereign, or principle: *allegiance to truth.* [< ME *alligeaunce* < OF *ligeance* < *lige* loyal subject < *leticus* < *letus* serf, of Germanic origin]

al li ga tor (al′ i gā′ tər), *n.* 1. A reptile with powerful jaws, sharp teeth, and thick skin, resembling the crocodile but having a shorter, flatter head. 2. Leather made from the skin of an alligator. [< Sp. *el lagarto* the lizard < L *lacertus* lizard]

al loy (*n.* al′ oi′, *v.* ə loi′), *n.* 1. A mixture of two metals or a metal and a nonmetal. 2. An addition which lowers the value and purity of a metal. —*v.* 1. To mix metals into an alloy. 2. To make a metal less valuable by mixing with a cheaper metal. [< MF *aloi* < *aloier* to alloy < L *alligāre* to bind to < *ad-* to + *ligāre* to bind. Doublet of ALLY.]

all right *adj.* 1. Satisfactory but not outstanding. 2. Correct. 3. Well; not sick.

al might y (ôl mī′ tē), *adj.* Supreme in power; all-powerful: *almighty strength* —*n.* **the Almighty,** God: *gifts from the Almighty.* [< ME *almighti* < OE *ealmihtig* < *eall* all + *mihtig* mighty]

al to (al′ tō), *n. pl.* **-tos** 1. In four-part singing, the low part sung by women. 2. A person who sings alto. —*adj.* Pertaining to the singing range between soprano and tenor. [< Ital. *alto* < L *altus* high]

am a teur (am′ ə tûr′, am′ ə chûr′), *n.* A person who engages in an activity as a pastime rather than as a profession. —*adj.* Having to do with an unprofessional level. [< F < L *amātor* lover < *amāre* to love]

am bi tious (am bish′ əs), *adj.* 1. Full of ambition, aspiration, or purpose. 2. Having a strong desire; eager. 3. Challenging; difficult: *ambitious project.* [< L *ambitiō* < *ambīre* to go around < *ambi-* around + *īre* to go]

am phib i an (am fib′ ē ən), *n.* 1. A cold-blooded, smooth-skinned animal that can live on land and in water. 2. Aircraft that takes off and lands either on land or on water. 3. A vehicle that can travel on land or on water. [< Gk. *amphibion* <

amphibios < amphi- on both sides *+ bios* life]

am ple (am´ pəl), *adj.* 1. More than what is needed: *an ample supply of wood.* 2. Sufficient for the need: *ample funds.* 3. Large: *an ample farmhouse.* [*< L amplus* large, abundant]

a muse (ə myüz´), *v.* **-mused, -mus ing** 1. To keep pleasantly occupied. 2. To cause a laugh or a smile by giving pleasure. [*< OF amuser* to stupefy *< a* to *+ muser* to stare]

a muse ment (ə myüz´ mənt), *n.* 1. The state of being pleasantly occupied. 2. That which amuses. [*< OF amuser*]

An a bap tist (an´ ə bap´ tist), *n.* A member of a religious group that observed believer's baptism and rejected infant baptism. [*< L anabaptista < Gk. ana-* again *+ baptizein* to baptize]

a nal y sis (ə nal´ i sis), *n. pl.* **-y ses** (-i sēs) 1. The separation of something complex into its different parts for study. 2. The stated findings of such a study. [*< Gk. analusis* a dissolving *< analuein* to undo *< ana* throughout *+ luein* to loosen]

an ar chy (an´ ər kē), *n. pl.* **-chies** 1. Absence of political law and order. 2. General disorder. [*< Gk. anarkhia < anarkhos < an-* without *+ arkhos* ruler]

a nat o my (ə nat´ ə mē), *n. pl.* **-mies** 1. The structure of a human body, a plant, or an animal. 2. The study of these structures by dissection, microscopic observation, etc. [*< Gk. anatomē* dissection *< ana-* up *+ tomē* a cutting]

an gel (ān´ jəl), *n.* A heavenly being who serves as an attendant in God's presence and as a messenger from God to man. [*< Gk. angelos* messenger]

a noint (ə noint´), *v.* 1. To apply oil, ointment, or a similar substance to. 2. To apply oil to as a sign of sanctification or consecration. [*< ME enointen < OF enoindre < L inunguere < in-* on *+ ungere* to smear]

Ant arc tic (ant ärk´ tik, ant är´ tik), *adj.* At or near the South Pole: *the Antarctic Circle.* [*< Gk. antarktikos < anti-* opposite *+ arktikos* northern]

an tic i pate (an tis´ ə pāt´), *v.* **-pat ed, -pat ing** 1. To look forward to; expect. 2. To accomplish before others do: *The Sumerians anticipated all other nations in writing.* [*< L anticipāre* to take

had, māde, cär; then, mē, hėrd; dim, hīde; not, hōme, ôr; oil, loud; sun, pùll, blüe; ch, such; ng, sing; sh, she; th, with; ŦH, the; zh, vision;

ə represents *a* in ago, *e* in open, *i* in pencil, *o* in wagon, *u* in cactus.

before *< antē* before *+ capere* to take]

an tic i pa tion (an tis´ ə pā´ shən), *n.* 1. A looking forward to. 2. Something looked forward to: *accomplished his anticipation.* [*< L anticipāre*]

an ti sep tic (an´ ti sep´ tik), *n.* A substance that prevents infection by killing harmful germs. —*adj.* Pertaining to the killing of germs: *antiseptic ointment.* [*< Gk. anti-* opposite *+ sēptikos* (*< sēptos* rotten)]

anx i e ty (ang zī´ i tē), *n. pl.* **-ties** Distress and uneasiness, esp. about the future. [*< L ānxietās < anxius* anxious]

a pol o gize (ə pol´ ə jīz´), *v.* **-gized, -giz ing** 1. To express regret or sorrow for a wrong action. 2. To offer reasons in defense of an idea or a belief. [*< L apologia*]

a pol o gy (ə pol´ ə jē), *n. pl.* **-gies** 1. The expression of regret or sorrow for a wrong action. 2. The defense of an idea or a belief by reasoning. [*< L apologia < Gk. apo-* away *+ -logy* study (*< logos* speech)]

a pos ta sy (ə pos´ tə sē), *n. pl.* **-sies** A departing from one's faith or principles. [*< L apostasia* defection *< Gk. aphistanai* to revolt *< apo-* away from *+ histanai* to stand]

ap os tol ic (ap´ ə stol´ ik), *adj.* Having to do with the faith, teachings, or time of the twelve apostles: *apostolic letters.* [*< Gk. apostolos* messenger *< apostellein < apo-* away from *+ stellein* to send]

a pos tro phe[1] (ə pos´ trə fē), *n.* The mark (') used to show the omission of letters in contractions, to make possessive forms, and to make the plural form of some numerals and letters. [*< L apostrophos < Gk. apostrophein < apo-* away *+ strephein* to turn]

a pos tro phe[2] (ə pos´ trə fē), *n.* A comment made aside to an absent or imaginary person. [*< Gk. apostrophein*]

ap pen di ci tis (ə pen´ di sī´ tis), *n.* Inflammation

adj.	adjective	*n.*	noun
adv.	adverb	*prep.*	preposition
conj.	conjunction	*pron.*	pronoun
interj.	interjection	*v.*	verb
sing.	singular	*pl.*	plural

of the appendix. [< APPENDIX < L *appendere* < *ad-* to + *pendere* to hang + -ITIS]

ap pe tite (ap′ i tīt′), *n.* A strong desire or urge. [< L *appetītus* strong desire < *appetere* < *ad-* toward + *petere* to seek]

ap pli cant (ap′ li kənt), *n.* An individual who applies for a job or a position. [< L *applicāns* < *applicāre* to affix < *ad-* to + *plicāre* to fold together]

ap pli ca tion (ap′ li kā′ shən), *n.* 1. The act of applying. 2. That which is applied, or put on: *Use an application of soda paste on your bee sting.* 3. The use of a rule in a practical way. [< L *applicāre*]

ap prox i mate ly (ə prok′ sə mit lē), *adv.* About; not exactly, but nearly. [< L *approximātus* < *approximāre* to approach < *ad-* to + *proximāre* to come near (< *proximus* nearest)]

a quar i um (ə kwer′ ē əm), *n. pl.* **-i ums** or **-i a** A tank or pool in which fish or other water animals are kept. [< L *aquārius* of water < *aqua* water]

ar chi tect (är′ ki tekt′), *n.* 1. A person who designs and supervises the construction of buildings and other large structures. 2. One who plans or creates: *the architect of this book.* [< L *architectus* < Gk. *arkhitektōn* < *archi-* chief + *tektōn* builder]

ar gue (är′ gyü), *v.* **-gued, -gu ing** 1. To give reasons for or against something. 2. To discuss reasons with someone who disagrees. 3. To quarrel or dispute. [< L *arguere* to make clear]

a rise (ə rīz′), *v.* **-rose, -ris en, -ris ing** 1. To get up or go up. 2. To come into being, as a river; originate. [< OE *ārīsan*]

ar mor (är′ mər), *n.* 1. A suit made of strong material worn to protect the body against weapons. 2. The protective, bony scales of some animals or plates on war equipment. 3. Something that protects: *Faith is part of the armor of God.*

[< L *armāre* to arm < *arma* arms] Also **armour** (British).

ar range ment (ə rānj′ mənt), *n.* 1. The act or process of arranging: *time for arrangement at market.* 2. Something put in order: *arrangement of books.* 3. Often **arrangements.** Plans made for an occasion: *arrangements to sing at the hospital.* [< OF *arengier* < *à-* to + *rengier* to put in a line (< *reng* line, of Germanic origin)]

ar thri tis (är thrī′ tis), *n.* Inflamation of joints. [< Gk. *arthron* joint + -ITIS]

ar ti fi cial (är′ tə fish′ əl), *adj.* 1. Manmade rather than natural: *artificial flowers.* 2. Pretended; not sincere: *artificial friendliness.* [< L *artificiālis* < *artificium* < *artifex* craftsman < *ars* art + *fex* maker (< *facere* to make)]

ar tis tic (är tis′ tik), *adj.* 1. Pertaining to art or artists. 2. Showing skill and good taste in color and design. [< Ital. *artista* < *arte* art < L *ars*] —**ar tis′ ti cal ly** *adv.*

as cend (ə send′), *v.* 1. To go up. 2. Climb: *ascend the ladder.* 3. To come to occupy: *Solomon ascended the throne after David.* [< L *ascendere* < *ad-* toward + *scandere* to climb]

as cen sion (ə sen′ shən), *n.* 1. An ongoing, upward movement. 2. **the Ascension** The lifting up of Christ from earth to heaven. [< L *ascendere*]

as cer tain (as′ ər tān′), *v.* To find out facts by examination and research; make sure of. [< OF *acertener* < *a-* to + *certain* (< *certus* < *cernere* to determine)]

as phalt (as′ fôlt′), *n.* 1. A dark, sticky substance found in natural deposits or obtained by refining petroleum, and used in waterproofing, paving, and roofing. 2. A mixture of asphalt with rock or sand used in paving. [< Gk. *asphaltos*]

as pi rin (as′ pə rin), *n.* 1. A chemical compound used to reduce pain and fever. 2. A tablet of aspirin. [Originally a trademark.]

as sess ment (ə ses′ mənt), *n.* 1. The estimation of the value of property. 2. A set amount to be paid in taxes, fine, or other payment. [< OF *assesser* < L *assidēre* to sit by (as an assistant judge) < *ad-* near to + *sedēre* to sit]

as so ci ate (*v.* ə sō′ shē āt′, ə sō′ sē āt′; *n.* ə sō′ shē it), *v.* **-at ed, -at ing** 1. To relate together in thought: *We associate citrus fruit with Florida.*

2. To keep company with: *Do not associate with the scornful.* —*n.* A partner in business or friendship. [< ME *associaten* < L *associāre* to join to < *ad-* to + *socius* companion]

as sur ance (ə shur′ əns), *n.* 1. The act of doing or saying something that brings confidence and freedom from doubt. 2. Too much boldness or confidence. [< OF *assurer* < L *assēcūrāre* < *ad-* to + *sēcūrus* secure]

as ter isk (as′ tə risk′), *n.* A small starlike figure (*) used in printed matter to call attention to footnotes, references, etc. [< Gk. *asteriskos* < *astēr* star]

a the ist (ā′ thē ist), *n.* 1. A person who denies that God exists. 2. A godless person. [< Gk. *atheos* godless < *a-* without + *theos* god]

ath let ic (ath let′ ik), *adj.* 1. Pertaining to an athlete. 2. Physically strong and vigorous. [< Gk. *athlētēs* contestant < *athlein* to contend < *athlon* prize]

a tone (ə tōn′), *v.* **-toned, -ton ing** 1. To make amends for a wrong. 2. To take away the condemnation: *Jesus' blood atones for our sin.* [< ME *atonen* to be reconciled < *at* + *one*]

at tach (ə tach′), *v.* 1. Fasten to: *attach two buttons.* 2. Feel close because of personal affection: *attached to his uncle.* [< OF *attachier,* of Germanic origin]

at ten dant (ə ten′ dənt), *n.* A person who attends, esp. as a helper or servant. —*adj.* Accompanying; following, as a consequence: *the attendant debt.* [< ME *attenden* < OF *atendre* < L *attendere* to heed < *ad-* to + *tendere* to stretch]

at tor ney (ə tėr′ nē), *n. pl.* **-neys** 1. One who is hired to act for another in business or legal matters. 2. Lawyer. [< OF *atorne* < *atorner* to assign to < *a-* to + *torner* to turn]

au di ence (ô′ dē əns), *n.* 1. A group of listeners. 2. A chance to be heard, esp. in a formal manner before a person of high rank: *audience with the king.* [< L *audientia* < *audiēns* < *audīre* to hear]

au di tor (ô′ di tər), *n.* 1. One who officially examines records or accounts for accuracy. 2. Hearer, listener. [< L *audīre* to hear]

au thor i ty (ə thôr′ i tē), *n. pl.* **-ties** 1. The right to require and enforce obedience. 2. A person or group with this right, esp. policemen and others who enforce law. 3. A person with superior knowledge about a subject; an expert. [< ME *autority* < OF *autorite* < L *auctōritās* < *auctor* creator]

au to graph (ô′ tə graf′), *n.* One's own signature or handwriting. —*v.* To sign one's name in or on: *autograph my cast.* [< Gk. *autographos* < *autos* self + *graphein* to write]

aux il ia ry (ôg zil′ yə rē), *adj.* 1. Giving help; assisting. 2. Additional; reserves: *auxiliary equipment.* —*n. pl.* **-ries** 1. A person who helps; assistant. 2. A verb that helps to express certain shades of meaning; helping verb. [< L *auxiliārius* < *auxilium* help]

a vail a ble (ə vā′ lə bəl), *adj.* At hand; able to be used. [< ME *availen* < *a-* (intensive) + OF *valoir* to be worth (< L *valēre*)]

av o ca do (av′ ə kä′ dō), *n. pl.* **-dos** 1. A tropical, oval-shaped fruit with a dark skin and a large seed. Its nutty-flavored pulp is used in salads. 2. The tree that bears this fruit. [< Sp. *aguacate* < Nahuatl *ahuacatl*]

B

ba nan a (bə nan′ ə), *n.* 1. A crescent-shaped yellow fruit with a firm, creamy flesh and thick, easily removed peel. 2. The treelike plant that bears this fruit. [Port. or Sp., of West Afr. origin]

bar ba rous (bär′ bər əs), *adj.* 1. Uncivilized; primitive. 2. Cruel; brutal. 3. Lacking refinement; crude. [Gk. *barbaros* foreign]

bar be cue (bär′ bi kyü′), *n.* 1. A meal including meat roasted over an open fire, usually eaten outdoors. 2. An outdoor facility for roasting meat, often over charcoal. 3. Meat prepared in this way. —*v.* **-cued, -cu ing** To do the work of roasting the meat. [< Am. Sp. *barbacoa* < Haitian, framework of sticks]

bass (bās), *n.* 1. In music, the lowest pitch for a male singer. 2. One who sings with such a voice. [ME *bas* low]

had, māde, cär; then, mē, hėrd; dim, hīde; not, hōme, ôr; oil, loud; sun, pull, blüe; ch, such; ng, sing; sh, she; th, with; ℔, the; zh, vision;

ə represents *a* in ago, *e* in open, *i* in pencil, *o* in wagon, *u* in cactus.

beaten   **118**   **brilliancy**

adj.	adjective	*n.*	noun
adv.	adverb	*prep.*	preposition
conj.	conjunction	*pron.*	pronoun
interj.	interjection	*v.*	verb
sing.	singular	*pl.*	plural

beat en (bēt′ ən), *adj.* 1. Worn and familiar through much use: *beaten path.* 2. Defeated: *a beaten runner.* 3. Exhausted; worn out. 4. Shaped or made thin by hammering: *beaten silver.* [< OE *bēaten*]

beg gar (beg′ ər), *n.* A person who makes his living by begging. —*v.* 1. To bring to want: *Careless spending will beggar you.* 2. To exhaust the resources of: *The beauty of heaven beggars description.* [< OF *begart*]

be hav ior (bi hāv′ yər), *n.* 1. The way in which one behaves. 2. The response of persons or things under special conditions: *Scientists studied the behavior of drug-fed cells.* [ME *behaven*] Also **behaviour** (British).

beige (bāzh), *n.* A soft, woolen dress material, originally beige in color. —*adj.* Light grayish brown or yellowish brown. [< F perhaps < Ital. *bambagia* cotton]

be liev a ble (bi lēv′ ə bəl), *adj.* Capable of being believed; credible. [< ME *bileven* < OE *belēfan*] —**be liev′ a bly** *adv.*

ben e dic tion (ben′ i dik′ shən), *n.* A prayer for blessing, esp. at the end of a worship service. [< L *benedictiō* < *benedicere* to bless < *bene* well + *dīcere* to say]

ben e fi cial (ben′ ə fish′ əl), *adj.* Producing good results. [< L *beneficium* < *beneficus* < *bene* well + *facere* to do]

be nign (bi nīn′), *adj.* 1. Of a kind nature. 2. Showing kindness and gentleness. 3. Mild; favorable: *a benign climate.* 4. Not malignant: *a benign growth or tumor.* [< L *benignus* < *bene* well + *genus* born]

be stow (bi stō′), *v.* 1. Give as a gift: *bestow a blessing.* 2. Use up: *bestow time on the flowers.* [ME *bestowen*]

bi cy cle (bī′ sik′ əl), *n.* A vehicle with a seat and handlebars on a frame with two wheels propelled by pedals. [< F < L *bi-* two + Gk. *kuklos* wheel]

bi en ni al (bī en′ ē əl), *adj.* Occurring once in two years. —*n.* A plant that normally requires two years to reach maturity. [< L *bi-* two + *annus* year]

bin oc u lars (bə nok′ yə lərz, bī nok′ yə lərz), *n.* A pair of telescopes joined together to use with both eyes at once. [< L *bīnī* two, double + *oculāris* of the eyes (< *oculus* eye)]

bi og ra phy (bī og′ rə fē, bē og′ rə fē), *n. pl.* **-phies** A written record of a person's life history, often in story form. [Gk. *biographia* < *bios* life + *graphia* (< *graphein* to write)]

bi ol o gy (bī ol′ ə jē), *n.* 1. The science of plant and animal life. 2. The plant and animal life of a certain area. [< Gk. *bios* life + *-logy* study]

book keep ing (bük′ kē′ ping), *n.* The work of recording the accounts and transactions of a business.

bore[1] (bôr, bōr), *v.* **bored, bor ing** To make a hole in or through, as by drilling. [< ME *boren* < OE *borian*]

bore[2] (bôr, bōr), *v.* **bored, bor ing** To make weary and uninterested with dullness or repetition. —*n.* That which bores. [Origin unknown]

bore[3] (bôr, bōr), *n.* A large wave rushing upstream because of the rising tide in a narrowing channel. [< ME *bare* wave < Old Norse *bāra*]

bore[4] Past tense of bear.

borne (bôrn), *v.* Past participle of **bear.** 1. Carry: *The news was borne by angels.* 2. To hold the weight: *Slender pillars had borne the balcony.* 3. Put up with; endure: *having borne hardships.* 4. Produce; bring forth: *The strawberries have borne well.* [< ME *beren* < OE *beran*]

boul e vard (bül′ ə värd′, bü′ lə värd′), *n.* A wide street often lined with trees. [< OF *boloart* originally the passage along a rampart. Doublet of BULWARK.]

bou quet (bō kā′, bü kā′), *n.* 1. A cluster of flowers, often in a vase. 2. An aroma typical of a wine. [< F *bosquet* thicket < *bosc* forest, of Germanic origin]

breadth (bredth), *n.* 1. The width of a surface. 2. A piece of something that is usually cut a certain width: *It took three breadths of carpet to do the room.* [< ME *brede* < OE *brǣd*]

bril lian cy (bril′ yən sē), *n.* Brightness. [< F

brillant < *briller* to shine < Ital *brillare* < *brillo*
beryl < L *beryllus*] Also **brilliance.**

bro chure (brō shûr′), *n.* A pamphlet or booklet.
[< F a stitched book < *brocher* to stitch < *broche*
knitting needle]

buf fa lo (buf′ ə lō′), *n. pl.* **-los, -loes,** or **buffalo**
1. The bison of North America, a member of the
cattle family that has a great, shaggy head and
short, curved horns. 2. One of several kinds of
oxen that live in Asia and Africa, as the water
buffalo. [Ital. or Port. *búfalo* < L *būfalus* <
bubalus < Gk. *boubalos*]

bum ble bee (bum′ bəl bē′), *n.* A large, hairy bee
that lives in a small colony and makes a loud
buzzing sound. [ME *bomblen* + OE *bēo*]

bu reau (byûr′ ō), *n. pl.* **-reaus, -reaux** (byûr′ ōz)
1. A piece of furniture resembling a chest of
drawers. 2. A certain part of government affairs:
Federal Bureau of Investigation. 3. An organization which handles business affairs or gives
information: *travel bureau.* [< F desk, cloth
cover for desks < OF *burel* woolen cloth < L
burra shaggy garment]

buy er (bī′ ər) *n.* 1. A person who buys something.
2. A person whose occupation is buying mer-
chandise for a store or other business. [OE
bycgan]

C

caf e te ri a (kaf′ i tēr′ ē ə), *n.* An eating place
where people help themselves instead of being
waited on. [< Mex. Sp. *cafetería* coffee shop <
café coffee]

cal o rie (kal′ ə rē), *n.* The unit used to measure the
amount of energy that foods produce. [< F < L
calor heat]

cam ou flage (kam′ ə fläzh′, kam′ ə fläj′), *n.* The
disguised appearance given to an object to hide
it from enemies. —*v.* To give an object a disguised appearance: *camouflage the nest with
grass.* [< F *camoufler* to disguise < Ital. *camuf-
fare*]

cam paign (kam pān′), *n.* A series of efforts planned
to gain a certain result. —*v.* To engage in a series
of battles for a desired end. [< F *campagne*
battlefield < Ital. *campagna* < L *campānia* open
country < *campus* field]

had, māde, cär; then, mē, hërd; dim, hīde; not, hōme, ôr;
oil, loud; sun, pùll, blüe; ch, such; ng, sing; sh, she; th, with;
ᵺ, the; zh, vision;

ə represents *a* in ago, *e* in open, *i* in pencil, *o* in wagon,
u in cactus.

can cel la tion (kan′ sə lā′ shən), *n.* 1. The act of
annulling or rendering void. 2. That which has
been canceled. 3. Marks made to cross out something that has been canceled. [< L *cancellāre* to
cross out < *cancelli* lattice]

can di date (kan′ di dāt′, kan′ di dit), *n.* Someone
who seeks or is suggested by others to fill a position or office: *candidate for teaching school.*
[L *candidātus* clothed in white (from the white
togas worn by Romans seeking office) < *candidus* white]

ca noe (kə nü′), *n.* A lightweight boat with pointed
ends used with paddles. —*v.* **-noed, -noe ing** To
paddle such a boat: *canoed ten miles.* [< Sp.
canoa, of Cariban origin]

can vass (kan′ vəs), *v.* 1. To examine thoroughly:
The prison guard canvassed all the cells. 2. To
go through an area asking for support, dona-
tions, etc.: *The Red Cross canvassed the whole
county.* —*n.* The act of canvassing or cam-
paigning for support. *The canvass took a week.*
[< *canvas* < ME *canevas* < F *canevaz* < L
cannabis hemp]

can yon (kan′ yən), *n.* A very deep chasm, often
with a stream running through and having high,
steep sides. [Sp. *cañon* < *caña* tube < L *canna*
reed]

ca pac i ty (kə pas′ i tē), *n. pl.* **-ties** 1. The amount
of space inside, which can be filled with people
or things: *capacity of 150 cubic feet.* 2. Talent;
gift: *a capacity for making friends.* 3. The greatest amount which can be done or produced:
loaded to capacity. 4. The qualities of an object:
the capacity of water to extinguish fires. 5. One's
role or position: *capacity as deacon.* [< L *capāc-
itās* < *capāx* spacious]

cap i tal ism (kap′ i təl iz′ əm), *n.* The system in
which individuals rather than the government
own establishments or services that produce
goods to be sold on a free market for whatever

adj.	adjective	*n.*	noun
adv.	adverb	*prep.*	preposition
conj.	conjunction	*pron.*	pronoun
interj.	interjection	*v.*	verb
sing.	singular	*pl.*	plural

profit they can get. [< L *capitālis* < *caput* head]

car bo hy drate (kär′ bō hī′ drāt′), *n.* A chemical compound containing carbon, hydrogen, and oxygen; sugars, starches, and cellulose are carbohydrates.

car di ac (kär′ dē ak′), *adj.* Pertaining to the heart: *cardiac medicine.* [< L *cardiacus* < Gk. *kardiakos* < *kardia* heart]

ca reer (kə rēr′), *n.* 1. One's occupation or profession: *a career in dentistry.* 2. Great speed; peak activity: *full career of a runaway team.* [< F *carrière* race course < *carriera* street < L *carrāria* cart road < *carra* cart]

car i bou (kar′ ə bü′), *n. pl.* **caribou** or **-bous** Reindeer of American Arctic. [Of Algonquian origin]

car ton (kär′ tən), *n.* 1. A cardboard or pasteboard box. 2. The amount that such a box holds: *a carton of juice.* [< Ital. *cartone* pasteboard < *carta* card < L *charta* leaf of papyrus]

cat a log (kat′ əl ôg′, kat′ əl og′), *n.* A publication of a list of items, often with a description of them. —*v.* To make such a list. [< Gk. *catalogos* < *katalegein* to list < *kata* down + *legein* to count] Also **catalogue.**

cat a ract (kat′ ə rakt′), *n.* 1. A steep waterfall. 2. A flood. 3. A darkening of the eye lens, often causing partial or total blindness. [< L *cataracta* < Gk. *katauraktēs* < *katarassein* to dash down < *kata* down + *rassein* to strike]

cat e go ry (kat′ i gôr′ ē, kat′ ə gōr′ ē), *n. pl.* **-ies** A division of people or things according to their similarities; classification. [< Gk. *katēgoria* to predicate < *kata-* against + *agora* assembly]

cau tion (kô′ shən), *n.* Carefulness so as to avoid injury or accident; wariness. —*v.* To advise to be careful; to warn. [< L *cautiō* < *cavēre* to take care]

cease (sēs), *v.* **ceased, ceas ing** To come to an end; discontinue. [< L *cessāre* to stop < *cēdere* to yield]

ce les tial (sə les′ chəl), *adj.* 1. Of the sky or heavens: *The moon is a celestial body.* 2. Pertaining to heaven as the dwelling place of God: *celestial home.* 3. Supremely good or beautiful: *celestial singing.* [< ML *celestiālis* < L *caelestis* < *caelum* sky] —**ce les′ tial ly** *adv.*

cen ti pede (sen′ tə pēd′), *n.* A wormlike arthropod having one pair of legs for each segment of its body. [< L *centipeda* < *centum* hundred + *pes* foot]

cer e mo ny (ser′ ə mō′ nē), *n. pl.* **-nies** 1. A special act or service performed for a special occasion such as at a Communion service, wedding, etc. 2. Very mannerly behavior: *opened the door with ceremony.* 3. Observance of tradition and form: *Do not let ceremony take the place of worship.* [< ME *cerimonie* < L *caerimonia* religious rite]

cer tain ty (sėr′ tən tē), *n. pl.* **-ties** 1. Freedom from doubt; conviction that something is certain or unquestionable. 2. An established fact: *Christ's return is a certainty.* [< L *certus* < *cernere* to determine]

cer tif i cate (sər tif′ i kit), *n.* 1. A written document to verify something: *birth certificate.* 2. A document stating that one is qualified to practice in a certain profession. [< L *certificātum* < *certificāre* < *certus* certain + *facere* to make]

cer ti fy (sėr′ tə fī′), *v.* **-fied, -fy ing, -fies** 1. To proclaim something to be true, often by a written statement. 2. To guarantee something. [< L *certificāre*]

chal lenge (chal′ ənj), *n.* 1. A difficulty that either stimulates determination to overcome or brings defeat. 2. A call to explain one's actions: *God's challenge humbled Job.* 3. A questioning or doubting of another's statements or beliefs: *The Anabaptists used Scripture to answer every challenge.* —*v.* **-lenged, -leng ing** To demand an answer, an explanation, or an action. [< ME *chalenge* < OF *chalenger* to accuse < L *calumniari* to accuse falsely < *calumnia* < *calvi* to deceive]

chap er on (shap′ ə rōn′), *n.* An older person who accompanies a younger person or a group of young people to keep vigilance. *v.* **-roned, -ron ing, -rones** To act as a chaperon. [< OF *chaperon* hood < *chape* covering] Also **chaperone.**

char ac ter is tic (kar′ ək tə ris′ tik), *adj.* Typical of one's character or quality: *characteristic humor.* —*n.* A special feature that makes one person or thing different from others: *absorbent characteristic of sponges.* [< L *charactēr* < Gk. *kharaktēr* < *kharassein* to inscribe]

chauf feur (shō′ fər, shō fėr′), *n.* 1. A person who is hired to drive a privately owned automobile. 2. A driver for someone. —*v.* To drive people around. [< F *chauffer* to heat, from the job of stoking a steam automobile]

chem i cal (kem′ i kəl), *adj.* 1. Pertaining to chemistry. 2. Made by using chemistry: *chemical fertilizer.* —*n.* Any substance that is made by using the science of chemistry: *explosive chemical.* [< L *chimicus* < *alchimicus* < *alchymia* alchemy]

choc o late (chô′ kə lit, chok′ lit), *n.* 1. A substance obtained by roasting and grinding cacao seeds. 2. Candy or drink made with chocolate. —*adj.* 1. Flavored with chocolate. 2. Dark brown. [< Sp. < Aztec *xocolatl* < *xococ* bitter + *atl* water]

chord[1] (kôrd), *n.* 1. Two or more notes of music sounded together in harmony. 2. An emotional feeling: *The story struck a compassionate chord.* [< *accord* agreement < OF *acorde* < *acorder* to agree < L *accordāre* < *ad-* to + *cor* heart]

chord[2] (kôrd), *n.* 1. A line that connects two points on a curve. 2. The string of a musical instrument. 3. A part of a bridge truss. [< OF *corde* < L *chorda* < Gk. *khordē* string of a musical instrument]

chron i cle (kron′ i kəl), *n.* 1. A record of happenings written in the order in which they took place. 2. **Chronicles** The thirteenth and fourteenth books of the Bible. —*v.* To put on record: *chronicle the accidents in the neighborhood.* [< ME *cronicle* < F *chronique* < Gk. *khronika* annals < *khronikos* of time < *khronos* time]

cir cu la tion (sėr′ kyə lā′ shən), *n.* 1. A moving around or through in a circular manner: *blood circulation.* 2. A spreading abroad, as of news or information: *circulation of rumors.* 3. The number of copies distributed, as of a newspaper or magazine: *This magazine has a circulation*

had, mādn, cär; then, mē, hėrd; dim, hīde; not, hōme, ôr; oil, loud; sun, půll, blüe; ch, such; ng, sing; sh, she; th, with; ŦH, the; zh, vision;

ə represents *a* in ago, *e* in open, *i* in pencil, *o* in wagon, *u* in cactus.

of five thousand. [< L *circulare, circulat-* to make round < *circulus* < *circus* circle]

ci vil ian (si vil′ yən), *n.* One who is not serving in a police, military, or firefighting force. —*adj.* Pertaining to civilians: *civilian labor.* [< L *cīvīlis* < *cīvis* citizen]

civ i lized (siv′ ə līzd′), *adj.* 1. Highly developed; not primitive. 2. Refined; mannerly. [< L *cīvīlis*]

clas si fi ca tion (klas′ ə fi kā′ shən), *n.* The act or result of arranging things into classes according to color, function, etc. [< L *classis* group, class]

clas si fy (klas′ ə fī′), *v.* **-fied, -fy ing, -fies** To arrange in classes or groups according to some system. [< L *classis*]

colo nel (kėr′ nəl), *n.* An officer in the U.S. Army, Air Force, or Marine Corps. [Alteration of obsolete *coronel* < O Ital. *colonello* < *colonna* column of soldiers < L *columna* pillar]

com men ta tor (kom′ ən tā′ tər), *n.* 1. One who writes comments. 2. A newswriter or broadcaster. [< L *commentum* interpretation < *comminīscī* to devise]

com merce (kom′ ərs), *n.* The business between states or nations; buying and selling of goods, esp. in large amounts. [< L *commercium* < *com* together + *merx* merchandise]

com mu ni cate (kə myü′ ni kāt′), *v.* **-cat ed, -cat ing** To transmit ideas or knowledge to another person by words or other symbols. [< L *commūnicāre* < *commūnicāt* < *commūnis* common]

com mun ion (kə myün′ yən), *n.* 1. An intimate sharing of thoughts and feelings; close fellowship. 2. **Communion** The Christian ordinance in which the bread and the cup are shared together in memory of Christ's suffering and death; the Lord's Supper. [< L *commūnio* multiple participation < *commūnis* common]

com mu nism (kom′ yə niz′ əm), *n.* A system in which the private ownership of property has

adj.	adjective	*n.*	noun
adv.	adverb	*prep.*	preposition
conj.	conjunction	*pron.*	pronoun
interj.	interjection	*v.*	verb
sing.	singular	*pl.*	plural

been partially or totally abolished by the government. The government also controls the production and distribution of goods and sometimes other rights of individuals, based on the idea that all goods will be shared equally by the people. [< F *communisme* < *commun* common]

com pan ion (kəm pan′ yən), *n.* 1. One who accompanies someone; comrade. 2. One of a pair, as of shoes; mate: *The companion to this sock is lost.* 3. Life companion; spouse. [< OF *compaignon* < L *compāniō* < *com-* together + *pānis* bread]

com pass (kum′ pəs, kom′ pəs), *n.* 1. An instrument for determining direction. 2. An instrument for drawing circles. 3. Area within specified boundaries; range, scope: *The salesman was outside the compass of his route.* —*v.* 1. To travel around (something); make a circuit of: *Nehemiah compassed the city wall.* 2. Hem in; surround: *Jerusalem was compassed about with armies.* [< OF *compasser* to measure < L *compassāre* < *com-* together + *passus* step (< *pandere* to stretch)]

com pe tent (kom′ pi tənt), *adj.* Having the proper qualifications for a job, a duty, etc.: *a competent doctor.* [< L *competēns* < *competere* to be suitable < *com-* together + *petere* to seek]

com pli ment (kom′ plə mənt), *n.* 1. Words of praise, admiration, or congratulation to another. 2. An act of courtesy or respect: *Grandfather appreciated the compliment of the offered chair.* 3. **compliments** Greetings; good wishes: *Take my compliments to your mother.* —*v.* To give words of praise or admiration to another: *Cornelius complimented Peter for coming.* [< Sp. *cumplimento* < *cumplir* to complete < L *complēre*]

com pro mise (kom′ prə mīz′), *n.* 1. Settlement of a disagreement in which both sides surrender some of their ideas. 2. The result of such a settlement. —*v.* **-mised, -mis ing** 1. To settle a disagreement by a partial yielding on both sides. 2. To expose oneself to dangerous or questionable practice. [< OF *compromis* < L *comprōmissum* mutual promise < *comprōmittere* < *com-* together + *prōmittere* promise]

con fer (kən fėr′), *v.* **-ferred, -fer ring** 1. To counsel together; to discuss; talk things over. 2. To give as a gift: *Jesus conferred healing on many lepers.* [< L *cōnferre* < *com-* together + *ferre* to bring]

con junc tion (kən jungk′ shən), *n.* 1. A part of speech that connects words, phrases, clauses, or sentences. 2. A combination: *heat in conjunction with drought.* 3. The position of two heavenly bodies in the same longitude. [< L *conjunctus* < *conjungere* to join together < *com-* together + *jungere* to join]

con sci en tious (kon′ shē en′ shəs), *adj.* 1. Careful to obey the conscience. 2. Careful and thorough; painstaking: *a conscientious pupil.* [< ML *cōnscientiōsus* < *cōnscientia* conscience < *cōnsciēns* < *cōnscīre* to know wrong < *com-* (intensive) + *scire* to know]

con spic u ous (kən spik′ yü əs), *adj.* 1. Easy to be seen; obvious: *a conspicuous hole.* 2. Drawing attention because of being remarkable or outstanding: *a conspicuous example of faithfulness.* [< L *cōnspicuus* < *cōnspicere* to observe < *com-* (intensive) + *specere* to look]

con stel la tion (kon′ stə lā′ shən), *n.* 1. An arrangement of stars, thought to resemble a figure. 2. The part of the heavens occupied by such a group. [< L *cōnstellātiō* < *com-* together + *stēlla* star]

con struc tion (kən struk′ shən), *n.* 1. The act or process of constructing something. 2. Something that is built; structure. 3. The manner in which something is put together: *sturdy construction.* [< L *cōnstrūct-* < *com-* together + *struere* to pile up]

con sult ant (kən sul′ tənt), *n.* 1. One who gives professional advice. 2. One who seeks advice in important matters. [< L *cōnsultāre* < *cōnsulere* to take counsel]

con sul ta tion (kon′ səl tā′ shən), *n.* 1. The act of seeking advice: *in consultation with the ministry.*

contemplate 123 crisis

2. A meeting where advice is given or things are talked over. [< L *cōnsultāre*]

con tem plate (kon′ təm plāt′), *v.* **-plat ed, -plat ing** 1. To look at carefully. 2. To consider thoughtfully. [< L *contemplat-* < *com-* (intensive) + *templum* a place for observing omens]

con tin u ous (kən tin′ yü əs), *adj.* Continuing; going or keeping on without interruption; constant. [< L *continuus* < *continēre* to hold together < *com-* together + *tenēre* to hold] —**con tin′ u ous ly** *adv.*

con trite (kən trīt′, kon′ trīt′), *adj.* Showing penitence: *a contrite expression.* [< L *contrītus* < *conterere* to crush < *com-* (intensive) + *terere* to grind] —**con trite′ ly** *adv.* —**con trite′ ness** *n.*

con tri tion (kən trish′ ən), *n.* Deep regret or sorrow for past sins or mistakes. [< L *contritus*]

con trol (kən trōl′), *v.* **-trolled, -trol ling** 1. To direct; regulate; govern. 2. Restrain, as an emotion: *control one's anger.* —*n.* 1. Power to keep (a person or thing) under one's command: *control of the classroom.* 2. That which controls, as a device on a machine. 3. A standard used to check the results of a scientific experiment. [< ME *countrollen* < OF *contrarotulare* < L *controretulare* to check by duplicate register < *contrarotulus* checklist < *contrā-* against + *rotulus* roll] —**con trol′ ler** *n.*

con ven ient (kən vēn′ yənt), *adj.* 1. Well suited to meet a need; handy. 2. Easily done with no problems: *Is it convenient for you to mail the letter?* 3. Within easy reach: *convenient file.* [< L *conveniēns* < *convenīre* to be suitable < *com-* together + *venīre* to come] —**con ven′ ient ly** *adv.*

con vey (kən vā′), *v.* 1. To move from one place to another. 2. Transmit: *Nerves convey impulses.* 3. To get a message across: *Her smile conveyed understanding.* 4. Move ownership to someone else: *The land was conveyed to his son.* [< ML *conviāre* to escort < *com-* with + *via* road. Doublet of CONVOY.]

cor re spon dence (kôr′ i spon′ dəns, kor′ i spon′ dəns), *n.* 1. Being in agreement: *in correspondence with God's Word.* 2. Similarity in structure or function: *correspondence of rice to potatoes in our diets.* 3. The practice of writing letters. 4. Letters written and received. [< L *correspondēre* < *com-* together + *respondēre* to respond]

cor sage (kôr säzh′), *n.* 1. An arrangement of flowers worn at the waist or shoulder. 2. Top part of a woman's dress. [< OF *cors* body < L *corpus*]

cos mic (koz′ mik), *adj.* 1. Having to do with the cosmos or universe: *cosmic elements.* 2. Vast; limitless. [Gk. < *kosmos* universe]

coun sel or (koun′ sə lər), *n.* 1. One who gives counsel. 2. Lawyer. 3. An instructor at a summer camp. [< ME *counseil* < OF *conseil* < L *cōnsilium*] Also **counsellor.**

coun te nance (koun′ tə nəns), *n.* 1. The face. 2. The expression of the face. —*v.* Support or approve: *cannot countenance tardiness.* **keep one's countenance** Not showing emotions. [< ME *contenaunce* < OF *contenir* to behave < L *continēre* < *com-* together + *tenēre* to hold]

cou ri er (kür′ ē ər, kėr′ ē ər), *n.* 1. A messenger in haste on an urgent errand. 2. One sent on official business. 3. One who secretly transfers information. [< OF *courrier* < Ital. *corriere* < *correre* to run < L *currere*]

coy o te (kī ō′ tē, kī′ ōt′), *n. pl.* **-tes** or **-te** A wolflike animal living on the prairies of western North America. [< Nahuatl *cóyotl*]

cran ber ry (kran′ ber′ ē, kran′ bər ē), *n. pl.* **-ries** 1. A creeping shrub, bearing tart red berries. 2. The berry of this shrub used for jelly, sauce, etc. [< Low G *Kraanbere* < *Kraan* crane + *-bere* berry]

cres cen do (krə shen′ dō), *n. pl.* **-dos** In music, a gradual increase in volume. [Ital. *crescere* to increase < L *crēscere*]

cri sis (krī′ sis), *n. pl.* **crises** (krī′ sēz′) 1. A situation or point that demands that a decision be made: *a financial crisis.* 2. A sudden change in the course of a disease, favorable or unfavorable. [< Gk. *krisis* < *krinein* to separate]

adj.	adjective	n.	noun
adv.	adverb	prep.	preposition
conj.	conjunction	pron.	pronoun
interj.	interjection	v.	verb
sing.	singular	pl.	plural

crit i cism (krit′ i siz′ əm), *n*. 1. Disapproving or faultfinding comments. 2. Skilled evaluation of art or writings. [< L *criticus* < Gk. *kritikos* able to discern < *krinein* to separate]

cro quet (krō kā′), *n*. An outdoor game in which mallets are used to hit wooden balls through wickets. [< F variant of *crochet* hook]

cru sade (krü sād′), *n*. 1. Often **Crusade.** One of the military expeditions by Europeans in the twelfth and thirteenth centuries in an effort to take the Holy Land from the Muslims. 2. A religious war. 3. A vigorous movement against an evil or for a cause: *a crusade against drugs.* —*v*. **-sad ed, -sad ing** To take part in a crusade. [< ML *cruciata* < *crux* cross] (The Crusaders wore the cross symbol.)

cu ri os i ty (kyür′ ē os′ i tē), *n. pl.* **-ties** 1. An intense desire to know. 2. Excessive eagerness to know; nosiness. 3. Something strange and unique: *A three-legged chick is a curiosity.* [< L *cūriōsus* careful, inquisitive < *cūra* care]

curse (kėrs), *v*. **cursed** or **curst, curs ing** 1. To ask that evil or injury would come upon (a person or thing). 2. To swear at. 3. To bring trouble or torment on. —*n*. 1. A prayer that harm or evil would fall. 2. Harm or evil that befalls as if in answer to prayer (perhaps superstitious). 3. One that is accursed. [< OE *curs* a curse]

cus tom ar y (kus′ tə mer′ ē), *adj*. 1. According to the usual procedure: *customary starting time.* 2. Based on custom or tradition rather than on a written law: *customary greeting.* [< ME *custume* < OF *costume* < L *cōnsuētūdō* < *cōnsuēscere* to accustom < *com-* (intensive) + *suēscere* to become accustomed]

cyl in der (sil′ ən dər), *n*. 1. Any object which is long and round with flat ends. It can be solid or hollow. 2. A part in some engines. 3. The rotating part in a revolver that holds the cartridges. 4. A rotating part in a printing press. [< L *cylindrus* < Gk. *kulindros* < *kulindein* to roll]

D

dachs hund (däks′ hünt′, däk′ sənt), *n*. A dog of a breed from Germany with a long body, short-haired coat, drooping ears, and very short legs. [< G *Dachs* badger + *Hund* dog]

deal (dēl), *v*. **dealt** (delt), **deal ing** 1. Having to do with: *Algebra deals with literal numbers.* 2. To act in a certain way toward others: *deal fairly.* 3. Take action: *deal with the offender.* 4. To do business: *He deals in lumber.* 5. Give, administer: *"Deal thy bread to the hungry" (Isaiah 58:7).* —*n*. 1. In a game, the distribution of cards. 2. Amount: *a great deal of time.* [< ME *delen* < OE *dāēlan* to divide, share]

Dec a logue (dek′ ə lôg′, dek′ ə log′), *n*. 1. The Ten Commandments in the Bible. 2. **decalogue** Any group of ten commandments. [< L *decalogus* < Gk. *dekalogos* < *deka* ten + *logos* word] Also **Dec a log** and **dec a log.**

dec i mal (des′ ə məl), *adj*. Pertaining to or based upon ten: *a decimal system of measures.* —*n*. A fraction or mixed number written in decimal form, as 0.25 or 8.76. [< ML *decimālis* of tithes < *decimus* tenth < *decem* ten]

dec o ra tion (dek′ ə rā′ shən), *n*. 1. An object or group of objects used to decorate. 2. A ribbon, badge, or other emblem of honor. 3. The act of decorating. [< L *decorāre* < *decus* ornament]

ded i cate (ded′ i kāt′), *v*. **-cat ed, -cat ing** 1. Set apart as sacred: *dedicate the house of God.* 2. To celebrate the opening of a bridge, building, etc., with an official ceremony. 3. To give up oneself to wholly serve some purpose or person: *dedicate my life.* 4. To inscribe a book or other written work to a person as a mark of affection or esteem. [< ME *dedicaten* < L *dēdicāre* < *dē-* apart + *dicāre* to say]

de duct (di dukt′), *v*. To take away (one amount from another); subtract. [< L *dēdūcere* < *dē-* away + *dūcere* to lead] —**de duct′ i ble** *adj*. —**de duc′ tion** *n*.

deem (dēm), *v*. To form an opinion; consider: *deem the bill settled.* [< OE *dēman* to judge]

deep (dēp), *adj*. 1. Going far down below a surface.

defendant · 125 · discrepancy

2. Going a long way from front to back: *a deep cupboard.* 3. Coming from far down: *a deep breath.* 4. Difficult to understand: *a deep sermon.* 5. Very absorbed or involved: *deep in thought.* 6. Rich and strong in color: *deep blue.* [OE *dēop*] —**deep′ ly** *adv.*

de fen dant (di fen′ dənt), *n.* One who is sued at law. [< ME *defenden* < OF *defendre* < L *dēfendere* to ward off]

de form (di fôrm′), *v.* Spoil the form or shape of; disfigure. [< L *dēformāre* < *dē-* off + *forma* form]

de hy drate (dē hī′ drāt′), *v.* **-drat ed, -drat ing** To dry by removing moisture from. [< *dē-* remove + HYDRATE (< Gk. *hudōr* water)]

de lin quent (di ling′ kwənt, di lin′ kwənt), *adj.* 1. Failing in one's duty. 2. Payment that is overdue: *delinquent taxes.* —*n.* An offender: *juvenile delinquent.* [< L *dēlinquēns* offending < *dē-* (intensive) + *linquere* to leave]

de moc ra cy (di mok′ rə sē), *n. pl.* **-cies** 1. Government in which the people are allowed to have a voice. 2. A country, state, or government so governed: *The U. S. is a democracy.* [< Gk. *dēmokratia* < *dēmos* people + *kratos* rule]

de sir a ble (di zīr′ ə bəl), *adj.* Of such quality as to be worthwhile; pleasing. [< OF *desirer* to long for < L *dēsīderāre*]

de sir ous (di zī′ rəs), *adj.* Having or expressing desire. [< OF *desirer*]

de struc tive (di struk′ tiv), *adj.* 1. Causing destruction: *a destructive storm.* 2. Tearing down; not upbuilding: *destructive influence.* [< L *dēstructus* < *dēstruere* to destroy] —**de struc′ tive ly** *adv.* —**de struc′ tive ness** *n.*

de ter gent (di tèr′ jənt), *n.* 1. A cleaning substance made from chemicals rather than from fats and lye. 2. Any soap. [< L *detergēre* < *dē-* off + *tergēre* to wipe]

de ter rent (di tèr′ ənt, di tur′ ənt), *adj.* Preventing or hindering: *deterrent price.* —*n.* That which deters. [< L *dēterrēre* < *dē-* away + *terrēre* to frighten]

de vo tion al (di vō′ shə nəl), *adj.* Pertaining to devotion: *devotional poem.* —*n.* A short worship service. [< L *devovēre* < *dē-* (intensive) + *vovēre* to vow]

di ag no sis (dī′ əg nō′ sis), *n. pl.* **-ses** (-sēz) 1. The process of identifying a disease through examination. 2. The results of a careful study. [< Gk. *diagnōsis* discernment < *diagignōskein* to distinguish < *dia-* apart + *gignōskein* to know]

di a gram (dī′ ə gram′), *n.* A sketch or drawing to show how something works or how parts are related. —*v.* **-gramed, -gram ing** or **-grammed, -gram ming** To make a drawing or sketch for explanation. [< L *diagramma* < Gk. *diagraphein* to mark out < *dia-* apart + *graphein* to write]

di am e ter (dī am′ i tər), *n.* 1. A straight line passing from side to side through the center of a circle or sphere. 2. The length of such a line. [< Gk. *diametros* < *dia-* through, apart + *metron* measure]

di a ry (dī′ ə rē), *n. pl.* **-ries** A book in which to record daily events; journal. [< L *diārium* < *diēs* day]

dic ta tor (dik′ tā′ tər, dik tā′ tər), *n.* 1. A ruler who has supreme authority in government. 2. One who dictates. [< L *dictāre* said often < *dīcere* to say]

die sel (dē′ zəl, dē′ səl), *n.* 1. An internal combustion engine that ignites fuel with the heat of highly compressed air. 2. A vehicle with a diesel engine. [< Rudolf Diesel, German engineer who invented the diesel engine]

diph the ri a (dif thēr′ ē ə, dip thēr′ ē ə), *n.* A contagious disease of the throat causing difficulty in breathing, high fever, and weakness. [< Gk. *diphthera* piece of leather]

dis cord (dis′ kôrd′), *n.* 1. Disagreement. 2. Disharmony in music tones. 3. A harsh sound. [< L *discordia* strife < *discors* < *dis-* apart + *cors* heart]

dis course (dis′ kôrs′), *n.* A speech or written discussion of a subject. —*v.* **-coursed, -cours ing** To speak or write at length: *We heard him discourse on tree grafting.* [< ME *discours* < L *discursus* discussion < *discurrere* to run about, to speak at length < *dis-* apart + *currere* to run]

dis crep an cy (di skrep′ ən sē), *n. pl.* **-cies**

had, māde, cär; then, mē, hèrd; dim, hīde; not, hōme, ôr; oil, loud; sun, pull, blüe; ch, such; ng, sing; sh, she; th, with; ŦH, the; zh, vision;

ə represents *a* in ago, *e* in open, *i* in pencil, *o* in wagon, *u* in cactus.

disqualify   **126**   **embroidery**

adj.	adjective	*n.*	noun
adv.	adverb	*prep.*	preposition
conj.	conjunction	*pron.*	pronoun
interj.	interjection	*v.*	verb
sing.	singular	*pl.*	plural

Disagreement between facts; inconsistency: *discrepancy between the exercises and the answer key.* [< L *discrepāns* < *discrepāre* to disagree < *dis-* apart + *crepāre* to rattle] Also **discrepance.**

dis qual i fy (dis kwol′ ə fī′), *v.* **-fied, -fy ing, -fies** 1. To render unfit; disable. 2. To declare something or someone unfit. [< L *dis* apart, asunder + *quālificāre* (< *quālis* of such a kind + *facere* to make)]

dis sat is fy (dis sat′ is fī′), *v.* **-fied, -fying, -fies** To fail to satisfy. [< L *dis* apart, asunder + *satisfacere* (< *satis* sufficient + *facere* to make)]

di vin i ty (di vin′ i tē), *n. pl.* **-ties** 1. A divine being; God. 2. The study of God and divine things. [< L *dīvīnus* < *dīvus* godhead; deity]

dor mi to ry (dôr′ mi tôr′ ē, dôr′ mi tōr′ ē), *n. pl.* **-ries** A building with many sleeping rooms, esp. at a school or college. [< L *dormītōrium* < *dormīre* to sleep]

dra mat ic (drə mat′ ik), *adj.* 1. Pertaining to drama or the theater. 2. Striking in appearance; forcefully effective: *dramatic storm.* [< Gk. *dramatikos* < *drama* < *dran* to do]

drea ry (drēr′ ē), *adj.* **drear i er, drear i est** Cheerless; gloomy. [< OE *drēorig* sad, bloody < *drēor* gore]

drown (droun), *v.* 1. To die under water because of suffocation. 2. To kill by putting in water or other liquid. 3. To overpower a sound by a louder sound: *Thunder drowned out my words.* [< ME *drounen,* of Scandinavian origin]

du al (dü′ əl, dyü′ əl), *adj.* Having two parts; double. [< L *duālis* < *duo* two] **—du' al ly** *adv.* **—du al′ i ty** *n.*

du plex (dü′ pleks′, dyü′ pleks′), *adj.* Having two parts; double: *duplex windows.* —*n.* A house divided into two living units. [< L < *duo* two + *plicāre* to fold]

dy nam ic (dī nam′ ik), *adj.* 1. Pertaining to energy or motion. 2. Active; very much alive: a *dynamic personality.* [< Gk. *dunamikos* < *dunamis* power]

E

e clipse (i klips′), *n.* A total or partial blocking of light when one heavenly body enters the shadow of, or is hidden by, another heavenly body. —*v.* **-clipsed, -clips ing** To surpass; outshine: *Daniel's wisdom eclipsed that of all the other wise men.* [< L *eclīpsis* < Gk. *ekleīpsis* < *ekleipein* to fail to appear < *ek-* out + *leipein* to leave]

ed i to ri al (ed′ i tôr′ ē əl, ed′ i tōr′ ē əl), *n.* A newspaper or magazine article expressing the views of the editor or publisher. —*adj.* Of or by an editor. [< L *editio* publication < *edere* to publish < *ex-* out + *dare* give]

ef fi cient (i fish′ ənt), *adj.* Able to produce the desired results without wasted time, energy, or expense: *efficient housewife.* [L < *efficiēns* < *efficere* to effect]

e lab o rate (*adj.* i lab′ ər it, *v.* i lab′ ə rāt′), *adj.* 1. Done with exactness; done with much attention to complicated details. 2. Having many fine details: *an elaborate building.* —*v.* **-rat ed, -rat ing** 1. To work out with great care and detail. 2. To explain in detail: *elaborate on your answer.* [< L *ēlabōrāre* < *ex-* out + *labōrāre* to work]

e lapse (i laps′), *v.* **-lapsed, -laps ing** To pass by; slip away: *before many minutes elapse.* [< L *ēlābī* < *ex-* away + *lābī* to slip]

el e ment (el′ ə mənt), *n.* 1. One of the parts that all matter is made of. 2. A substance made of atoms that are chemically alike and cannot be separated into different substances by chemical means: *Gold and carbon are elements.* 3. The forces of the atmosphere, esp. in unpleasant weather. 4. A part in an electrical device. 5. Something basic that must be learned before one can advance; rudiment. [< L *elementum*]

el i gi ble (el′ i jə bəl), *adj.* Having the proper qualifications for a certain position or job: *eligible for mayor.* [< L *ēligere* to select < *ex-* out + *legere* to choose]

em broi der (em broi′ dər), *v.* To ornament with stitches on cloth, leather, etc. [OF *embroder* < *en-* in + *broder* to embroider, of Germanic origin]

em broi der y (em broi′ də rē), *n.* 1. The art of

embroidering. 2. A piece of embroidered cloth, leather, etc.

e mer gen cy (i mėr′ jən sē), *n. pl.* **-cies** A serious, unexpected situation that demands immediate action. [(Originally an emerging) < L *ēmergere* < *ex-* out + *mergere* to immerse]

em pha sis (em′ fə sis), *n. pl.* **-pha ses** (-fə sēz) 1. Special importance placed upon something: *emphasis on correct posture.* 2. Stress of voice on a syllable or word. [< Gk. *emphainein* to indicate < *en-* in + *phainein* to show]

em pha size (em′ fə sīz), *v.* **-sized, -siz ing** To stress; attach importance to: *emphasize the need to study.* [< Gk. *emphainein* to indicate < *en-* in + *phainein* to show]

em ploy ee (em ploi′ ē, em′ ploi ē′), *n.* Person who works for another for pay. [< *employ* < OF *emploier* < L *implicāre* < *in-* in + *plicāre* to fold]

em ploy ment (em ploi′ mənt), *n.* 1. Work done for another for pay. 2. An activity one is engaged in.

en coun ter (en koun′ tər), *v.* 1. To meet without prearrangement. 2. To be faced with: *encounter difficulties.* —*n.* 1. An unplanned meeting. 2. A meeting of enemies. [< OF *encontrer* to meet < L *incontrāre* < *in-* in + *contrā* against]

en cour age (en kėr′ ij), *v.* **-aged, -ag ing** 1. Inspire with courage, cheer, etc.; hearten. 2. Be favorable to; promote: *encourage rapid growth.* [< ME *encouragen* < OF *encoragier* < *en-* in + *corage* courage (< L *cor* heart)]

en dure (en dür′, en dyür′), *v.* **-dured, -dur ing** 1. Continue existing; last. 2. To put up with patiently or firmly (as pain or hardship). [< OF *endurer* < L *indūrāre* to make hard < *in-* (intensive) + *durare* harden (< *dūrus* hard)]

en er gy (en′ ər jē), *n. pl.* **-gies** 1. Strength of body or mind. 2. Power from resources: *steam energy.* [< Gk. *energeia* < *energos* active < *en-* at + *ergon* work]

en gage ment (en gāj′ mənt), *n.* 1. The act of being occupied or in use. 2. Betrothal. [< ME *engagen* to pledge something as security for repayment of debt < OF *engager* < *en-* in + *gage* pledge, of Germanic origin]

en gi neer (en′ jə nēr′), *n.* 1. One who takes care of or runs engines. 2. A member of a military corps engaged in construction work, etc. —*v.* 1. Plan, build, or manage as an engineer. 2. Manage skillfully: *He engineered three remodeling jobs.* [< ML *ingeniātor* contriver < *ingenium* skill]

en light en (en līt′ ən), *v.* To instruct with truth and light that frees one from ignorance: *enlighten the heathen.* [ME *lēoht* light]

e nor mous (i nôr′ məs), *adj.* 1. Very great in size or number; immense. 2. *Archaic* Very wicked; shocking; abominable. [< L *ēnormis* < *ē* out + *norma* norm] —**e nor′ mous ly** *adv.*

en thu si as tic (en thü′ zē as′ tik), *adj.* Full of eagerness and zeal. [< Gk. *entheos* godpossessed < *en-* in + *theos* god]

en vi ron ment (en vī′ rən mənt), *n.* Surrounding conditions or circumstances. [< OF *environ* round about < *en-* in + *viron* circle (< *virer* to circle)]

ep i dem ic (ep′ i dem′ ik), *n.* 1. The rapid spread of a contagious disease, causing many people to have it at the same time. 2. The rapid growth of an idea, fashion, etc. [< Gk. *epidēmia* < *epidēmos* prevalent < *epi-* on + *dēmos* people]

ep i der mis (ep′ i dėr′ mis), *n.* The outer layer of the skin, consisting of nonsensitive cells. [< Gk. *epi-* on + *derma* skin]

ep i lep sy (ep′ ə lep′ sē), *n.* A disorder of the nervous system shown by attacks of convulsions and unconsciousness. [< L *epilēpsia* < *epilambanein* to lay hold of < *epi-* on + *lambanein* to take]

e pis tle (i pis′ əl), *n.* A usually long, instructive letter written in formal language. [< Gk. *epistolē* < *epistellein* to send to < *epi-* to + *stellein* to send]

es teem (i stēm′), *v.* 1. To value highly. 2. Consider: *esteem fame of little worth.* —*n.* A very favorable attitude; respect: *held in high esteem.* [< ME *estemen* to appraise < OF *estimer* < L *aestimāre*]

e van gel ist (i van′ jə list), *n.* One who preaches the Gospel, esp. at revival meetings. [< Gk.

---

had, māde, cär; then, mē, hėrd; dim, hīde; not, hōme, ôr; oil, loud; sun, pùll, blüe; ch, such; ng, sing; sh, she; th, with; ŦH, the; zh, vision;

ə represents *a* in ago, *e* in open, *i* in pencil, *o* in wagon, *u* in cactus.

adj.	adjective	*n.*	noun
adv.	adverb	*prep.*	preposition
conj.	conjunction	*pron.*	pronoun
interj.	interjection	*v.*	verb
sing.	singular	*pl.*	plural

euangelos bringing good news < *eu-* good + *angelos* messenger]

ev i dent (ev′ i dənt), *adj.* Clearly seen or understood; plain. [< L *ēvidēns* < *ex-* out + *videns* (< *vidēre* to see)] —**ev i dent ly** (ev′ i dənt lē, ev′ i dent′ lē) *adv.*

ex am ple (ig zam′ pəl), *n.* 1. A sample; representative; specimen: *an example of patience.* 2. A person or thing worthy of imitation: *"Be thou an example."* 3. An arithmetic problem: *a division example.* [< L *exemplum* < *eximere* to take out < *ex-* out + *emere* to take]

ex ceed ing ly (ik sē′ ding lē), *adv.* To a very great degree; extremely: *exceedingly cold.* [< L *excēdere* < *ex-* out + *cēdere* to go]

ex cep tion al (ik sep′ shə nəl), *adj.* Not ordinary; unusual. [< L *excipere* < *ex-* out + *capere* to take] —**ex cep′ tion al ly** *adv.*

ex claim (ik sklām′), *v.* Speak suddenly and strongly; cry out. [< L *exclāmāre* < *ex-* out + *clāmāre* cry out]

ex cur sion (ik skėr′ zhən), *n.* 1. A usually small journey or tour made for pleasure. 2. Sideline or digression from the main topic. [< L *escurrere* to run out < *ex-* out + *currere* to run]

ex haust (ig zôst′), *v.* 1. Use up completely; drain: *exhaust his patience.* 2. Wear out physically; tire. 3. Deal with thoroughly, covering everything of importance: *You will never exhaust the Bible.* —*n.* 1. Waste material that escapes from an engine. 2. A pipe or other outlet through which waste material passes from an engine. [< L *exhaurīre* < *ex-* out + *haurīre* to draw]

ex hi bi tion (ek′ sə bish′ ən), *n.* 1. Demonstration: *an exhibition of diligence.* 2. A public display: *the antique exhibition.* 3. Objects shown publicly. [< L *exhibēre* < *ex-* out + *habēre* to hold]

ex ile (eg′ zīl′, ek′ sīl′), *v.* **-iled, -il ing** 1. To remove a person by force from his country or home as a punishment; banish. 2. To choose to leave one's home or country for a long time. —*n.* One who is exiled: *John was an exile on Patmos.* [< L *exilium* < *exul* exiled person]

ex o dus (ek′ sə dəs), *n.* 1. A departure, usually of a multitude from a place or country. 2. **Exodus** The departure of the Israelites from Egypt. 3. The second book of the Bible containing this account of the Israelites' departure. [< Gk. *exodos* < *ex-* out + *hodos* way]

ex or bi tant (ig zôr′ bi tənt), *adj.* Much too high, as a price: *an exorbitant fee.* [< L *exorbitāre* to deviate < *ex-* out of + *orbita* track]

ex plore (ik splôr′, ik splōr′), *v.* **-plored, -plor ing** 1. To examine systematically; investigate. [< L *explōrāre*]

ex tinct (ik stingkt′), *adj.* 1. No longer alive: *The homing pigeon is extinct.* 2. Inactive: *an extinct volcano.* [< L *extinguere* to extinguish]

ex traor di nar y (ik strôr′ dən er′ ē, ek′ strə ôr′ dən er′ ē), *adj.* Beyond the ordinary; very unusual; exceptional. [< L *extrā* outside + *ōrdinārius* (< *ōrdō* order)]

F

faith ful ly (fāth′ fəl ē), *adv.* In a faithful, or devoted, manner; conscientiously and loyally. [< OF *feid* < L *fidēs* < *fidere* to trust]

fas ci nat ing (fas′ ə nā′ ting), *adj.* Captivating; holding the attention of; attractive: *a fascinating story.* [< L *fascināre* to enchant < *fascinum* witchcraft]

fa tigue (fə tēg′), *n.* 1. Physical or mental weariness due to hard work or effort. 2. An activity that causes weariness. 3. Weakness in metal or other material caused by continued stress. 4. Menial work assignments to soldiers in training. —*v.* **-tigued, -tig uing** Make weary; tire. [< OF < *fatiguer* to tire < L *fatīgāre*]

fa vor ite (fā′ vər it, fāv′ rit), *n.* One that is preferred above others. —*adj.* Most favored. [< Ital. *favorita* < *favorire* to favor < *favore* < L *favēre* to be favorable]

fi nan cial (fə nan′ shəl, fī nan′ shəl), *adj.* Having to do with money: *financial records.* [< ME *finaunce* money supply < OF *finance* gift < *finer* to pay ransom < *fin* end < L *fīnis*]

fis sion (fish′ ən), *n.* The process of splitting into

flammable   129   guarantee

parts; division: *atomic fission.* [< L *fissiō* a cleaving < *fissus* split]

flam ma ble (flam′ ə bəl), *adj.* Easily ignited; inflammable. [< L *flammāre* to flame < *flamma* flame]

flan nel (flan′ əl), *n.* 1. A soft, warm cloth made of wool or cotton. 2. **flannels** A garment made of flannel, as pajamas. [< ME *flannel* a kind of woolen cloth]

flour ish (flėr′ ish), *v.* 1. Grow well; thrive: *flourishing business.* 2. To make showy, sweeping movements; wave: *He flourished the ten-dollar bill.* —*n.* A fancy curve in handwriting: *many flourishes in the signature.* [OF *floriss-* to bloom < L *florere* < *flos* flower] —**flour′ ish ing ly** *adv.*

for mal (fôr′ məl), *adj.* 1. With strict attention to outward forms and ceremonies: *a formal court hearing.* 2. According to set customs or rules: *a formal letter.* [L *formalis* < *fōrma* form] —**for′ mal ly** *adv.*

for mu la (fôr′ myə lə), *n. pl.* **-las** or **-lae** 1. Directions giving the amounts of the ingredients needed for making something; recipe; prescription. 2. A mixture of milk or milk substitute for feeding a baby. 3. The chemical makeup of a substance shown by symbols: *The formula for water is H_2O.* 4. In arithmetic, a rule expressed with symbols: *The formula for the volume of a cylinder is $v = Bh$.* [< L *formalis* < *fōrma* shape]

fraud (frôd), *n.* 1. Dishonesty, trickery, or cheating in dealing. 2. A falsehood used to take money, rights, etc., away from another. 3. A statement, act, etc., that is not what it seems to be; trick. [< OF *fraude* < L *fraus* deceit]

fre quent (frē′ kwənt), *adj.* Happening or coming often. —*v.* Visit often; be present (at a place) regularly: *He frequents the bookstore.* [< L *frequēns* numerous] —**fre′ quent ly** *adv.*

G

gal lop (gal′ əp), *n.* 1. The gait of an animal in which all four feet are off the ground together once in each stride. 2. A ride at a gallop. —*v.* 1. Ride or go at a gallop. 2. Go at a fast pace. 3. Cause to go at a gallop: *gallop a horse.* [< OF *galoper,* of Germanic origin. Doublet of WALLOP.]

had, māde, cär; then, mē, hėrd; dim, hīde; not, hōme, ôr; oil, loud; sun, pull, blüe; ch, such; ng, sing; sh, she; th, with; ᴛH, the; zh, vision;

ə represents *a* in ago, *e* in open, *i* in pencil, *o* in wagon, *u* in cactus.

gal va nize (gal′ və nīz′), *v.* **-nized, -niz ing** 1. To use an electric current to stimulate or shock. 2. To arouse to awareness; startle. 3. To cover iron or steel with zinc to prevent rust. [< Luigi Galvani (an Italian physician)]

ga rage (gə räzh′, gə räj′), *n.* A building in which motor vehicles are parked or serviced. [< F *garer* to protect]

gen er ate (jen′ ə rāt′), *v.* **-rat ed, -rat ing** Bring into being; produce; create: *Friction generates heat.* [< L *generāre* to produce < *genus* birth]

ge ol o gy (jē ol′ ə jē), *n. pl.* **-gies** 1. Study of rocks in the earth's crust. 2. The structure (rocks, rock formation, etc.) of a specific region: *the geology of the West.* [< Gk. *geō-* (< *gē* earth) + *-logy* study]

ge om e try (jē om′ i trē), *n.* The study of angles, lines, points, and the measurement of squares, cubes, spheres, and other plane and solid figures. [< Gk. *geōmetrein* to measure land < *gē* earth + *metron* measure]

gla cier (glā′ shər), *n.* A huge mass of snow compressed into ice, which slides slowly down a mountain. [< F *glace* ice < L *glaciēs*]

gour met (gur mā′, gur′ mā′), *n.* A person skilled in judging fine food and drink. [< OF *gourmet* wine merchant's servant]

grad u a tion (graj′ ü ā′ shən), *n.* 1. The receiving of a degree or a diploma showing that studies have been completed at a school or college. 2. A ceremony at which diplomas are given; commencement. 3. A scale showing degrees for measuring: *The cup was marked in graduation of ounces.* [< L *graduare* < *gradus* step, degree]

grippe (grip), *n.* A flu with inflammation of the respiratory tract, fever, muscular pain, and irritation in the intestinal tract. [< F *gripper* to seize, of Germanic origin]

guar an tee (gar′ ən tē′), *n.* 1. A promise or pledge that a purchased product will function as claimed

hammock   **130**   **immigrant**

adj.	adjective	*n.*	noun
adv.	adverb	*prep.*	preposition
conj.	conjunction	*pron.*	pronoun
interj.	interjection	*v.*	verb
sing.	singular	*pl.*	plural

or the buyer's money will be returned: *The clock has a one-year guarantee.* 2. Person who gives a guarantee. —*v.* **-teed, -tee ing** 1. To give a promise for: *The bakery guarantees fresh bread.* 2. To give security; protect: *Money does not guarantee health.* [OF *guarant* warrant, of Germanic origin. Doublet of WARRANTY.]

H

ham mock (ham′ ək), *n.* A bed consisting of a fabric suspended by the head and foot ends. [< Sp. *hamaca* < Arawak Indian]

han gar (hang′ ər), *n.* A building for housing or repairing airplanes. [< ML *angarium* shed for shoeing horses]

hast y (hā′ stē), *adj.* **hast i er, hast i est** 1. Done or made quickly. 2. Done in a hurry without taking time to think: *a hasty decision.* 3. Easily angered; irritable: *a hasty disposition.* [Of Germanic origin] —**hast′ i ly** *adv.* —**hast′ i ness** *n.*

ha tred (hā′ trid), *n.* Very strong dislike; bitterness. [OE *hatian*]

hel i cop ter (hel′ i kop′ tər), *n.* An aircraft without wings, deriving its lift from the ground and support in the air by propellers or rotors. [< F *hélicoptère* < Gk. *helix* spiral + *pteron* wing]

her e sy (her′ i sē), *n. pl.* **-sies** A religious belief held as false and contrary to the established belief: *The anabaptists were accused of heresy.* [< L *haeresis* < Gk. *hairesis* faction < *haireisthai* to choose]

he ro ic (hi rō′ ik), *adj.* Pertaining to a hero; marked by courage and nobleness: *heroic deed.* [< L < Gk. *hērōs*]

hu mid i ty (hyü mid′ i tē), *n.* Moisture in the air. [< L *hūmidus* be moist]

hu mil i ty (hyü mil′ i tē), *n.* Lowliness of self-esteem; absence of pride. [< L *humilitās* < *humilis* humble < *humus* ground]

hur ri cane (her′ i kān′), *n.* A large whirling storm that develops over the tropic Atlantic Ocean and has winds of 74 miles per hour (119 km/hr.) or more. [< Sp. *huracán* < Arawak]

hy drant (hī′ drənt), *n.* A pipe or cylinder with a valve for drawing water from a water main. [< Gk. *hudōr* water]

hy drau lic (hī drô′ lik), *adj.* 1. Having to do with water or other fluids. 2. Operated by forcing liquid through a small opening. 3. Hardening under water: *hydraulic cement.* [< Gk. *hudraulis* water organ < *hudōr* water + *aulos* pipe]

hy dro gen (hī′ drə jən), *n.* A colorless gas lighter than air, highly flammable, and very abundant in the universe. [< F *hydrogène* < Gk. *hudōr* water + *gène* (< Gk. *genēs* born)]

hyp not ic (hip not′ ik), *adj.* Pertaining to a sleep-like trance called hypnotism. [< Gk. *hupnōtikos* < *hypnoun* to put to sleep < *hupnos* sleep]

I

i ci cle (ī′ si kəl), *n.* A hanging stick of ice formed from water freezing as it drips. [ME *isikle* < OE *is* ice + *ikel* icicle]

i den ti fy (ī den′ tə fī′), *v.* **-fied, -fy ing, -fies** 1. Recognize or verify the identity of a person or thing. 2. Consider oneself as sharing the circumstances or feelings of another person; put oneself in another's situation: *identify with his sorrow.* 3. Consider the same; equate: *identify evil with darkness.* [< ML *identificāre* < *identitās* identity + *facere* to make] —**i den′ ti fi′ er** *n.*

i gua na (i gwä′ nə), *n.* Any of various tropical American lizards often having spiny crests along their backs. [< Sp. < Arawak *iwana*]

il lu mi nate (i lü′ mə nāt′), *v.* **-nat ed, -nat ing** 1. Shed light on: *illuminate the closet.* 2. To make clear by explaining: *Diagrams illuminate the instructions.* 3. To decorate letters or pages with colors and designs: *Old books were often illuminated.* [< L *illūmināre* < *in-* in + *lūmināre* to light up (< *lūmin* light)] —**il lu′ mi na′ tor** *n.*

im mense (i mens′), *adj.* Very large in size or degree: *immense relief.* [< L *immēnsus* < *in-* not + *mēnsus* (< *mētīrī* to measure)]

im mi grant (im′ i grənt), *n.* A person who comes into a foreign country to live. [< L *immigrāre* < *in-* in + *migrāre* to move]

immortal   131   intelligence

im mor tal (i môr′ təl), *adj.* 1. Living forever; death-less. 2. Having to do with deathless beings: *immortal love.* [< L *immortālis* < *in-* not + *mortālis* (< *mors* death)]

in cense[1] (in′ sens′), *n.* 1. A substance giving off a fragrant smell when burned. 2. Any pleasant smell or aroma: *the incense of autumn.* [< L *incēnsum* < *incendere* to set on fire]

in cense[2] (in sens′), *v.* **-censed, -cens ing** Fill with anger; enrage. [< OF *incénser* < L *incēnsus* < *incendere* to set on fire]

in con ven ience (in′ kən vēn′ yəns), *n.* Something that is not convenient; a hindrance. —*v.* **-ienced, -ienc ing** To cause trouble; hinder: *Will a change of schedule inconvenience you?* [< L *inconveniens* < *in-* not + *conveniens* (< *convenire* to be suitable < *com-* together + *venīre* to come)]

in def i nite (in def′ ə nit), *adj.* 1. Not clearly specified or stated: *indefinite plans.* 2. Not limited or set: *an indefinite amount of time.* [< L *indefinitus* < *in-* not + *definitus* (< *dēfīnīre* to define)] —**in def′ i nite ly** *adv.* —**in def′ i nite ness** *n.*

in di vid u al (in′ də vij′ ü əl), *n.* One person or thing. —*adj.* 1. Separate from the rest: *each individual petal.* 2. For one only: *individual servings.* 3. Peculiar to one person or thing: *individual preferences.* [< L *indīviduus* indivisible < *in-* not + *dīviduus* divisible (< *dīvidere* to divide)]

in fal li ble (in fal′ ə bəl), *adj.* 1. Without fault; free from error: *infallible example.* 2. Unfailing; reliable: *The Bible is an infallible guide.* [< L *infallibilis* < *in-* not + *fallibilis* fallible (< *fallere* to deceive)] —**in fal′ li bly** *adv.*

in fe ri or i ty (in fēr′ ē ôr′ i tē), *n.* Condition of being lower in rank or quality. [< L *īnferus* low]

in fi nite (in′ fə nit), *adj.* Without limits or termination: *God's infinite love.* [< L *infinitus* < *in-* not + *finitus* (< *fīnīre* to limit < *fīnis* end)]

in hab i tant (in hab′ i tənt), *n.* One who lives in a place; resident; dweller. [< L *inhabitāre* < *in-* in + *habitāre* to dwell]

in iq ui ty (i nik′ wi tē), *n. pl.* **-ties** A great sin; wicked deed; injustice. [< L *inīquitās* < *inīquus* unjust < *in-* not + *aequus* equal]

in i ti a tion (i nish′ ē ā′ shən), *n.* 1. A beginning; introduction: *initiation of ZIP codes.* 2. The

had, māde, cär; then, mē, hërd; dim, hīde; not, hōme, ôr; oil, loud; sun, pull, blüe; ch, such; ng, sing; sh, she; th, with; TH, the; zh, vision;

ə represents *a* in ago, *e* in open, *i* in pencil, *o* in wagon, *u* in cactus.

admission of a person into a group or society with a ceremony, test, or instruction. [< L *initium* beginning < *inire* to enter < *in-* in + *ire* to go]

in som ni a (in som′ nē ə), *n.* Chronic sleeplessness. [< L *īnsomnis* sleepless < *in-* not + *somnus* sleep]

in spec tion (in spek′ shən), *n.* The act of looking carefully; examination. [< L *inspectare* < *in-* in + *specere* to look]

in spi ra tion (in′ spə rā′ shən), *n.* 1. A stimulation of thoughts and feelings that leads to creative action: *inspiration to write a poem.* 2. A sudden bright idea: *Your note gave me an inspiration.* 3. Direction and guidance from God: *"All Scripture is given by inspiration" (2 Timothy 3:16).* 4. The act of taking air into the lungs; inhalation. [< L *īnspīrāre* < *in-* in + *spīrāre* to breathe]

in stal la tion (in′ stə lā′ shən), *n.* 1. The act of putting in place and preparing for use. 2. A military base or camp. [< ML *installāre* < *in-* in + *stallum* place]

in stinct (*n.* in′ stingkt′, *adj.* in stingkt′), *n.* 1. A natural tendency to act in a certain way: *Birds fly south by instinct.* 2. Natural talent or ability. —*adj.* Charged or impelled with inner force: *an expression instinct with curiosity.* [< L *īnstīnctus* impulse < *īnstinguere* to incite < *in-* on + *stinguere* to prick]

in struc tion (in struk′ shən), *n.* 1. The act of teaching. 2. Rule, lesson, or factual matter that is taught. 3. **instructions** Directions; orders. [< L *instructus* < *instruere* to prepare < *in-* on + *struere* to build]

in tel li gence (in tel′ ə jəns), *n.* 1. The ability to receive and apply knowledge. 2. Received information; news: *intelligence of the accident.* 3. A group employed in finding out secret information. [< L *intellegens* < *intellegere* to perceive < *inter-* between + *legere* to choose]

adj.	adjective	*n.*	noun
adv.	adverb	*prep.*	preposition
conj.	conjunction	*pron.*	pronoun
interj.	interjection	*v.*	verb
sing.	singular	*pl.*	plural

in ter val (in′ tər vəl), *n.* 1. A space of time between events or instances: *an interval in the training.* 2. Space between objects: *Plant the bushes at three-foot intervals.* 3. **at intervals** Now and then. 4. The difference between two tones in music. [< L *intervallum* originally, space between palisades < *inter-* between + *vallum* rampart]

in tes tine (in tes′ tin), *n.* The lower part of the digestive canal where most of the food digests, and where waste material passes through to be discharged. [< L *intestīnus* internal < *intus* within]

Is ra el ite (iz′ rē ə līt′), *n.* A descendant of Israel. —*adj.* Pertaining to Israel or the Jews: *an Israelite tent.* [< Gk. *Israēl* < Heb. *Yisrā′ēl*]

i tem ize (ī′ tə mīz′), *v.* **-ized, -iz ing** To list each item. [< L *ita* thus]

J

jag uar (jag′ wär′, jag′ yü är′), *n.* A large, cat-like animal of the tropical American forests. [< Portuguese < Guarani *jaguá* dog]

jeal ous (jel′ əs), *adj.* 1. Spiteful through the fear of losing one's position to (a rival): *Saul was jealous of David.* 2. Demanding total love and obedience; not tolerating worship of another person or thing: *The Lord is a jealous God.* [< L *zelos* zeal < Gk. *zēlos*] —**jeal′ ous ly** *adv.*

jus ti fy (jus′ tə fī′), *v.* **-fied, -fy ing, -fies** 1. To clear of accusation: *Sickness justifies his absence.* 2. To cause to be guiltless before God: *Jesus' blood will justify the repentant.* 3. To adjust lines of type with spaces of the right size so that the lines are of equal length. [< OF *justifier* < L *justificare* < *justus* just + *facere* to do]

ju ve nile (jü′ və nīl′, jü′ və nəl), *adj.* 1. Young; youthful; also childish; immature. 2. Of or for young people: *juvenile interests.* —*n.* A young person, esp. one who is not of legal age; minor. [< L *juvenis* young]

K

ki mo no (kə mō′ nə, kə mō′ nō), *n. pl.* **-nos** 1. A loose outer garment with wide sleeves and a broad sash worn by Japanese men and women. 2. A dressing gown worn chiefly by women. [< Japanese *ki* to wear + *mono* object]

kin der gar ten (kin′ dər gär′ tən), *n.* A school or class for children four to six years old. [< G *Kinder* children + *Garten* garden]

L

la bel (lā′ bəl), *n.* 1. A slip of paper or other material attached to an item to identify or describe it. 2. A word or phrase used to describe a person, thing, etc.: *Honest Abe was the label given to Abraham Lincoln.* —*v.* 1. To attach a label: *label the box.* 2. To call someone or something a certain name: *label dishonesty sin.* [< OF] —**la′ bel er** *n.*

lab o ra to ry (lab′ rə tôr′ ē, lə bor′ ə trē), *n. pl.* **-ries** 1. A place where scientific tests and experiments are done. 2. A place where drugs, chemicals, explosives, etc., are manufactured. [< ML *labōrātōrium* < *labōrāre* to labor]

lan guage (lang′ gwij), *n.* Human speech, spoken or written. [< L *lingua*]

lei sure (lē′ zhər, lezh′ ər), *n.* A time of freedom from work in which a person may do whatever he wants to. —*adj.* Free; not occupied with the usual duties: *leisure moments.* **at leisure** or **at one's leisure** Not busy; without hurry; when one pleases. [< OF *leisir* < L *licēre* be allowed]

lei sure ly (lē′ zhər lē, lezh′ ər lē), *adj.* Unhurried: *a leisurely breakfast.* —*adv.* In an unhurried manner; slowly: *walked leisurely away.* [< OF *leisir*]

lieu ten ant (lü ten′ ənt), *n.* 1. A military officer who ranks below a captain. 2. A police or fire department officer. [< OF < *lieu* in place of + *tenir* to hold]

lime stone (līm′ stōn′), *n.* Rock containing magnesium carbonate and quartz. It is much used in building and in manufacturing. [OE *līm* + *stān*]

lit er ar y (lit′ ə rer′ ē), *adj.* 1. Pertaining to literature or writers: *literary meeting.* 2. Educated in or fond of literature or learning: *literary*

literature   133   manuscript

opinion. [< L *litterārius* < *littera* letter]

lit er a ture (lit′ ər ə chür′, lit′ ər ə chər), *n.* 1. Writings of a certain period, language, or country, kept because of their beauty or other outstanding quality. 2. Information on a certain subject: *travel literature.* 3. The study of literature. [< L *litterātūra* < *litterae* writing < *littera* letter]

live ly (līv′ lē), *adj.* **-li er, -li est** 1. Full of life and vigor; active. 2. Bright; colorful. 3. Happy; cheerful: *a lively classroom.* 4. Bouncing well: *a lively ball.* [< OE *līflīc* < *līf* life] —**live′ li ness** *n.*

lla ma (lä′ mə), *n. pl.* **-mas** or **-ma** A hoofed, woolly-haired, South American animal used as a beast of burden. [< Sp. < Quechua]

log i cal (loj′ i kəl), *adj.* Reasonable; sound; sensible: *a logical answer.* [< Gk. *logikos* of reason < *logos* reason < *legein* speak] —**log′ i cal ly** *adv.* —**log′ i cal ness** *n.*

loy al ty (loi′ əl tē), *n. pl.* **-ties** The state of being loyal, or faithful; feelings of devoted attachment and affection. [< OF *loial* < L *lēgālis* legal]

lu mi nous (lü′ mə nəs), *adj.* 1. Radiant; shining of itself. 2. Easy to understand; clear: *a luminous lecture.* [< L *lūminōsus* < *lūmen* light]

lunch eon (lun′ chən), *n.* 1. A formal lunch. 2. A light lunch served at an afternoon party. [< Obsolete *nuncheon* light snack > *none* noon + *schench* drink]

M

Mad am (mad′ əm), *n. pl.* **-ams, Mes dames** (mā däm′) A polite title used in addressing a woman. [< OF *ma dame* < *ma* my + *dame* lady]

mag nif i cence (mag nif′ i səns), *n.* Splendor; grandeur. [< L *magnificus* < *magnus* great + *facere* to make]

mag nif i cent (mag nif′ i sənt), *adj.* 1. Very beautiful; splendid. 2. Grand or noble; exalted. [< L *magnificus*] —**mag nif′ i cent ly** *adv.*

mag ni fy (mag′ nə fī′), *v.* **-fied, -fy ing, -fies** 1. Enlarge the size: *Magnify the small picture.* 2. Exaggerate; cause to seem greater: *He magnifies his troubles.* 3. Praise highly: *Magnify the Lord.* [< L *magnificus*]

maid en (mād′ ən), *n.* An unmarried woman. —*adj.* 1. Pertaining to a maiden: *maiden*

had, māde, cär; then, mē, hërd; dim, hīde; not, hōme, ôr; oil, loud; sun, pùll, blüe; ch, such; ng, sing; sh, she; th, with; ŦH, the; zh, vision;

ə represents *a* in ago, *e* in open, *i* in pencil, *o* in wagon, *u* in cactus.

dimples. 2. First or earliest: *maiden voyage.* [OE *mægden*]

main te nance (mān′ tə nəns), *n.* 1. The work of maintaining; upkeep. 2. Means of living; support; livelihood. [< OF *maintenir* < L *manū tenēre* to hold in one's hand < *manus* hand + *tenēre* to hold]

ma lar i a (mə ler′ ē ə), *n.* A disease carried by mosquitoes, with symptoms of chills, fever, and sweating. [< Ital. *mal'aria* < *mala aria* bad air]

mal ice (mal′ is), *n.* A desire to harm or to make others suffer; ill will. [< L *malitia* < *malus* bad]

ma li cious (mə lish′ əs), *adj.* Showing ill will or spite. [< L *malitia*]

ma lig nant (mə lig′ nənt), *adj.* 1. Exceedingly hateful or malicious. 2. Evil in influence: *malignant companions.* 3. Dangerous to one's health; threatening to cause death: *a malignant tumor.* [< L *malignus* evil]

man da to ry (man′ də tôr′ ē), *adj.* Required by (or as if by) a mandate, or command; compulsory. [< L *mandātum* < *mandāre* to order] —**man′ da to′ ri ly** *adv.*

ma neu ver (mə nü′ vər, mə nyü′ vər), *n.* 1. A move designed to steer or control someone or something. 2. A skilled physical motion: *fancy skating maneuver.* —*v.* 1. To make a move to achieve some purpose. 2. To attempt something by scheming; manipulate. [< OF *maneuvre* manual work < ML *manuopera* < *manu* by hand + *operārī* to work]

man u fac tur er (man′ yə fak′ chər ər), *n.* A person or an establishment that makes something; a factory or a factory owner. [< L *manufactus* < *manus* hand + *facere* to make]

man u script (man′ yə skript′), *n.* A book, article, etc., prepared for publication. —*adj.* Written by hand rather than typed. [< L *manūscrīptus* handwritten < *manus* hand + *scrīptus* (< *scrībere* to write)]

materially   **134**   **minister**

adj.	adjective	n.	noun
adv.	adverb	prep.	preposition
conj.	conjunction	pron.	pronoun
interj.	interjection	v.	verb
sing.	singular	pl.	plural

ma te ri al ly (mə tēr′ ē ə lē), *adv.* 1. With regard to the material or physical world: *materially poor.* 2. Pertaining to matter or substance rather than form: *Snow is materially water.* [< L *māteriālis* of matter < *māteria* matter < *māter* mother]

math e mat ics (math′ ə mat′ iks, math mat′ iks), *n.* The study of numbers, quantities, and measurements. Mathematics includes arithmetic, geometry, algebra, etc. [< Gk. *mathēmatikos* < *mathēma* science < *manthanein* to learn]

ma tur i ty (mə tyür′ i tē, mə tür′ i tē, mə chür′ i tē), *n.* 1. The condition of being mature; being fully developed. 2. The time when a note or debt is payable. [< L *mātūrus* ripe]

max i mum (mak′ sə məm), *n. pl.* **-mums** or **-ma** 1. The greatest amount or degree: *borrowed the maximum.* 2. An upper limit established by authority: *lowered the maximum.* 3. The moment during which a variable star is at its greatest brilliance. *—adj.* Being of the greatest amount or degree: *maximum rainfall.* [< L *maximus* greatest < *magnus* great]

mea sles (mē′ zəlz), *n. sing.* or *pl.* A contagious disease caused by a virus, characterized by symptoms of a bad cold, fever, and a breaking out of small red spots on the skin. [ME *maseles* plural of *masel* measles spot]

mel an chol y (mel′ ən kol′ ē), *n. pl.* **-chol ies** 1. Sadness or depression; gloominess. 2. Deep thoughtfulness. *—adj.* 1. Sad; gloomy: *a melancholy mood.* 2. Suggesting or promoting sadness: *a melancholy story.* [< Gk. *melankholia* < *melas* black + *kholē* bile] (It was once believed that black bile was responsible for depression.)

met a phor (met′ ə fôr′, met′ ə fər), *n.* A figure of speech in which something is called by a name that indicates a comparison but usually means something else, as in *I am the vine.* [< L *metaphora* < Gk. *metapherein* to transfer < *meta-* change + *pherein* to bear]

me te or (mē′ tē ər, mē′ tē ôr′), *n.* A mass of rock or other material that enters the earth's atmosphere, where friction may cause it to glow and burn up before reaching the earth's surface. [< Gk. *meteōros* high in the air > *meta-* after + *aoros* lifted]

me te or ite (mē′ tē ə rīt′), *n.* A meteor that is not burned up before it reaches the earth's surface. [< Gk. *meteōros*]

me ter[1] (mē′ tər), *n.* Rhythm in poetry or music: *iambic meter.* [< OF *metre* < L *metrum* < Gk. *metron* measure]

me ter[2] (mē′ tər), *n.* A unit of length in the metric system, equal to about 39.37 inches. [< F *mètre* < Gk. *metron*]

me ter[3] (mē′ tər), *n.* A device for measuring something (time, distance, speed) or regulating and recording: *electric meter.* *—v.* 1. To measure with a meter. 2. To imprint with a postage meter. [< ME *meten* to measure]

me trop o lis (mə trop′ ə lis), *n.* 1. The chief city of a country or region. 2. A city important because of a specific activity: *a manufacturing metropolis.* 3. The mother city or state of an ancient Greek colony. [< Gk. *mētropolis* mother city < *mētēr* mother + *polis* city]

mi cro film (mī′ krə film′), *n.* A film on which information is stored in microscopic form. [< Gk. *mikros* small + OE *filmen*]

mi cro phone (mī′ krə fōn′), *n.* An instrument that magnifies sounds by converting sound waves into an electric current. [< Gk. *mikros* small + *phōno* voice, sound]

mi gra to ry (mī′ grə tôr′ ē), *adj.* 1. Migrating, or relocating, periodically: *migratory species.* 2. Pertaining to migration: *migratory instinct.* 3. Wandering; nomadic: *migratory herders.* [< L *migrare* to move]

min i a ture (min′ ē ə chür′, min′ ə chür′), *n.* 1. A model of something much reduced in size from the original. 2. A small painting done with great detail. *—adj.* In a very small scale: *miniature train.* [< Italian *miniatura* picture in an illuminated manuscript < L *miniāre* to paint red < *minium* red lead]

min is ter (min′ i stər), *n.* 1. One who is ordained to preach and conduct worship services in a church. 2. A person at the head of a government department: *the minister of foreign affairs.* 3. One sent to another country as a representative of his government: *the United States minister to Italy.* 4. A person or thing serving another: *Joshua was Moses' minister.* —*v.* To be helpful; give aid: *minister to the bereaved.* [< ME *ministre* < L *minister* attendant]

mis cel la ne ous (mis' ə lā' nē əs), *adj.* Characterized by an assortment; varied. Commonly abbreviated **misc.** [< L *miscellāneus* < *miscēre* to mix]

mis sion ar y (mish' ə ner' ē), *n. pl.* **-ar ies** A person who helps to spread the Gospel. —*adj.* Of or about missionaries: *missionary stories.* [< L *missiō* < *mittere* to send]

moc ca sin (mok' ə sin), *n.* 1. A soft leather shoe with no heel and the sole and sides made of one piece, originally worn by the Indians. 2. The water moccasin, a poisonous snake. [< Natick *mohkussin*]

mod er ate (*adj.* mod' ər it, *v.* mod' ə rāt'), *adj.* Not extreme: *moderate breeze.* —*v.* 1. To make less severe or extreme. 2. To direct a meeting or activity. [< L *moderātus* < *moderare* to reduce]

mod est (mod' ist), *adj.* 1. Having a moderate view of oneself and one's abilities: *a modest attitude.* 2. Not bold or forward; reserved in a proper way. 3. Showing decency in thought, conduct, and dress: *a modest sister.* 4. Not extravagant or gaudy; humble in appearance: *a modest home.* [< L *modestus* in due measure] —**mod' est ly** *adv.*

mood y (mü' dē), *adj.* **mood i er, mood i est** 1. Given to a gloomy disposition. 2. Enveloped in sadness; gloomy. [ME *mod* < OE *mōd*]

mort gage (môr' gij), *n.* 1. A pledge of property to be given to a person or a firm in case money lent to the owner is not paid when due. 2. A contract stating the terms of such a claim. —*v.* **-gaged, -gag ing** To give a lender claim to one's property. [< ME *morgage* < OF *mort* death + *gage* pledge, of Germanic origin]

mos qui to (mə skē' tō), *n. pl.* **-toes** or **-tos** A small insect, the female of which pierces the skin of man and animals and draws blood. [< Sp.

had, māde, cär; then, mē, hėrd; dim, hīde; not, hōme, ôr; oil, loud; sun, pull, blüe; ch, such; ng, sing; sh, she; th, with; ᴛH, the; zh, vision;

ə represents *a* in ago, *e* in open, *i* in pencil, *o* in wagon, *u* in cactus.

mosquito small fly < *mosca* fly < L *musca*]

mot to (mot' ō), *n. pl.* **-toes** or **-tos** 1. A short expression giving a rule of conduct, such as *"Look before you leap."* 2. An appropriate word, sentence, or phrase written or engraved on some object. [< Ital. *motto* word < L *mōttum* < *muttum* grunt < *muttire* to mutter]

mu si cal (myü' zi kəl), *adj.* 1. Having to do with music: *musical instruction.* 2. Characteristic of or resembling music: *a musical doorbell.* [L *mūsica* < Gk. *mousikē* < *mousikos* of the Muses]

mu si cian (myü zish' ən), *n.* One skilled in writing, singing, or playing music. [< ME *musicien* < L *mūsica*]

mut ton (mut' ən), *n.* The meat of a mature sheep. [< OF *moton,* of Celtic origin]

mu tu al (myü' chü əl), *adj.* 1. Having the same feelings each toward the other: *mutual understanding.* 2. Shared by two or more at the same time: *mutual concern.* [< ME *mutuall* < OF *mutuel* < L *mutuus* < *mutare* to change] —**mu' tu al ly** *adv.*

N

ne ces si ty (nə ses' i tē), *n. pl.* **-ties** 1. That which is needed or indispensible: *Water is a necessity.* 2. A condition of desperate need: *Trust God in your necessity.* [< L *necessitās* < *necesse* necessary (< *ne* not + *cedere* to withdraw)]

nine teenth (nīn tēnth'), *adj.* Next after eighteenth. —*n.* One part out of nineteen equal parts. [< ME *nintene* < OE *nigontēne* < *nigon* nine]

ni tro gen (nī' trə jən), *n.* A gas with no color, odor, or taste that makes up about 80 percent of the atmosphere and forms a part of all living tissues. [< Gk. *nitron* + *-genēs* born]

non sense (non' sens'), *n.* 1. Foolish words or doings. 2. Worthless things; junk. [< L *nōn* not + *sēnsus* (< *sentīre* perceive, know, feel)]

no tice a ble (nō' ti sə bəl), *adj.* 1. Likely to be

oblige   136   **parable**

adj.	adjective	*n.*	noun
adv.	adverb	*prep.*	preposition
conj.	conjunction	*pron.*	pronoun
interj.	interjection	*v.*	verb
sing.	singular	*pl.*	plural

seen. 2. Worthy of notice: *a noticeable improvement.* [< L *nōtitia* < *nōtus* known < *nōscere* to come to know]

O

o blige (ə blīj′), *v.* **-bliged, -blig ing** 1. To constrain or bind: *Joseph was obliged to go to prison.* 2. To place one under a debt of thanks for some favor shown: *I was obliged to him for changing the tire.* 3. Do a favor or service: *Oblige us with a visit.* [< OF *obligier* < L *obligāre* < *ob-* to + *ligāre* to bind]

ob sta cle (ob′ stə kəl), *n.* Something that stands in the way of progress; hindrance. [< L *obstāculum* < *obstāre* < *ob-* against + *stāre* to stand]

oc ca sion (ə kā′ zhən), *n.* 1. A time or event, usually one that is special. 2. A cause; reason: *no occasion to worry.* —*v.* Be the reason for; bring about: *an accident occasioned by carelessness.* [< L *occāsiō* < *occidere* to fall < *ob-* down + *cadere* to fall]

oc ca sion al (ə kā′ zhə nəl), *adj.* 1. Happening now and then: *occasional visit.* 2. Suitable for a particular occasion: *occasional poetry.* 3. A piece of furniture that is not part of a set: *occasional chair.* [< L *occāsiō*] **—oc ca' sion al ly** *adv.*

oc cur (ə kėr′), *v.* 1. To happen; take place. 2. To come to mind: *Did it occur to you?* [< L *occurrere* < *ob* toward + *currere* to run]

oc ta gon (ok′ tə gon′), *n.* An eight-sided plane figure. [< Gk. *okta-* eight + *gōnia* angle]

oc to pus (ok′ tə pəs), *n. pl.* **-pus es** or **-pi** (ok′ tə pī′) A water animal with a saclike body and eight tentacles lined with suckers. [< Gk. *oktōpous* eight-footed < *oktō* eight + *pous* foot]

o mis sion (ō mish′ ən), *n.* 1. The act of omitting, or leaving something out. 2. Something that is omitted, or excluded. [< L *omissiō* < *omittere* < *ob* away + *mittere* to send]

o mit (ō mit′), *v.* **-mit ted, -mit ting** 1. Leave out: *Omit the salt.* 2. Neglect: *Nine lepers omitted their thanks.* [< L *omittere*]

on ion (un′ yən), *n.* The bulb of a plant in the lily family, having a sharp, strong odor and flavor. [< OF *oignon* < L *uniō*]

o pin ion (ə pin′ yən), *n.* A personal judgment or conclusion about a matter; what one thinks about something. [< ME *opinioun* < L *opinio* < *opinari* to suppose]

o pos sum (ə pos′ əm, pos′ əm), *n. pl.* **-sums** or **-sum** A small American animal that lives mostly in trees and is active at night. [< *aposoum,* of Algonquian origin]

op por tu ni ty (op′ ər tü′ ni tē, op′ ər tyü′ ni tē), *n. pl.* **-ties** A favorable time; a convenient occasion or circumstance. [< L *opportūnus* (a wind) blowing toward port and thus favorable < *ob-* toward + *portus* harbor]

or di nar y (ôr′ dən er′ ē), *adj.* Common; everyday; usual. —*n. pl.* **-nar ies** Something that is common or usual: *out of the ordinary.* [< L *ōrdinārius* < *ōrdō* order]

or na ment (ôr′ nə mənt), *n.* Something added for decoration. —*v.* To decorate: *ornament the fence with roses.* [< L *ōrnāmentum* < *ōrnāre* to embellish]

out stand ing (out stan′ ding), *adj.* 1. Noticeable; standing out, esp. because of importance or excellence: *outstanding artwork.* 2. Still standing; unpaid: *an outstanding check.* [OE *ūt* + *standan*]

o ver re ac tion (ō′ vər rē ak′ shən), *n.* Response that is extreme. [OE *ofer* + L *re* + L *actum*]

ox y gen (ok′ si jən), *n.* A gas that forms 21 percent of the atmosphere and that is necessary for the existence of life. [< F *oxygène* < Gk. *oxus* sharp, acid + *-gène* born, produced (because it was once considered essential to all acids)]

P

pam phlet (pam′ flit), *n.* A booklet with paper covers; brochure. [< ME *pamflet* < L *Pamphilus* title of a popular poem published in this form in the 1100s]

par a ble (par′ ə bəl), *n.* A short story that teaches a spiritual truth through natural examples. [< Gk.

parachute   137   perish

parabolē < *paraballein* to compare < *para-* beside + *ballein* to throw]

par a chute (par′ ə shüt′), *n.* A folding, umbrella-shaped canopy that breaks the fall of something descending through the air, esp. from an airplane. —*v.* **-chut ed, -chut ing** To come down with a parachute. [< F *parare* to shield + *chute* fall]

par a dise (par′ ə dīs′, par′ ə dīz′), *n.* 1. The place where righteous souls are after death. 2. A place of beauty and delight. 3. Often **Paradise.** The Garden of Eden. [< Gk. *paradeisos* < Iranian *pairi-daēza* < *pairi* around + *daēza* wall]

par a lyze (par′ ə līz′), *v.* **-lyzed, -lyz ing** 1. To cause a loss or partial loss of motion or feeling. 2. To make helpless: *paralyzed by fright.* [< Gk. < *paraluein* to disable < *para-* in an injurious way + *luein* loosen. Doublet of PALSY.]

par a site (par′ ə sīt′), *n.* 1. A plant or animal that lives on another living thing and gets food from it. 2. A person who lives at the expense of another. [< Gk. *parasitos* feeding beside < *para* beside + *sitos* food]

par lia ment (pär′ lə mənt), *n.* An assembly that is the highest lawmaking body in some countries. [< OF *parlement* < *parler* to talk]

par tial (pär′ shəl), *adj.* 1. Incomplete; not total: *a partial fracture.* 2. Favoring one side more than another; prejudiced: *A judge must not be partial.* 3. Favorably inclined toward; fond of: *I am partial to licorice.* [< L *partiālis* < *pars* part] —**par′ tial ly** *adv.*

pas sage (pas′ ij), *n.* 1. A means of passing through, as a hallway. 2. The process of passing or changing from one place or condition to another: *the passage from adolescence to adulthood.* 3. A ticket or other means that gives one the right to pass through: *We have passage for ten people.* 4. A brief piece of a speech or writing: *a passage from the Bible.* [< OF *passer* < L *passus* step]

pat i o (pat′ ē ō′, pä′ tē ō′), *n. pl.* **-i os** 1. An inner part of a house without a roof, esp. in houses with Spanish design. 2. A paved area next to a house used for eating, relaxing, etc. [< Sp. < L *patēre* to be open]

peace a ble (pē′ sə bəl), *adj.* Having a tranquil

had, māde, cär; then, mē, hėrd; dim, hīde; not, hōme, ôr; oil, loud; sun, pull, blüe; ch, such; ng, sing; sh, she; th, with; ͭH, the; zh, vision;

ə represents *a* in ago, *e* in open, *i* in pencil, *o* in wagon, *u* in cactus.

tendency; keeping peace: *a peaceable encounter.* [< ME *pees* < OF *pais* < L *pāx*] —**peace′ a ble ness** *n.* —**peace′ a bly** *adv.*

peas ant (pez′ ənt), *n.* 1. A farmer of a small scale or poorer class. 2. An uneducated or rude person. —*adj.* Pertaining to peasants: *peasant dwellings.* [< OF *paisant* < *pais* country < L *pāgēnsis* living in a district < L *pāgus* district]

pe cu liar (pi kyül′ yər), *adj.* 1. Strange; odd: *a peculiar odor.* 2. Distinct from others: *a peculiar people.* [< L *peculium* private property < *pecus* cattle]

pen i cil lin (pen′ i sil′ in), *n.* An antibiotic that is made from a mold and is used against certain disease-causing bacteria. [< L *Pēnicillium* the name of a mold < *pēnicillus* brush]

Pen ta teuch (pen′ tə tük′, pen′ tə tyük′), *n.* The first five books of the Old Testament: Genesis, Exodus, Leviticus, Numbers, and Deuteronomy. [< Gk. *Pentateukos* < *penta-* five + *teukhos* scroll]

per il (per′ əl), *n.* 1. The state of being exposed to danger: *"in perils of robbers."* 2. A source of danger: *Icy roads are a peril to travelers.* [< L *perīculum*]

pe rim e ter (pə rim′ i tər), *n.* 1. The boundary line of a plane figure or area: *planted the perimeter of the garden in tulips.* 2. The measure of a line around: *a perimeter of twenty feet.* [< L *perimetros* < Gk. *peri* around + *metron* measure]

pe ri od i cal (pir′ ē od′ i kəl), *adj.* Happening at regular intervals: *periodical pruning.* —*n.* A magazine published at regular intervals but less often than daily. [< Gk. *periodos* circuit < *peri* around + *hodos* way] —**pe′ ri od′ i cal ly** *adv.*

per ish (per′ ish), *v.* **-ished, -ish ing** 1. To die, esp. untimely or because of violence. 2. To cease to be; disappear gradually: *his dreams perished.* [< ME *perishen* < OF *periss-* < L *perīre* < *per-* away + *īre* to go]

adj.	adjective	*n.*	noun
adv.	adverb	*prep.*	preposition
conj.	conjunction	*pron.*	pronoun
interj.	interjection	*v.*	verb
sing.	singular	*pl.*	plural

per suade (pər swād′), *v.* **-suad ed, -suad ing** To convince; cause to think or do. [< L *persuādēre* < *per-* (intensive) + *suādēre* to urge]

pe ti tion (pə tish′ ən), *n.* 1. A request made to authority for a right, privilege, etc. 2. Prayer; supplication: *Daniel made his petition three times a day.* —*v.* To make a formal request: *Rehoboam's subjects petitioned for lower taxes.* [< L *petītiō* < *petere* to request] —**pe ti′ tion er** *n.*

Phi le mon (fi lē′ mən, fī lē′ mən), *n.* The book in the New Testament consisting of Paul's letter to Philemon.

phi los o phy (fi los′ ə fē), *n. pl.* **-phies** 1. Ideas about life, such as what is right and wrong; system of values: *philosophy of child training.* 2. Love and pursuit of wisdom: *vain philosophies.* [< Gk. *philosophos* loving wisdom < *philos* loving + *sophia* wisdom]

pho to graph (fō′ tə graf′), *n.* A picture made by using a camera. —*v.* To take a picture with a camera. [< Gk. *phōt-* light + *graphein* to write]

phys i cal (fiz′ i kəl), *adj.* 1. Of the body, as opposed to mental or spiritual: *physical harm.* 2. Of natural matter and the laws that govern it: *physical forces.* [< L *physica* < Gk. *phusis* nature] —**phys′ i cal ly** *adv.*

pic tur esque (pik′ chə resk′), *adj.* 1. Having an appearance suitable to be used in a picture. 2. Forming a picture in the mind: *picturesque words.* [< F *pittoresque* < Ital. *pittoresco* < *pittore* painter < L *pictor* < *pingere* to paint] —**pic′ tur esque′ ly** *adv.* —**pic′ tur esque′ ness** *n.*

pi rate (pī′ rit), *n.* 1. One who robs ships on the sea. 2. One who makes something available to the public without the owner's permission. —*v.* **-rat ed, -rat ing** To rob a ship or to illegally use or reproduce another's work. [< L *pīrāta* < Gk. *peiratēs* < *peiran* to attempt]

plac id (plas′ id), *adj.* 1. Peaceful; calm. 2. Complacent; unexcitable. [< L *placidus* < *placēre* to please]

pla za (plä′ zə, plaz′ ə), *n.* An open area such as a square or marketplace in a town or city. [< Sp. < L *platea* broad street]

please (plēz), *v.* **pleased, pleas ing** 1. To satisfy; make glad. 2. To have the will or desire: *however you please.* [< ME *plesen* < OF *plaisir* < L *placēre*]

plen te ous (plen′ tē əs), *adj.* 1. Available in plenty; abundant. 2. Producing in abundance; fertile. [< OF *plentiveus* < *plente* plenty < L *plēnitās* < *plēnus* full] —**plen′ te ous ly** *adv.* —**plen′ te ous ness** *n.*

plen ty (plen′ tē), *n.* 1. Abundance; more than required. 2. General prosperity: *land of plenty.* [< L *plēnitās* < *plēnus* full]

plun der (plun′ dər), *v.* To rob openly and by force. —*n.* 1. Goods taken in plundering; loot. 2. The act of robbing by force. [< G *plündern* < *Plunder* household goods]

pneu mo nia (nù mōn′ yə, nyù mōn′ yə), *n.* A disease of the lungs, causing them to be inflamed because of the entrance of bacteria, viruses, chemicals, or foreign particles. [< Gk. *pneumōn* lung]

pol i ti cian (pol′ i tish′ ən), *n.* 1. Someone who spends much time in matters of politics or government affairs. 2. Someone with a political office. [< L *polīticus* < Gk. *politikos* < *politēs* citizen < *polis* city]

poo dle (püd′ əl), *n.* A breed of intelligent dogs with thick, curly hair of solid color. [< G *Pudel* short for *Pudelhund* < *pudeln* to splash + *Hund* dog]

pop u la tion (pop′ yə lā′ shən), *n.* The number of people living in a certain area, as in a country, state, county, etc. [< L *populatio* < *populus* the people]

pos ses sion (pə zesh′ ən), *n.* 1. The state of possessing; ownership. 2. Something owned; property. [< ME *possessen* < L *possidēre* < *potis* capable + *sedēre* to sit]

po ta to (pə tā′ tō), *n. pl.* **-toes** 1. A plant with a starchy tuber used as a vegetable. 2. This vegetable, which is round or oval, hard, and has a very thin skin. [< Sp. *patata* < Caribbean *batata* sweet potato]

prac ti cal (prak′ ti kəl), *adj.* 1. Active in work instead of only theory: *practical gardening.* 2. Having good sense; efficient: *a practical reason.* 3. Useful; serving a purpose without being elaborate: *a practical fence.* [< L *prācticus* < Gk. *praktikos* < *prattein* to act] —**prac' ti cal ness** *n.*

prai rie (prer′ ē), *n.* A vast, level or rolling grassland, esp. the region in central North America. [< OF *praerie* < L *pratum* meadow]

pre cau tion (pri kô′ shən), *n.* Something done in advance to avoid possible danger or failure. [< L *praecautiō* < *praecavēre* to guard against < *prae-* before + *cavēre* to beware]

pre cede (pri sēd′), *v.* **-ced ed, -ced ing** Be or go before. [< L *praecedere* < *prae-* before + *cedere* to go]

pre cious (presh′ əs), *adj.* 1. Very valuable. 2. Greatly loved; dear: *a precious friend.* 3. Overrefined: *precious speech.* 4. *Informal* Very great: *a precious loss.* —*adv. Informal* Used as an intensifier: *a precious little amount.* [< OF *precios* < L *pretiōsus* < *pretium* price] —**pre' cious ly** *adv.* —**pre' cious ness** *n.*

pre cip i ta tion (pri sip′ i tā′ shən), *n.* 1. A headlong fall or rush. 2. Moisture that falls from the sky in the form of snow, rain, etc. [< L *praecipitāre* to throw headlong < *praeceps* headlong < *prae-* in front + *caput* head]

pref er ence (pref′ ər əns, pref′ rəns), *n.* 1. A special liking of one thing rather than another. 2. Showing favor to one more than to another: *Who gets preference in your visiting?* [< L *praeferentia* < *praeferre* to prefer < *prae-* before + *ferre* to carry]

prep a ra tion (prep′ ə rā′ shən), *n.* 1. The act of preparing, or getting ready. 2. That which is done beforehand to make ready for something. 3. Something made or prescribed for a special purpose: *Spread this preparation on the sore.* [< L *praeparāre* < *prae-* before + *parāre* to make ready]

pre scribe (pri skrīb′), *v.* **-scribed, -scrib ing** 1. To set down as a rule or guide; order: *The governor prescribed a price change.* 2. Give an order for or direct the use of a remedy: *The doctor prescribed penicillin three times daily.* [< L *praescrībere* write before < *prae-* before + *scrībere* to write]

had, māde, cär; then, mē, hėrd; dim, hīde; not, hōme, ôr; oil, loud; sun, pull, blüe; ch, such; ng, sing; sh, she; th, with; ŦH, the; zh, vision; ə represents *a* in ago, *e* in open, *i* in pencil, *o* in wagon, *u* in cactus.

pres sur ize (presh′ ə rīz′), *v.* **-ized, -iz ing** 1. To keep normal air pressure in (an aircraft compartment, etc.). 2. To put under high pressure. [< L *pressūra* < *premere* to press] —**pres' sur i za' tion** *n.* —**pres' sur iz' er** *n.*

pre vi ous (prē′ vē əs), *adj.* 1. Happening or going before in time or order. 2. *Informal* Too hasty; quick: *Do not be previous with your answer.* [< L *praevius* going before < *prae-* before + *via* way] —**pre' vi ous ly** *adv.* —**pre' vi ous ness** *n.*

priv i lege (priv′ ə lij), *n.* A special right, favor, or benefit. [< L *prīvilēgium* a law affecting one person < *prīvus* individual + *lēx* law]

pro ce dure (prə sē′ jər), *n.* 1. A manner by which to proceed or carry out something; way of doing things. 2. The usual way of conducting business: *hospital procedure.* [F *procédure* < OF *proceder* to proceed < L *prō-* forward + *cēdere* to go]

proc ess (pros′ es′, prō′ ses′), *n.* 1. A system of actions or operations done in a special order, which produces something: *the building process.* 2. Ongoing movement; progression: *lost his shoe in the process.* —*v.* **-cessed, -cess ing** 1. To prepare or change by going through special steps: *process the grapes.* 2. To put through the steps of a standard procedure: *process the order.* [< L *prōcessus* < *prōcēdere*]

prop a gan da (prop′ ə gan′ də), *n.* 1. An organized way of spreading certain opinions or beliefs. 2. Ideas spread in this way: *newspapers full of propaganda.* [< Ital. short for the Latin title *Sacra Congregātiō dē Prōpagandā Fide* (Sacred Congregation for Propagating the Faith) L *prōpāgāre* propagate < *propages* offspring < *pro* before + *pangare* to fasten cuttings of plants]

proph e sy (prof′ i sī), *v.* **-sied, -sy ing, -sies** To speak under divine inspiration, esp. in foretelling the future. [< OF *prophecie* < L *prophētia* < Gk. *prophētēs* < *pro-* before + *phanai* to speak] —**proph' e si' er** *n.*

protein   **140**   **referee**

adj.	adjective	*n.*	noun
adv.	adverb	*prep.*	preposition
conj.	conjunction	*pron.*	pronoun
interj.	interjection	*v.*	verb
sing.	singular	*pl.*	plural

pro tein (prō′ tēn′, prō′ tē in), *n.* An important nutrient that contains nitrogen and is necessary for the growth and repair of cells in the body. [< F *protéine* < Gk. *prōteios* primary < *prōtos* first]

psy chol o gy (sī kol′ ə jē), *n. pl.* **-gies** The study of the mind and its processes as actions, feelings, thoughts, etc. [< Gk. *psukhē* spirit, life + *-logia* (< *-logy* study)]

pur sue (pər sü′), *v.* **-sued, -su ing** 1. To follow in order to catch or kill. 2. To seek; keep on with a goal in view: *pursue a closer walk with God.* 3. To follow persistently with annoyances, trouble, etc.: *The Pharisees pursued Jesus.* [< F *pursuer* < L *prosequi* < *prō-* forward + *sequī* to follow] —**pur su′ a ble** *adj.* —**pur su′ er** *n.*

Q

qual i ty (kwol′ i tē), *n. pl.* **-ties** 1. That which makes something what it is; a characteristic: *An important quality of clay is its pliability.* 2. Degree of excellence: *high quality.* [< L *quālitās* < *quālis* of what sort]

quan ti ty (kwon′ ti tē), *n. pl.* **-ties** 1. A definite number or amount. 2. An indefinite amount (usually large): *buy in quantity.* [< L *quantitās* < *quantus* how much]

quar tet (kwôr tet′), *n.* A group of four persons or things; esp. a group of four singers. [< Ital. *quartetto* < *quarto* fourth < L *quārtus*] Also **quartette.**

quo ta tion (kwō tā′ shən), *n.* 1. That which someone said or wrote, repeated exactly by another person. 2. The current price of something: *the quotation for beef.* [< L *quotāre* < *quotus* which or what number (in a sequence) < *quot* how many]

R

rac coon (ra kün′), *n. pl.* **rac coons** or **rac coon** 1. A small, nocturnal, flesh-eating mammal with a bushy, ringed tail. 2. The fur of this animal. [< Algonquian *arathkone*] Also **racoon.**

re al i ty (rē al′ i tē), *n. pl.* **-ties** The state of being real; actuality: *Heaven is a reality.* [< L *reālis* < *rēs* thing]

re al ize (rē′ ə līz′), *v.* **-ized, -iz ing** 1. Understand fully; be aware of: *I realize the predicament.* 2. Make real; accomplish: *realize his goal.* 3. Obtain as gain or profit: *He realized $5,000 from his investment.* [< L *reālis* < *rēs* thing]

rec og nize (rek′ əg nīz′), *v.* **-nized, -niz ing** 1. To know and remember (someone or something) upon seeing again. 2. To acknowledge willingly; accept; admit: *recognize my error.* 3. To make known (as with a nod) that one acknowledges an acquaintance. 4. To acknowledge status and agree to deal with. [< L *recognoscere* < *re-* again + *cognoscere* to know. Doublet of RECONNOITER.]

rec om mend (rek′ ə mend′), *v.* 1. To speak well of. 2. Suggest; advise: *I recommend that you see a doctor.* 3. To draw favorable attention to: *Diligence recommended him in the community.* [< L *recommendāre* < *re-* (intensive) + *commendāre* to entrust (< *com-* together + *mandāre* to order)] —**rec′ om mend′ a ble** *adj.*

rec on cile (rek′ ən sīl′), *v.* **-ciled, -cil ing** 1. Reestablish a friendship after a quarrel, etc.: *reconcile your brother.* 2. Settle, as a quarrel or disagreement: *reconcile the inheritance dispute.* 3. To bring into agreement with something else; harmonize: *reconcile actions and words.* 4. To bring oneself to give in or accept; submit: *reconciled to his handicap.* [< L *reconciliāre* < *re-* back + *conciliāre* to regain friendship (< *concilium* meeting)]

re cov er (ri kuv′ ər), *v.* 1. To get back after losing; regain. 2. To make up for (something that has been lost): *recover lost time.* 3. To regain health or normal condition or position. 4. To gain a favorable court ruling: *recover all his privileges.* 5. To get back into a useful condition: *recover land that was strip-mined.* 6. *Archaic* Get to; reach. [< OF *recoverer* < L *recuperāre* < *re-* back + *capere* to take] —**re cov′ er er** *n.* —**re cov′ er a ble** *adj.*

ref e ree (ref′ ə rē′), *n.* 1. One to whom something

is referred to be settled or decided. 2. An official supervising a game; umpire. [< L *referre* < *re-* back + *ferre* to carry]

re fresh ment (ri fresh′ mənt), *n.* 1. A time of renewing and reviving. 2. Something that refreshes. 3. **refreshments** Something to eat or drink: *refreshments after pulling weeds.* [< OF *refreschir* < *re-* anew + *fres* fresh, of Germanic origin]

re frig er a tor (ri frij′ ə rā′ tər), *n.* A box or room to keep food cold. [< L *refrigerāre* < *re-* anew + *frigerāre* to make cool (< *frigus* cold)]

ref u gee (ref′ yů jē′, ref′ yü jē′), *n.* One who flees because of war, persecution, etc., to a place of safety. [F *réfugié* < *réfugier* to take refuge < *refuge* < L *refugium* < *refugere* to run away < *re-* back + *fugere* to flee]

re gret (ri gret′), *v.* **-gret ted, -gret ting** To look back with sorrow or dissatisfaction: *regret my words.* —*n.* 1. A sorrowful feeling: *filled with regret.* 2. **regrets** A polite reply stating why one cannot accept an invitation: *send my regrets.* [< OF *regretter* to lament] —**re gret′ ter** *n.*

reign (rān), *n.* 1. The time during which a ruler exercises his authority. 2. The rule of a monarch: *a demanding reign.* 3. Widespread influence: *a reign of peace.* —*v.* 1. To rule; exercise authority: *God reigns over all the earth.* 2. To be predominant; prevalent: *when kindness reigns.* [< OF *reigne* < L *regnum* < *rēx* king]

re mem brance (ri mem′ brəns), *n.* 1. The act of recalling; memory. 2. Something observed to honor the memory of a person or event: *"This do in remembrance of me."* 3. A token kept for memory's sake; souvenir. [< OF *remembrer* < L *rememorārī* < *re-* again + *memorari* to be mindful of (< *memor* mindful)]

re pen tance (ri pen′ təns), *n.* Sorrow for wrongdoing and turning from it to a different course. [< OF *repentir* < L *re-* in response + *pentir* to be sorry (< *paenitēre* to repent)]

rep re sen ta tive (rep′ ri zen′ tə tiv) *n.* 1. A person who acts or speaks for others: *a representative of the feed company.* 2. One who belongs to the House of Representatives in Washington D.C. 3. An example of: *Noah is a representative of obedience.* —*adj.* 1. Serving to show

had, māde, cär; then, mē, hėrd; dim, hīde; not, hōme, ôr; oil, loud; sun, půll, blüe; ch, such; ng, sing; sh, she; th, with; ŦH, the; zh, vision;

ə represents *a* in ago, *e* in open, *i* in pencil, *o* in wagon, *u* in cactus.

something: *a representative slice of the melon.* 2. Involving the people through elected officers: *representative government.* [< L *repraesentāre* to show < *re-* again + *praesentāre* to present] —**rep′ re sen′ ta tive ly** *adv.* —**rep′ re sen′ ta tive ness** *n.*

res er voir (rez′ ər vwär′, rez′ ər vôr′), *n.* 1. A place for storing water, as for use in a city. 2. A container in which to store liquid. 3. A storage place for anything: *Grandmother's chest is a reservoir of memories.* 4. An extra supply of anything: *a reservoir of wheat.* [< F *réservoir* < *réserver* to reserve]

res i dence (rez′ i dens′), *n.* 1. The act of dwelling at a place: *took up residence last week.* 2. The place where one resides, or lives; home. 3. The length of time that a person lives at one place. [< L *residēre* to sit back < *re-* back + *sedēre* to sit]

re sign (ri zīn′), *v.* 1. To give up a position, job, etc.; quit. 2. To submit patiently without complaint; accept: *resigned to the task.* [< L *resignāre* to unseal < *re-* back + *signāre* to seal (< *signum* mark)]

re sis tance (ri zis′ təns), *n.* 1. The act of resisting: *Jesus made no resistance at the cross.* 2. Ability to resist: *the body's resistance to sickness.* 3. A force that hinders: *Air resistance made it hard to fly.* [< L *resistere* < *re-* against + *sistere* to place]

res o lu tion (rez′ ə lü′ shən), *n.* 1. Something that a person decides to do: *a resolution to read the Bible through.* 2. The act of resolving or determining: *Our resolution led to renewed efforts.* 3. Holding to a purpose with determination: *hoed thistles with resolution.* [< L *resolūtus* < *resolvere* to untie < *re-* back + *solvere* to untie]

re source (rē′ sôrs′, ri sôrs′), *n.* 1. Something that gives support or help: *A Bible dictionary is a resource of information.* 2. A supply that can be

adj.	adjective	*n.*	noun
adv.	adverb	*prep.*	preposition
conj.	conjunction	*pron.*	pronoun
interj.	interjection	*v.*	verb
sing.	singular	*pl.*	plural

drawn from in time of need: *the resource of canned food.* 3. The means used that help one out of trouble or help him to success: *Crying is a baby's resource.* 4. **resources** Financial worth in money or assets: *the resources of the nation.* [< F *ressource* < *resourdre* to rise again < L *resurgere* < *re-* again + *surgere* to rise]

re spon si bil i ty (ri spon′ sə bil′ i tē), *n. pl.* **-ties** 1. The state of being responsible, or accountable: *Responsibility aged him.* 2. Dependability; trustworthiness. 3. That for which one is responsible: *His debts are his responsibility.* [< L *respondēre* to respond]

re spon si ble (ri spon′ sə bəl), *adj.* 1. Accountable for the welfare of people or things put into one's care. 2. Having the ability to perform without supervision; reliable. 3. Getting the credit or blame: *responsible for the damage.* [< L *respondēre* to respond]

res tau rant (res′ tər ənt, res′ tə ränt′), *n.* A place where meals can be bought and eaten. [< F *restaurer* to restore < L *restaurāre*]

rev e nue (rev′ ə nü, rev′ ə nyü), *n.* 1. Money received from investments or property; income. 2. Money that the government collects from the public. 3. An item or source of income. [< F *revenir* to return < L *revenīre* < *re-* back + *venīre* to come]

rheu ma tism (rü′ mə tiz′ əm), *n.* A disease of the joints that causes them to become stiff and swollen. [< Gk. *rheuma* a flowing < *rhein* to flow]

ri dic u lous (ri dik′ yə ləs), *adj.* Not sensible; absurd. [< L *ridiculus* laughable < *ridēre* to laugh] —**ri dic′ u lous ly** *adv.* —**ri dic′ u lous ness** *n.*

room mate (rüm′ māt′, rüm′ māt′), *n.* One who shares a room or an apartment with another. [OE *rūm* + G *ge-* together + *mat* meat, food]

ru in (rü′ in), *n.* 1. Destruction; decay; collapse: *the*

ruin of the land. 2. That which causes destruction, etc.: *Covetousness was Achan's ruin.* 3. Often **ruins.** The remains of something that has been demolished, destroyed, or decayed. —*v.* To demolish; spoil. [< L *ruina* < *ruere* to fall]

S

Sab bath (sab′ əth), *n.* Day of the week used for rest and worship. Sunday is the Sabbath for Christians; Saturday is the Jewish Sabbath. [< L *sabbatum* < Gk. *sabbaton* < Hebrew *shabbāth* < *shābhath* he rested]

sab o tage (sab′ ə täzh′), *n.* Destruction done to machinery, tools, etc., by an enemy to hinder war efforts, stop production, or be a threat: *The train was stalled because of sabotage to the tracks.* —*v.* **-taged, -tag ing** To deliberately hinder: *Rebellious workers sabotaged the conveyor.* [< F < *saboter* to bungle < *sabot* wooden shoe, from damage done to machinery with sabots]

sac ri lege (sak′ rə lij), *n.* The act of profaning something sacred; disrespectful treatment of something holy. [< L *sacrilegus* temple robber < *sacer* sacred + *legere* to pick up] —**sac′ ri le′ gious** *adj.* —**sac′ ri le′ gi ous ly** *adv.*

sales man (sālz′ mən), *n. pl.* **sales men** A man hired to sell something.

sanc ti fy (sangk′ tə fī′), *v.* **-fied, -fy ing, -fies** 1. To make holy. 2. To set apart as sacred; consecrate: *sanctified the vessels in the temple.* 3. To make binding by religious authority: *sanctify the vows.* [< L *sānctificāre* < *sānctus* holy + *facere* to make]

sand wich (sand′ wich, san′ wich), *n.* A food combination consisting of two pieces of bread with meat, cheese, or some other item between them. —*v.* **-wiched, -wich ing** To place between two parts of something else: *a row of petunias sandwiched between vegetable plots.* [After an 18th century official from Sandwich, England.]

sat el lite (sat′ əl īt′), *n.* 1. A small heavenly body revolving around a planet: *The moon is a satellite of the earth.* 2. A manmade object which revolves around a heavenly body. [< L *satelles* attendant]

sat is fac to ry (sat′ is fak′ tə rē), *adj.* Of a quality that satisfies, or pleases; adequate; acceptable.

[< L *satisfacere* < *satis* enough + *facere* to make] —**sat' is fac' tor i ly** *adv.*

sau er kraut (sour′ krout′), *n.* Finely cut salted cabbage that has cured by fermentation. [< G *sauer* sour + *Kraut* cabbage]

sched ule (skej′ ül; *British* shed′ yül), *n.* A written or printed form on which details are listed, esp. a table listing things that are to take place and the time when each thing is to happen. —*v.* **-uled, -ul ing** To appoint a certain time to do something. [< L *schedula* < *scheda* sheet of papyrus]

scheme (skēm), *n.* 1. A plan of action: *a scheme to tunnel through the mountain.* 2. A secret plan: *a scheme to avoid paying taxes.* 3. An organized system of things, thoughts, parts, etc.: *a color scheme.* —*v.* To make a scheme; to plan. [< L *schēma* figure < Gk. *skhēma* form]

sci en tist (sī′ ən tist), *n.* 1. One who knows much about science and does scientific experiments. 2. **Scientist** A person of the Christian Scientist religion. [< L *scientia* knowledge < *scīre* know]

scratch y (skrach′ ē), *adj.* **scratch i er, scratch i est** 1. Marked by scratches. 2. Making a scratching noise. 3. Irregular; scanty: *scratchy clouds.* 4. Rough; irritating: *a scratchy voice.* [ME *scracchen* probably a blend of *scratten* to scratch, and *cracchen* to scratch (< Mid Dutch *cratsen* to scrape)] —**scratch' i ly** *adv.* —**scratch' i ness** *n.*

sec re tar y (sek′ ri ter′ ē), *n. pl.* **-tar ies** A person who writes letters, keeps records, etc., for a company. [< ML *sēcrētārius* confidential officer < *sēcrētus* secret]

se cu ri ty (si kyur′ i tē), *n. pl.* **-ties** 1. The state of feeling or being secure; safety; confidence. 2. Something that gives security: *Love of the truth is security against deception.* 3. Something given as a guarantee that a person will fulfill a promise, payment, etc.: *His car serves as security for the loan.* (In the Old Testament [Deuteronomy 24] it was called a pledge.) [< L *sēcūrus* < *se-* free from + *cūra* care. Doublet of SURETY.] —**se cur' a ble** *adj.* —**se cure' ly** *adv.* —**se cure' ment** *n.* —**se cure' ness** *n.* —**se cur' er** *n.*

sen si ble (sen′ sə bəl), *adj.* Having good judgment; showing or exercising common sense;

had, māde, cär; then, mē, hėrd; dim, hīde; not, hōme, ôr; oil, loud; sun, pull, blüe; ch, such; ng, sing; sh, she; th, with; ŦH, the; zh, vision;

ə represents *a* in ago, *e* in open, *i* in pencil, *o* in wagon, *u* in cactus.

discreet. [< L *sēnsibilis* < *sēnsus* < *sentīre* to feel, perceive] —**sen' si bly** *adv.* —**sen' si ble ness** *n.*

sep a rate (*v.* sep′ ə rāt′, *adj.* sep′ ər it), *v.* **-rat ed, -rat ing** 1. Be between; keep apart: *The Atlantic Ocean separates America and Europe.* 2. Go apart: *David and Jonathan separated.* —*adj.* Apart from others: *a separate shipment.* [< ME *separaten* < L *sēparāre* < *sē-* apart + *parāre* to make ready] —**sep' ar ate ly** *adv.*

ser geant (sär′ jənt), *n.* 1. A military officer. 2. A police officer ranking just above an ordinary policeman. [< OF *sergent* < L *serviēns* < *servīre* to serve < *servus* slave]

se ri al (sēr′ ē əl), *n.* A story appearing (as in a publication) one chapter or part at a time. —*adj.* 1. Published one part at a time: *a serial account.* 2. Arranged in a series: *serial encyclopedias.* [< L *serere* to join] —**ser' i al ly** *adv.*

sheer[1] (shēr), *adj.* 1. Fine and very thin: *sheer tablecloth.* 2. Unmixed; pure: *sheer joy.* 3. Very steep; almost perpendicular: *sheer canyonside.* [< ME *schir* clear of guilt] —**sheer' ly** *adv.* —**sheer' ness** *n.*

sheer[2] (shēr), *v.* **sheered, sheer ing** To swerve; turn aside. —*n.* 1. A curving or a swerving of a ship from its route. 2. The amount of upward curve of a ship's body. 3. The position of a ship at anchor in order to keep it clear of the anchor. [Probably < Dutch *scheren*]

shout (shout), *n.* A loud cry often expressing joy, anger, etc., or used in commanding or calling. —*v.* **shout ed, shout ing** To utter a shout; cry out loudly. [< ME *shoute*] —**shout' er** *n.*

sig nif i cant (sig nif′ i kənt), *adj.* 1. Meaningful: *a significant gesture.* 2. Of importance; large or extensive enough to be worthy of notice: *a significant difference.* [< L *significāns* < *significāre* < *signum* sign + *facere* to make]

sil hou ette (sil′ ü et′), *n.* The representation of an

adj.	adjective	*n.*	noun
adv.	adverb	*prep.*	preposition
conj.	conjunction	*pron.*	pronoun
interj.	interjection	*v.*	verb
sing.	singular	*pl.*	plural

object by outline filled in with one solid color. —*v.* **-et ted, -et ting** To give an appearance like a silhouette: *silhouetted on the sunset sky.* [< Étienne de *Silhouette,* French finance minister]

sim pli fy (sim′ plə fī′), *v.* **-fied, -fy ing, -fies** Make simple or easy. [< ML *simplificāre* < *simplus* simple + *facere* to make]

sin cere (sin sēr′), *adj.* **-cer er, -cer est** Free from pretense or deceit. [< L *sincērus*] —**sin cere' ly** *adv.*

sketch (skech), *n.* 1. A rough drawing or painting. 2. A brief outline as of a book or other writing. 3. A brief account. —*v.* To make a sketch or rough drawing. [< Dutch *schets* < Ital. < L < Gk. *schedios*] —**sketch' er** *n.*

ski ing (skē′ ing), *n.* The sport of gliding over snow on long, flat runners on one's feet. [Norwegian < Old Norse *skīo*]

small pox (smôl′ pox′), *n.* A contagious disease with fever and blisterlike skin eruptions. [< OE *smœl* + *pocc* pock]

so-called (sō′ kôld′), *adj.* Falsely or improperly named: *The so-called free gifts are not really free.* [< OE *swā* + ME *callen* (< Old Norse *kalla*)]

sol vent (sol′ vənt), *n.* A liquid in which something can be dissoved. [< L *solvere* to loosen]

soph ist (sof′ ist), *n.* One skilled in clever, misleading argument. [< Gk. *sophistēs* expert < *sophizesthai* to play tricks < *sophos* wise]

soph o more (sof′ ə môr′), *n.* A student in the second year of high school or college. [< Gk. *sophos* wise + *mōros* foolish]

so pran o (sə pran′ ō, sə prä′ nō), *n. pl.* **-os** 1. Music in the higher singing range for women and children. 2. A singer who has the high part. [< Ital. *sopra* above < L *suprā*]

sou ve nir (sü′ və nēr′, sü′ və nēr), *n.* Something that serves as a remembrance; keepsake. [< L *subvenīre* come to mind < *sub-* under + *venīre* to come]

spe cif ic (spi sif′ ik), *adj.* 1. Set forth clearly and exactly: *specific instructions.* 2. Distinctive of a certain species: *Fins are specific to water animals.* [< L *specificus* < *speciēs* sort]

spe cif i cal ly (spi sif′ ik lē), *adv.* In a precise way; definitely; particularly: *David specifically requested gentleness toward Absalom.* [< L *specificus*]

spec i fi ca tion (spes′ ə fi kā′ shən), *n.* 1. The act of specifying, or explaining in detail: *Make your specification clearly.* 2. Often **specifications.** Detailed description of work and materials needed in a building project: *carefully fulfilled specifications.* [< L *specificus*]

spec i fy (spes′ ə fī′), *v.* **-fied, -fy ing, fies** Refer to in particular; mention specific information. [< L *specificus*]

speed om e ter (spē dom′ i tər), *n.* An instrument to indicate the speed of an automobile or other vehicle, and often the distance traveled. [< OE *spēd* success + L *metrum* (< Gk. *metron* measure)]

spir i tu al ize (spir′ i chü ə līz′), *v.* **-ized, -iz ing** 1. To make spiritual: *spiritualize his thought life.* 2. To give spiritual meaning or interpretation to: *spiritualize the laws of nature.* [< L *spīritus* breath]

stam pede (stam pēd′), *n.* 1. A sudden wild flight of animals caused by fright. 2. A general rush or flight of a large group: *a stampede for bargains.* —*v.* To rush in a sudden, senseless manner. [< Sp. *estampida* < *estampier* to stamp]

sta tis tics (stə tis′ tiks), *n.* A collection of numerical information. [< G *Statistik* political science < L *statisticus* of state affairs < *status* position < *stare* to stand]

stren u ous (stren′ yü əs), *adj.* 1. Taking much energy and exertion: *strenuous climb.* 2. Zealous; energetic: *strenuous farmer.* [< L *strenuus*] —**stren' u ous ly** *adv.* —**stren' u ous ness** *n.*

strict (strikt), *adj.* 1. Permitting no deviations from following the rules: *strict obedience.* 2. Exactly defined; accurate: *strict measurement.* [< L *strictus* < *stringere* to bind tightly. Doublet of STRAIT.] —**strict' ly** *adv.* —**strict' ness** *n.*

struc ture (struk′ chər), *n.* 1. Something constructed, or assembled, as a building. 2. Anything made of parts fit together: *human structure.* 3. The way something is put together: *structure of the government.* —*v.* To build; form: *How would you structure a dog house?* [< L *strūctūra* < *struere* to construct]

sub ma rine (sub′ mə rēn′, sub′ mə rēn′), *n.* An underwater boat. —*v.* **-rined, -rin ing** To attack another boat with a submarine. —*adj.* Being underwater: *submarine cliffs.* [< L *sub* under + *marīnus* of the sea (< *mare* sea)]

sub scrip tion (səb skrip′ shən), *n.* 1. The signing of one's name, as on an important paper. 2. A contribution of money: *a subscription to the Red Cross.* 3. A contract to receive something as a periodical for a specified amount of time by paying a certain sum: *Our subscription expired.* 4. *Archaic* Submission; obedience. [< L *subscrībere* < *sub-* under + *scrībere* to write]

sub stan tial (səb stan′ shəl), *adj.* 1. Having substance, or reality; not imaginary; real: *substantial assets.* 2. Solid; firm; well built. 3. Considerable amount: *substantial evidence.* 4. Sufficiently nourishing: *a substantial meal.* [< L *substantia* substance]

sub tle (sut′ əl), *adj.* **-tler, -tlest** 1. Difficult to detect or discern because of being only slightly obvious; elusive: *a subtle fragrance.* 2. Sly; crafty; deceptive: *The devil works in subtle ways.* 3. Working in a hidden and usually harmful way: *subtle erosion.* [< L *subtilīs* woven underneath]

sub urb (sub′ ėrb′), *n.* 1. A town or village near or adjacent to a large city. 2. **suburbs** The area of homes near the boundary of a city; outskirts. [< L *suburbium* < *sub-* below + *urbs* city]

suc ces sor (sək ses′ ər), *n.* A person who takes the place of another, esp. in office or position: *Solomon was David's successor.* [< L *successus* < *sub-* after + *cēdere* to go]

suf fi cient (sə fish′ ənt), *adj.* As much as is needed; enough to fill a need. [< L *sufficiēns* < *sufficere* to suffice < *sub-* under + *facere* to make] —**suf fi' cient ly** *adv.*

su i cide (sü′ ə sīd′), *n.* 1. The intentional killing of oneself. 2. A person who kills himself intentionally. [< L *suī* of oneself + *-cīdium* (< *caedere* to kill)]

sum ma ry (sum′ ə rē), *n. pl.* **-ries** A brief statement

had, māde, cär; then, mē, hėrd; dim, hīde; not, hōme, ôr; oil, loud; sun, pùll, blüe; ch, such; ng, sing; sh, she; th, with; ᴛʜ, the; zh, vision;

ə represents *a* in ago, *e* in open, *i* in pencil, *o* in wagon, *u* in cactus.

of the main points. —*adj.* 1. Covering much in a brief way: *a summary lecture.* 2. Done without delay or formality: *a summary dismissal.* [< L *summārius* < *summa* sum]

sum mon (sum′ ən), *v.* 1. To call (a person) to come, esp. with authority: *summoned to appear in court.* 2. To call forth; arouse: *summon your courage.* [< L *summonēre* to suggest < *sub-* under + *monēre* to warn]

sun set (sun′ set′), *n.* 1. The setting of the sun below the horizon. 2. The final stage: *sunset of his reign.* [OE *sunne* + *settan*]

su per in ten dent (sü′ pər in ten′ dənt, sü′ prin ten′ dənt), *n.* A director; manager. [< L *superintendere* < *super-* above + *intendere* to direct]

sup ple ment (*n.* sup′ lə mənt, *v.* sup′ lə ment′), *n.* 1. Something added to give completion: *a supplement to the story.* 2. Something added where there is a lack: *a food supplement.* 3. The amount added to an angle or arc to make a total of 180°. —*v.* To supply a supplement: *Carving supplements his income.* [< L *supplēre* to complete < *sub-* from below + *plēre* to fill]

sup port (sə pôrt′), *v.* 1. Hold in position; keep from falling: *Posts support the roof.* 2. To provide strength; help: *God's grace supported the martyrs.* 3. To supply with money or necessities: *He supports his parents.* 4. To favor; approve: *I support your decision.* 5. To supply proof for: *The facts support his story.* —*n.* 1. The act of giving support: *Jonathan's support saved David.* 2. Person or thing that supports, or holds something up. 3. Means of existence; provision: *life support.* [< L *supportāre* to carry < *sub-* from below + *portāre* carry]

sur geon (sėr′ jən), *n.* A doctor who specializes in surgery. [< ME *surgien* < F *serurgein* < *serurgie* surgery < L *chīrūrgia* < Gk. *kheirurgos* working by hand < *kheir* hand + *ergon* work]

sur plus (sėr′ pləs, sėr′ plus′), *n.* The amount that

adj.	adjective	*n.*	noun
adv.	adverb	*prep.*	preposition
conj.	conjunction	*pron.*	pronoun
interj.	interjection	*v.*	verb
sing.	singular	*pl.*	plural

is left above the needed amount; excess. —*adj.* Left over; excess: *surplus crops.* [< L *superplūs* < *super-* over + *plūs* more]

sur ren der (sə ren′ dər), *v.* Yield to (another person); give up, as in defeat. —*n.* The act of yielding; a giving up. [< OF *surrendre* < *sur-* over + *rendre* to deliver (< L *rendere* < *re-* back + *dare* to give)]

sus cep ti ble (sə sep′ tə bəl), *adj.* 1. Easily influenced or impressed; sensitive: *susceptible moods.* 2. Having a nature apt to permit; capable of receiving: *Language is susceptible to change.* 3. Having little or no resistance; open to: *susceptible to sickness.* [< L *susceptibilis* receivable < *suscipere* < *sub-* from below + *capere* to take] —**sus cep' ti ble ness** *n.* —**sus cep' ti bly** *adv.*

sus pi cion (sə spish′ ən), *n.* 1. The act or condition of suspecting; imagination of blame without proof. 2. The state of being suspected: *The stranger was under suspicion.* 3. A slight hint; small amount: *a suspicion of pink in the white petals.* [< L *suspicere* to watch < *sub-* from below + *specere* to look at]

sus pi cious (sə spish′ əs), *adj.* 1. Giving reason to suspect; questionable: *He was seen at a suspicious place.* 2. Showing or feeling suspicion; mistrust: *a suspicious glance.* [< L *suspicere*] —**sus pi' cious ly** *adv.* —**sus pi' cious ness** *n.*

swamp (swomp, swômp), *n.* Wet, spongy lowland; marsh. —*v.* 1. To drench or sink with water or other liquid: *swamp the boat.* 2. Overcome, as with a flood: *swamped with mail.* [Low G *swampen* to quake]

sym bol (sim′ bəl), *n.* A sign or object that represents something else: *The eagle is a symbol of power. X is a symbol for multiplication.* [< L *symbolum* < Gk. *sumbolon* token, mark < *sumballein* to compare < *sun-* together + *ballein* to throw]

sym pa thet ic (sim′ pə thet′ ik), *adj.* 1. Having a feeling of kindness toward others; compassionate. 2. Being in agreement with: *sympathetic to the building code.* [< L *sympathīa* < Gk. *sumpatheia*]

sym pa thy (sim′ pə thē), *n. pl.* -**thies** 1. A feeling of understanding and sorrow for the trouble or grief of another. 2. Agreement; likemindedness: *in sympathy with the idea.* [< Gk. *sumpathētikos* < *sumpatheia* sympathy < *sumpathēs* affected by like feelings < *sun-* together + *patho* feeling]

symp tom (sim′ təm, simp′ təm), *n.* 1. An indication of something: *a symptom of poverty.* 2. An abnormal change in the body showing sickness: *symptoms of appendicitis.* [< L *symptoma* < Gk. *sumptōma* < *sumpiptein* to coincide < *sun-* together + *piptein* to fall]

syn a gogue (sin′ ə gog′), *n.* A building used by Jews for religious services. [< L *synagoga* < Gk. *sunagōgē* to bring together < *sun-* together + *agein* to bring] Also **synagog.**

syn thet ic (sin thet′ ik), *adj.* 1. Made artificially by using chemicals: *synthetic vitamins.* 2. Artificially devised; not genuine: *synthetic friendliness.* [< Gk. *sunthetikos* component < *suntithenai* to combine < *sun-* together + *tithenai* to put]

T

tap i o ca (tap′ ē ō′ kə), *n.* A starchy food obtained from the root of the cassava plant, used in puddings and as a thickening. [< Tupi (Indian) *tipiog*]

tar get (tär′ git), *n.* 1. An object for shooting at to test aim. 2. A person or thing used as an object of scorn, ridicule, etc.: *Jesus was a target for criticism.* 3. A goal one desires to achieve: *His memorization target this year is three hundred verses.* 4. A plate in an x-ray tube. [< OF *targette* < *targe* shield]

tel e graph (tel′ ə graf′), *n.* A communication system that transmits electric impulses by wire. —*v.* To wire a message. [< Gk. *tēle* at a distance + *graphein* to write]

tem po ral[1] (tem′ pər əl, tem′ prəl), *adj.* 1. Pertaining only to time as opposed to eternity: *"The things which are seen are temporal."*

2. Enduring for a short while: *temporal fads.* [< L *temporālis* < *tempus* time] —**tem′ po ral ly** *adv.*

tem po ral[2] (tem′ pər əl, tem′ prəl), *adj.* Having to do with the temples of the forehead: *temporal wrinkles.* [< L *temporālis* < *tempora* the temples]

tem po rar y (tem′ pə rer′ ē), *adj.* Lasting or used for only a short time: *temporary living quarters.* [< L *temporārius* < *tempus* time] —**tem′ po rar′ i ly** *adv.* —**tem′ po rar′ i ness** *n.*

ten den cy (ten′ dən sē), *n. pl.* -**cies** A natural inclination to think or act in a certain way: *a tendency to wander.* [< L *tendēns* < *tendere* to tend]

ten der[1] (ten′ dər), *adj.* 1. Not tough; soft: *tender steak.* 2. Not strong; easily crushed: *tender seedlings.* 3. Expressing kindness and love: *God's tender mercies.* 4. Young and undeveloped: *tender youth.* 5. Painful to the touch; sore: *tender skin.* [< OF *tendre* < L *tener*] —**ten′ der ly** *adv.* —**ten′ der ness** *n.*

ten der[2] (ten′ dər), *n.* 1. A formal offer for a business contract or to fulfill an obligation. 2. Something offered in payment: *legal tender.* —*v.* 1. To present formally, as a resignation. 2. To offer something in payment of a debt or other obligation. [< F *tendre* < L *tendere* to stretch, extend]

ten der[3] (ten′ dər), *n.* 1. A person who tends something: *blower tender.* 2. A boat used for transportation to and from larger ships. 3. A railroad car that carries coal and water attached to the rear of a steam locomotive. [< ME *tenden* < *attenden* to attend < OF *atendre* < L *attendere* to heed < *ad-* to + *tendere* to stretch]

ten or (ten′ ər), *n.* 1. The general tendency: *the violent tenor of the multitude.* 2. The highest male voice in music. [< L *tenor* uninterrupted course < *tenēre* to hold on]

tes ti mo ny (tes′ tə mō′ nē), *n. pl.* -**nies** 1. A statement or declaration used for proof, esp. in court. 2. Proof: *Improved scores are testimony of her diligence.* 3. An open confession of one's faith. 4. **Testimony** The Law of God. [< L *testimōnium* < *testari* to testify]

theme (thēm), *n.* 1. The topic or subject on which one writes or speaks: *His theme was obedience.*

had, māde, cär; then, mē, hërd; dim, hīde; not, hōme, ôr; oil, loud; sun, pull, blüe; ch, such; ng, sing; sh, she; th, with; ℋ, the; zh, vision;

ə represents *a* in ago, *e* in open, *i* in pencil, *o* in wagon, *u* in cactus.

2. A short article, esp. one written as an assignment. 3. A basic melody. [< L *thema* < Gk. proposition < *tithenai* to place]

the ol o gy (thē ol′ ə jē), *n. pl.* -**gies** 1. Teachings about God and man's relationship to Him: *The best theology book is the Bible.* 2. A study of religious beliefs. [< L *theologia* < Gk. *theos* god + -*logy* science, study (< *logos* word)]

ther a pist (ther′ ə pist), *n.* A person who gives therapy treatments for an illness or disability. [< Gk. *therapeia* < *therapeuein* to cure, treat < *theraps* attendant]

ther mom e ter (thər mom′ i tər), *n.* An instrument for measuring temperature. [< Gk. *thermē* heat + *metron* measure]

ther mo stat (ther′ mə stat′), *n.* A device for regulating temperature. [< Gk. *thermē* heat + -*statēs* one that causes to stand]

threat en (thret′ ən), *v.* 1. To utter a threat, or promise of harm; express an intention to do (something undesirable). 2. Be a sign of something dangerous, unpleasant, etc.: *That little leak threatens to sink the ship.* [< OE *thrēatnian* to compel, urge]

to bac co (tə bak′ ō), *n. pl.* -**cos** or -**coes** 1. A plant native to tropical America but cultivated widely for its leaves, which are dried and used in making cigarettes, cigars, etc. 2. The use of tobacco: *He never practiced tobacco.* [< Sp. *tabaco* < Carib]

tom a hawk (tom′ ə hôk′), *n.* A hatchetlike weapon used by early American Indians. [< Algonquian *tamahaac*]

tor na do (tôr nā′ dō), *n. pl.* -**does** or -**dos** A violent whirlwind accompanied by dark clouds and appearing as a twisting funnel moving across the land in a destructive path. [< Sp. *tronada* thunderstorm < *tronar* to thunder < L *tonāre*]

tour ist (tur′ ist), *n.* One who makes a tour or travels for pleasure. —*adj.* Pertaining to tourists:

adj.	adjective	*n.*	noun
adv.	adverb	*prep.*	preposition
conj.	conjunction	*pron.*	pronoun
interj.	interjection	*v.*	verb
sing.	singular	*pl.*	plural

tourist bus. [< F *touriste* turn < L *tornus* lathe. Related to TURN.]

tran scend (tran send′), *v.* To go beyond or above: *Rockets transcend the atmosphere.* [< L *trān-scendere* < *trāns* over + *scandere* to climb]

tran scribe (tran skrīb′), *v.* **-scribed, -scrib ing** 1. To write out in full as from shorthand notes: *transcribe a sermon.* 2. To make a recording of. [< L *trānscrībere* < *trāns* over + *scrībere* to write] —**tran scrib′ er** *n.*

trans fer (*n.* trans′ fər, *v.* trans fėr′), *n.* 1. A change or assignment to a different place or position: *a transfer from secretary to manager.* 2. A ticket that allows a person to change from one vehicle to another in traveling. —*v.* **-ferred, -fer ring** 1. Pass or cause to pass from one place to another: *transfer information.* 2. Change from one vehicle to another in traveling. [< L *trans-ferre* < *trāns* across + *ferre* to carry]

tri fle (trī′ fəl), *n.* 1. Something insignificant or of little importance: *The scratch was only a trifle.* 2. A small amount: *a trifle of molasses.* —*v.* 1. Talk or act in a lighthearted way. 2. To handle something absent-mindedly; toy: *trifle with a pen.* 3. Act without purpose; waste time: *He trifled away the hours.* [< OF *trufle* trickery] —**tri′ fler** *n.*

trip let (trip′ lit), *n.* 1. One of a set of three children who are born to the same mother at the same time. 2. In music, a group of three notes that are sung in the time of two notes having that value. [< L *triplus* < Gk. *triplous* < *tres* three]

tri umph (trī′ əmf), *n.* 1. Victory; success. 2. Exultation because of a success: *triumph on his face.* —*v.* 1. To be victorious: *Christ triumphed over death.* 2. To rejoice over a victory: *Christians triumph when a sinner is converted.* [< L *triumphus*]

triv i al (triv′ ē əl), *adj.* Of small importance; too little to be concerned with. [< L *triviālis* ordinary < *trivium* public square < *tri-* three + *via* road]

tu ber cu lo sis (tů bėr′ kyə lō′ sis, tyů bėr′ kyə lō′ sis), *n.* A communicable disease affecting various body tissues, but most commonly the lungs. [< L *tūberculum* < *tūbercle* lump + -OSIS]

ty ing (tī′ ing), *v.* Progressive form of *tie.* [< OE *tīgan* to bind]

typ i cal (tip′ i kəl), *adj.* Showing characteristics or traits belonging specifically to that type or group: *a typical letter from Grandmother.* [< L *typicus* < Gk. *tupikos* impressionable < *tupos* impression]

typ ist (tī′ pist), *n.* Person who types, esp. as a regular occupation. [< L *typus* figure < Gk. *tupos*]

tyr an ny (tir′ ə nē), *n. pl.* **-nies** 1. Cruelty or harshness practiced by one who is in power. 2. A government in which a single ruler has absolute power. 3. The administration of a tyrant. [< L *tyrannia* < Gk. *turannia* < *turannos* tyrant]

U

u nan i mous (yü nan′ ə məs), *adj.* 1. Being of one mind; agreed: *unanimous friends.* 2. Showing complete agreement: *unanimous vote.* [< L *ūnanimus* < *ūnus* one + *animus* mind] —**u nan′ i mous ly** *adv.* —**u nan′ i mous ness** *n.*

un be liev er (un′ bi lē′ vər), *n.* A person who does not believe, esp. one who does not have religious beliefs. [< OE *ond-* against + *belēfan*]

un der rate (un′ dər rāt′), *v.* **-rat ed, -rat ing** Value or rate too low; underestimate: *Do not underrate the power of prayer.* [< OE *under* + L *rata* proportion]

un doubt ed ly (un dou′ tid lē), *adv.* Without a doubt; certainly. [< OE *ond-* against + *douten* (< OF *douter* < L *dubitāre* to waver)]

u ni form (yü′ nə fôrm′), *adj.* Unchanging; regular; consistent: *uniform speed.* —*n.* Distinctive clothes that identify members of a particular group or organization. [< L *ūniformis* < *unus* one + *forma* shape]

u nique (yü nēk′), *adj.* 1. Different from anything else; being the only one of its kind. 2. Uncommon; unusual; rare: *a unique privilege.* [< L *ūnicus* < *unus* one] —**u nique′ ly** *adv.*

u ni ver si ty (yü′ nə vėr′ si tē), *n. pl.* **-ties** An institution of higher learning including schools of law, medicine, etc. [< L *ūniversitās* a society < *universus* < *ūnus* one + *versus* (< *vertere* to turn)]

un like ly (un līk′ lē), *adj.* Not likely to happen or succeed. [< OE *ond-* against + *gēlic* similar] —**un like' li ness** *n.*

un nec es sar y (un nes′ i ser′ ē), *adj.* Not necessary; needless. [< *un-* not + *necessary* (< L *necesse* unavoidable < *ne* not + *cedere* to withdraw)] —**un nec' es sar' i ly** *adv.*

un re gen er ate (un′ ri jen′ ər it), *adj.* Not born again; ungodly; unrepentant. [< OE *ond-* against + L *regenerāre* to reproduce (< *re-* again + *generāre* to beget < *genus* birth)]

un u su al (un yü′ zhü əl), *adj.* Not usual or ordinary; uncommon. [< OE *ond-* against + L *ūsuālis* custom] —**un u' su al ly** *adv.* —**un u' su al ness** *n.*

ur gent (ėr′ jənt), *adj.* 1. Demanding immediate action; very necessary: *an urgent need.* 2. Persistent; repeatedly demanding: *urgent questions.* [< L *urgēns* < *urgēre* to urge] —**ur' gent ly** *adv.*

u til ize (yüt′ əl īz′), *v.* **-lized, -liz ing** To put to use. [< F *utiliser* < Ital. *utilizzare* < *utile* useful < L *ūtilis* < *ūtī* to use] —**u' til iz' a ble** *adj.* —**u' til i za' tion** (yüt′ əl īzā′ shən) *n.* —**u' til iz' er** *n.*

V

vac cine (vak sēn′, vak′ sēn′), *n.* A preparation of dead or weakened bacteria or viruses used to make a person or animal immune to a disease. [< L *vaccīnus* of cows < *vacca* cow] (The first successful vaccine consisted of cowpox germs used to immunize against smallpox.)

vac u um (vak′ yü əm, vak′ yüm), *v.* 1. The absence of matter or air. 2. An empty feeling or sense of lack. [< L *vacuus* empty < *vacāre* to be empty]

vague (vāg), *adj.* **vagu er, vagu est** 1. Not definite or clear: *a vague idea.* 2. Without definite shape or form: *a vague outline of the bridge through the mist.* [< L *vagus* wandering]

val u a ble (val′ yü ə bəl, val′ yə bəl), *adj.* Having much value; precious in terms of money or some other standard: *valuable time.* —*n.* Often **valuables.** Something that has value, as an article of gold or silver: *All the valuables were stolen.*

had, māde, cär; then, mē, hėrd; dim, hīde; not, hōme, ôr; oil, loud; sun, púll, blüe; ch, such; ng, sing; sh, she; th, with; ᵺH, the; zh, vision;

ə represents *a* in ago, *e* in open, *i* in pencil, *o* in wagon, *u* in cactus.

[< OF *valoir* to be worth < L *valēre*] —**val' u a ble ness** *n.* —**val' u a bly** *adv.*

ven geance (ven′ jəns), *n.* Punishment; revenge: *Vengeance belongs to God.* **with a vengeance** Done with violence or great force; extremely; excessively. [< OF *vengier* to avenge < L *vindicāre* < *vindex* avenger]

ver bal (vėr′ bəl), *adj.* 1. Spoken rather than written words; oral: *verbal confession.* 2. Word for word: *verbal inspiration of the Bible.* 3. Having the nature of or derived from a verb: *verbal suffix.* [< L *verbālis* < *verbum* word] —**ver' bal ly** *adv.*

vi o lence (vī′ ə ləns), *n.* 1. Physical force intended to injure or destroy: *arrested for violence.* 2. Intensity; fury: *violence of the storm.* 3. Misrepresentation; distortion of meaning: *did violence to the song.* [< L *violentus* < *vīs* force]

vi o lent (vī′ ə lənt), *adj.* 1. Showing strong, rough force: *violent waves.* 2. Brought about by force rather than by natural causes: *violent death.* 3. Severe; extreme: *violent pain.* [< L *violentus*] —**vi' o lent ly** *adv.*

vis i ble (viz′ ə bəl), *adj.* Capable of being seen. [< L *vīsibilis* < *vidēre* to see] —**vis' i bly** *adv.* —**vis' i ble ness** *n.*

vis i tor (viz′ i tər), *n.* Person who visits; guest. [< L *vīsitāre* to go to see < *visere* to view < *vidēre* to see]

vi tal (vīt′ əl), *adj.* 1. Pertaining to life: *vital statistics.* 2. Necessary to sustain life: *Respiration is a vital function.* 3. Causing death; fatal: *vital injuries.* 4. Full of life; lively: *vital personality.* [< L *vītālis* < *vīta* life] —**vi' tal ly** *adv.*

vi ta min (vī′ tə min), *n.* An organic substance that is needed to maintain the normal functions of man and animals. [< G *Vitamine* < L *vīta* life + *-amine* an organic compound]

vol ca no (vol kā′ nō), *n. pl.* **-noes** or **-nos** A mountain with a vent at or near the peak from which

adj.	adjective	*n.*	noun
adv.	adverb	*prep.*	preposition
conj.	conjunction	*pron.*	pronoun
interj.	interjection	*v.*	verb
sing.	singular	*pl.*	plural

ashes, molten rock, and gases are expelled. [Named after the Roman god of fire.]

vol un tar y (vol′ ən ter′ ē), *adj.* 1. Done of one's own free will and not out of constraint: *voluntary labor.* 2. Done on purpose: *voluntary destruction.* [< L *voluntārius* < *voluntās* will < *vol-* < *velle* to wish]

voy age (voi′ ij), *n.* 1. A journey by water, usually of some distance. 2. A journey through the air or through space. —*v.* To go on a voyage, or journey. [< OF *veyage* < L *viāticum* provisions for a journey < *viāticus* of a journey < *via* road]

W

war rant (wôr′ ənt, wor′ ənt), *n.* 1. That which gives authority or right: *a warrant to hunt on his property.* 2. A document giving authority to do something: *a search warrant.* 3. Good reason; grounds: *a warrant for his beliefs.* 4. A guarantee. —*v.* 1. To give authority to someone: *He was warranted to keep order.* 2. To make a guarantee: *The dealer warranted the safety of the product.* 3. Show to be right; justify: *Nothing warrants such driving habits.* [< OF *warant*, of Germanic origin]

war ri or (wôr′ ē ər, wor′ ē ər), *n.* A soldier experienced in fighting. [< OF *werreier* wage war < *werre* war]

wretch ed (rech′ id), *adj.* 1. Unhappy; miserable: *wretched tramp.* 2. Disgraceful; despicable: *wretched manners.* 3. Of poor quality: *wretched equipment.* [< ME *wrecched* < *wrecche* wretch < *wrecca* outcast < *wrecan* to drive] —**wretch′ ed ly** *adv.* —**wretch′ ed ness** *n.*

Z

ze ro (zir′ ō, zē′ rō), *n. pl.* **-ros** or **-roes** 1. The figure or digit (0) representing the quantity of none. 2. Nothing. [Ital. < Arabic *sifr* empty. Doublet of CIPHER.]